AMERICAN BAND

AMERICAN BAND

★

Music, Dreams,
and Coming of Age
in the Heartland

KRISTEN LAINE

GOTHAM BOOKS

GOTHAM BOOKS
Published by Penguin Group (USA) Inc.
375 Hudson Street, New York, New York 10014, U.S.A.
Penguin Group (Canada), 90 Eglinton Avenue East, Suite 700, Toronto, Ontario M4P 2Y3,
Canada (a division of Pearson Penguin Canada Inc.); Penguin Books Ltd, 80 Strand,
London WC2R 0RL, England; Penguin Ireland, 25 St Stephen's Green, Dublin 2, Ireland
(a division of Penguin Books Ltd); Penguin Group (Australia), 250 Camberwell Road,
Camberwell, Victoria 3124, Australia (a division of Pearson Australia Group Pty Ltd);
Penguin Books India Pvt Ltd, 11 Community Centre, Panchsheel Park, New Delhi –
110 017, India; Penguin Group (NZ), 67 Apollo Drive, Rosedale, North Shore 0745,
Auckland, New Zealand (a division of Pearson New Zealand Ltd); Penguin Books
(South Africa) (Pty) Ltd, 24 Sturdee Avenue, Rosebank, Johannesburg 2196, South Africa

Penguin Books Ltd, Registered Offices: 80 Strand, London WC2R 0RL, England

Published by Gotham Books, a division of Penguin Group (USA) Inc.

First printing, August 2007

10   9   8   7   6   5   4   3   2   1

Grateful acknowledgment is made to the following for permission to reprint previously published material:

OCP Publications: excerpts from the lyrics to "On Eagle's Wings" by Michael Joncas.
© 1979 OCP Publications, 5536 NE Hassalo, Portland, OR 97213. All rights reserved. Used
with permission.

Music Services: excerpts from the lyrics to "Undignified" by Matt Redman. © 1995
Thankyou Music. All rights reserved. Used with permission.

Cameron Bradley: excerpts from the lyrics to "The Cry." © 2004 Cameron Bradley. All
rights reserved. Used with permission.

Photo credits: Darrel Yoder: insert page 1, top and bottom; page 2; page 3, top; page 4, top
and bottom; page 6, top and bottom; page 7, top and bottom; page 8. Jeff Longenbaugh: insert page 3, bottom; page 5, top and bottom.

Gotham Books and the skyscraper logo are trademarks of Penguin Group (USA) Inc.

LIBRARY OF CONGRESS CATALOGING-IN-PUBLICATION DATA HAS BEEN
APPLIED FOR.

ISBN 978-1-592-40319-6

Printed in the United States of America
Set in Sabon
Designed by Victoria Hartman

For Jim

★

Contents

AMERICAN BAND

Prelude

They knew they would win.

Even as the Concord Marching Minutemen heeled-and-toed onto the artificial turf, holding their instruments at attention and their chins so high they couldn't see the ground in front of them, they carried themselves with the certainty of champions.

Two hundred and sixteen teenagers raised resolute, sure faces to three drum majors, and beyond, to thousands of spectators who filled one side of the massive RCA Dome, where the Indianapolis Colts would play football the next day. They knew, each of them, that they would march in long lines that turned to the right and then snaked back left, that they would follow each other backward through curves, that they'd bring three and four and more rows together on the field and rotate them, keeping each line and each diagonal straight, and do all of this so precisely that the judges watching from boxes high above the field couldn't find a single foot out of step. They'd thought about, and practiced, every move and every sound they made on the field so many times that they could perform the routine on command, with their eyes shut, and now, when it counted.

They knew they had the power of a community behind them. They would form their lines on a brightly painted cubist tarp in the shape of a guitar, the neck of which led to a stylized scroll through a series of ramps and platforms. The set had been built and painted over hundreds of hours by band dads now standing on the sidelines in matching green jackets. The dads had run onto the field to assemble the set before the Minutemen went on, and they'd swarm out afterward to take it down. Band moms who all season had tended to blisters, sunburn, thirst, tears; sewed uniforms and served food; dispensed hundreds, thousands of hugs; now stood in a block and shouted, "Give me a C! Give me an O! . . ."

For eight minutes, the high school students would play a sophisticated medley that their director called "Guitarras Españolas." First, a concert-band fanfare led by the crack trumpet section, followed by a technically difficult piece that sped up as it progressed, requiring the horn players to double-tongue while they marched nearly three steps every second. Crashing cymbals would herald an edgy concerto for electric guitar and wind orchestra, a composition so new that it had premiered in concert only the year before. Their finale: a swing-band chestnut so familiar no one played it anymore, and therefore shocked with both recognition and surprise.

And then they went out and did it.

Amanda Bechtel played fast triplets on piccolo while striding backward on tiptoe in a different rhythm. Cameron Bradley swung his saxophone toward the back sideline, and thought, *Perfect so far*. Brent Lehman marched along the front with the trombones, sending every rapid note straight up to the judges' boxes, daring them to find a single mistake.

Nick Stubbs sidestepped along the back of the field, his hands flashing above his snare. He rolled thunder from his sticks, and the long lines atomized, fragmented. The small groups played faster, and the music grew more dissonant. Matt Tompkins's solo guitar joined the argument, moving from acoustic Spanish flamenco into rock concert wail and screaming to a final distended high note.

And then, tension released and unity re-established, the entire band played "Malagueña." Grant Longenbaugh leaned back on the fifty-yard line and blew his horn. He'd kept the trumpets together during the final dissonant notes of "Chaos Theory," kept them driving to the end, as he'd kept the entire high-brass section together during the past season. All the kids in his section, and in others, too, watched Grant, copied Grant, believed because Grant believed. He never doubted they'd win.

After the results were announced, the drum majors swigged milk beneath a sign that said, "Winners Drink Milk," and carried the tall trophy between them as they led the band outside, past a cheering crowd. The 2003 Indiana Class B state champions celebrated on the plaza outside the Dome, surrounded by more than a thousand supporters. Veteran director Max Jones said, in front of everyone gathered there, "You have been a special band from day one."

He could have stopped then, stopped talking, stopped working, even, called that win the cap of a long career. But Max Jones had one more mission. He was on the brink of creating one last dynasty: not just a band that brought home trophies but a music program so top-to-bottom strong—from the high school's top jazz and concert bands to the elementary-school band—that it would give thousands more their own shots at becoming champions. He wanted to institutionalize the notion, for every student who came through the Concord music program, that greatness emerged only when all, together, strove for perfection. Along with many in the band and the community—and indeed, along with the students themselves—he thought the upcoming seniors, the Class of 2005, were the ones who could help him finish his task.

IT WAS DURING the fall, after the band had won every one of its contests and then the state championship, that Kathy Greene decided to teach *Paradise Lost* to her eleventh-grade honors English class. She regarded October a cruel month for the students who marched in the band, which usually meant most of her students. (It was understood around Concord that the students in honors and AP classes also filled the rows of the band and the orchestra.) Greene knew about the Saturdays that began with seven a.m. rehearsals, flowed into daylong performances, and ended back at the school twelve or sixteen hours later. She knew the directors expected the musicians to hold additional practices on their own, and the older students, like her juniors, to teach the younger ones. During the last weeks of October, when the push was on for state finals, the band kids dragged themselves into Kathy Greene's first-period class with dark circles under their eyes, not fully prepared for the day's assignments, but jumpy, too, running on the adrenaline of competition.

As it did every year, a letdown followed the finals. The kids in the band sat half-asleep at their desks, morose and withdrawn. Kathy Greene watched the best student she'd ever taught slouch down in a chair by the doorway, the hood of his sweatshirt pulled low over his face, and worried that she was losing him. Grant Longenbaugh ranked first in his class, as he had since first grade. He'd won awards for his artwork. As a sophomore, he'd sat first-chair trumpet in the top concert band and had helped two of Concord's academic bowl teams to the state finals. He was a once-in-a-lifetime student for so many of his teachers that they teased each other about it in the faculty lounge.

Unlike other very smart kids Greene had taught or gotten to know, Grant wasn't cynical or arrogant, or dismissive of Concord, Elkhart (the bigger town across Concord's suburban borders), or the Midwest. Earlier in the fall, he'd often stopped by her classroom after school, first to talk about books, then increasingly about love and God and purpose.

But since the state finals, what had first struck Greene as exhaustion had edged into apathy and then into what seemed like depression. So when Grant responded brightly to one of her guided discussions, a "Socratic seminar," one day near the end of the first trimester, she took note. It wasn't the book that Grant seemed to respond to, but her questions: "Is suffering necessary?" "Does modern man need God?" He seemed to wake up and then to energize everyone else in the room.

Kathy Greene thought the Class of 2005 was strong enough to handle the rigors of Milton. But she put the new lesson plan together for Grant Longenbaugh. She wanted him to be engaged as fully every day as he was on that day. She wanted to challenge him, and she wanted Milton's language and Milton's ideas inside his head when he thought about heaven and hell.

And so she assigned the entire class all ten thousand five hundred and twenty-five lines of John Milton's epic blank verse: ten thousand lines of dense allusions to Greek mythology, pre-Copernican cosmology, and musty religious debates; ten thousand lines that described man's fall from grace using backward-facing metaphors and verbs that clung to the tail ends of long-nested phrases. She didn't stop with Milton. On top of his Protestant hell, she piled Dante's Catholic *Inferno*, and extended the whole hellish morass into the modern world with T.S. Eliot's *The Waste Land*.

It was by far the most demanding month of coursework Kathy Greene had ever developed. She wasn't sure if she was asking too much of her students. Milton's language was just as difficult as Shakespeare's, his concerns widely considered irrelevant to modern American teenagers. Furthermore, it was impossible to teach *Paradise Lost* without talking about God and Satan, sin and grace. Teachers wary of crossing the boundary between church and state often chose to teach other books. But talking about God and Satan was exactly what Kathy Greene wanted her students to do.

On the first day of the spring trimester, she stood at the door to greet each student. One of her four children was already in college, but Greene was trim and wore body-hugging clothes and jangling jewelry, and her frosted brown hair moved in long, curling waves against her shoulders. Boys fantasized about her. Girls compared themselves to her. Every Friday she handed out upbeat musings on life that were known around the school as "Mrs. Greene's love letters." Her very presence asked her students to react on several levels at once, so it added only a slight dissonance when she hugged the juniors that March and welcomed them to hell.

Greene counted on the students from the band to be her most committed workers. Amanda Bechtel had read *Paradise Lost* all the way through once and the CliffsNotes twice, and had some questions about Milton's soul. Cameron Bradley arrived at class saying Milton could have written just as good a book using half the words. Trombone player Brent Lehman carried printouts from an online readers' guide. Nick Stubbs had liked the epic's battle scenes, but took his place with the skeptics against the back wall.

Greene was also counting on one of the strong students not in the band, Leandra Beabout, a pretty, dark-haired junior new to Concord. Leandra was doubly exotic in a class where most of the kids had known one another for years, because she had come to Elkhart from Slovakia. At first, Leandra had seemed overwhelmed by the bigger, noisier, looser American system, but Kathy Greene could tell she was very bright. When the class took a statewide English test, Leandra received a perfect score—several points higher, even, than Grant Longenbaugh's.

The student for whom Kathy Greene had created the class did not

arrive that first day having completed the assignment. A week before
the new trimester started, on a warm, springlike day after church,
Grant Longenbaugh had propped his feet up on his front porch and
opened the marked-up edition of *Paradise Lost* that his older sister,
Anne, had used at Purdue. He'd become used to pulling off his homework at the last moment. He was quickly pulled into the story; it reminded him of *The Lord of the Rings*. He read eagerly, absorbed in
Milton's attempt to "justify the ways of God to men," but began the
class a few pages short of finishing.

In Milton's calling, Grant thought he might be seeing his own. If
Milton's central theme was man's fall from grace, Grant had personally
sensed the grace. He'd nearly forgotten the abyss of the previous fall.
From his present vantage, his junior year was a series of leaps from
high peak to high peak. He now prayed before school in the quiet trophy hallway by the band room with Cameron, Amanda, Leandra, and
several other students who attended the same evangelical church.
Sometimes on those mornings, as he bowed his head beneath the glass
cases of trophies and banners, he wanted to share his persistent feeling
of standing under a shower of God's love.

He kept that feeling to himself, though, along with something else.
Recently, a phrase had started sounding inside him, saying, *I am well-
pleased with you.* He wouldn't have said it out loud, but he was sure
that the voice came from God. He felt certain, pure, perfect—ready for
what God had in store for him.

One day, Greene led the class to a passage in *Paradise Lost*, the end
of a conversation between Adam and the angel Raphael, who had been
sent by God to warn Adam and Eve that Satan had found his way into
Eden. Greene read Adam's final question to the angel:

> Love not the heav'nly Spirits, and how thir Love
> Express they. . . . ?

Then she read Raphael's reply, ending with the lines:

> Easier than Air with Air, if Spirits embrace,
> Total they mix, Union of Pure with Pure
> Desiring; nor restrain'd conveyance need
> As Flesh to mix with Flesh, or Soul with Soul.

"Why is Raphael blushing here?" Kathy Greene asked the class, blushing herself. Students bent to their books, puzzling out the words and the unfamiliar grammar. Grant burst out, "It's angel sex!"

Sex, even disembodied sex, even described in Latinate phrases, had the desired effect. Everyone in the class now wanted to understand the poetry. "Angel sex" would become a running joke between Grant and Cameron Bradley. "That's what I'd like sex to be," Grant whispered to his friend. *Union of Pure with Pure.*

Two weeks later, Greene put her students into groups to wrestle with *The Waste Land.* Greene didn't make much of the fact that T. S. Eliot was a Midwesterner; to many of the students, he seemed the epitome of East Coast or British elite: all mind, no heart. Leandra was assigned the first section of the poem, with its famous line, "April is the cruelest month." For her, spring had been anything but. She'd started to make friends. She loved the sense the poem gave, like a scent, of struggle and learnedness, and found it beautiful. Afterward, she would associate *The Waste Land* with the smell of wet earth and the feeling of a new life beginning.

Brent Lehman, in one of the other sections, heard Grant throwing out ideas, making connections between lines of the poem and big themes, and felt a stab of envy, then anger at himself. He didn't want to be jealous of Grant. But most of the things that Brent cared about came to Grant so easily: grades, music, art, leadership, friends, even family. And Grant seemed to exist comfortably in the middle of things, while Brent often felt on the outside. He was a liberal in a conservative community, and an activist. When he traveled to anti-war demonstrations, he felt the excitement of being part of a group and the shared sense that he could even change the world. When he returned to Concord, he immdiately felt isolated again, and frustrated that he couldn't get even one classmate to listen to him. Seeing the others lean in as Grant talked stirred those same feelings.

The discussions on Eliot's poem of modern life marked the class as youth who could not accurately be called modern. Most of Greene's students resisted its depiction of fragmentation and loss, and they didn't accept the notion that their world sat on uncertain or shifting ground. They believed that the certainties of their faith were already granting them safe passage through the wasteland of the modern world.

Even more than she'd hoped, Greene's class served her purposes. It had challenged Grant and showed the other students how far they could stretch. Most of all, she'd encouraged her students to think for themselves. As someone who'd been raised in Elkhart, she knew how subversive that could be.

WITH WARMER DAYS the juniors became restless and eager for the school year to end. For the band kids, though, summer would be a beginning: the new marching season that would give them a two-month jump on their senior year. As a class, they knew they'd been the engine behind the previous year's championship. They wore their new championship rings and put championship patches on letter jackets. Soon it would be their turn to lead.

Even with the championship, Brent Lehman carried a vague sense of shame for some of the ways he'd acted as a junior. He had no clear idea how he'd lead the trombone section, only that he would do things differently in the coming year.

Amanda Bechtel, who would take over the flute section, was preparing just then to go to Israel with a Christian-scholar group. She'd been driving four hours each way to Ohio several times a month, despite her parents' misgivings, to attend lectures on Jewish and biblical history. As stubbornly independent in her approach to leadership, Amanda had definite ideas about how she would change the culture of the flute section, which at times seemed like a girly-girl mafia where the weapon of choice was backstabbing.

Back in October, Nick Stubbs had sat on the bus outside the RCA Dome before state finals, certain of winning, and thought, *Omigod, what about next year?* He knew he'd be captain of the drumline, the elite corps inside the band. And now next year was almost there.

At the band tables in the lunchroom that spring, Grant worked quietly to psyche up his classmates. His stature inside the band was growing. After two years of leading from below, he would soon have the opportunity—be expected—to lead from above. His director had also commissioned Grant to paint portraits of Concord's band directors through the years, about fifteen paintings; he was to keep the project to himself. Grant kept quiet about a more personal goal. He wanted to use his position in the band to leave a legacy of faith and leadership, an example of how to live one's life.

Grant had one more reason to feel growing excitement. One day in April, Kathy Greene took Grant aside and suggested he ask Leandra to the prom. "She's your intellectual equal," she told him.

The notion pleased Grant, and got inside him. He gave Leandra a story he'd written for the class. On an inner page, far enough in to tell him she'd actually read it, he placed a sticky note: "Enjoy this and come to prom with me!" When she returned the story, he saw that she'd penned "OK!" below his invitation.

Soon after the prom, Kathy Greene held a bonfire for her junior honors English class. At the party, Grant sat between Mrs. Greene and Cameron, but was keenly aware of Leandra talking to Brent Lehman on the other side of the flames. It looked to Grant like Brent was flirting with her, and he felt a surge of emotion. The feeling was so foreign to him that he didn't know to call it jealousy.

In one of their final classes of the year, Kathy Greene had given her juniors a rare honor: She wanted them to choose lines from their reading for a wall of her classroom, joining Emerson's "Concord Hymn" and lines from *Macbeth*. In the flickering light of the bonfire, Grant told his teacher what lines he thought they should paint on the wall. Even though the students and their teacher were already calling their shared experience "the Milton class," and would count reading all of *Paradise Lost* as one of their most memorable academic achievements, the lines weren't from Milton's epic, but from the last section of *The Waste Land*, "What the Thunder Said." Grant quoted the lines to her, his face in shadow and light, looking across the flames at Leandra.

> *Datta*: What have we given?
> My friend, blood shaking my heart
> The awful daring of a moment's surrender
> Which an age of prudence can never retract
> By this, and this only, we have existed

"In the Hindu fable," Eliot had written in his notes to the poem, "beings on earth—gods, men, and demons—asked their father, 'Speak to us O Lord.' To each he replied with one syllable, '*DA*.'" Each group interpreted the syllable in a different way: one heard *datta*, which meant to give to the poor; another heard the Hindu word for self-control; a third heard the word for compassion. Eliot's note quoted the concluding lines: "This is what the divine voice, the Thunder, repeats when he says: *DA, DA, DA* . . ." Grant was intrigued by what the foreign fable might be saying about God and man, and how man hears the voice of God. He liked how "*DA*" sounded like thunder. The word was so simple, only two letters, but he could imagine it containing all God's power and mystery.

Marching band would start in a little more than a month. Of all the adults around them, only Kathy Greene might have truly understood what her students were marching into the season with. She'd taken their ideas and yearnings seriously and let them express what was in their hearts and on their minds. Amanda Bechtel, Brent Lehman, Cameron Bradley, Nick Stubbs—all of them had a vision of how they should be in the world. Grant Longenbaugh also had a vision, and a mission. Kathy Greene had given them the room to speak.

Band would give them the room to act.

1 ⋆ The Voice of God

M ax Jones woke ahead of his alarm. The pain relief capsule he took like a sleeping pill had worn off too early, as it always did during marching season. He tried to sleep, but his mind churned with thoughts of what needed to be done. Shortly after six a.m., he pulled his convertible into the parking lot across Minuteman Way from the music department entrance. He sniffed the air, as practiced as an old farmer at sensing a turn in the weather: muggy already, storms likely. His was the only car at the school. It was the middle of July, summer vacation for students and teachers alike. But for Max, the day marked the beginning of another cycle of waking before dawn, working late into the night, and spending entire weekends away from home, all in the service of his obsession and his gift: teaching music to teenagers.

Max Jones. It was a great name for a band director, or a general. But the students all called him Mr. Jones, in deference to his authority as an adult and a teacher; many of the parents did, too. Other band directors turned his name into one word, *MaxJones*—the legendary director who'd won state championships in each of four decades; the icon who'd adapted to changes in his craft and the world around him for nearly forty years; the master teacher who could take any group of kids and mold them into fine musicians, and do it year after year after year. His name had spread across the state and across state lines—though, like many intimidating people, he appreciated those who simply called him Max.

Four of his assistants had started the week before at the junior high, showing sixth graders how to assemble their instruments; how to clean them; what a head joint was, and a ligature. The directors had greeted each of the students by name and made games out of learning what the boys and girls had eaten for breakfast ("nothing" was not acceptable). They'd reminded the young musicians to bring notebooks and pencils to every class. Steve Peterson had dimmed the lights and set a disco ball spinning while his beginning woodwinds played their first notes. Scott Spradling had led his new brass players in buzzing competitions with their mouthpieces. In a few hours, Max would meet students three years beyond similar humble beginnings. He needed to help them make a crucial transition, for them and himself.

He unlocked the doors to the music offices upstairs, the band room downstairs, the multipurpose room with floor-to-ceiling mirrors for the color guard, the percussion room, the classroom where he held staff meetings, and the trophy hall. With twelve soundproof practice rooms, two piano labs, and an auditorium that seated nearly a thousand, the music facilities in this modest community—Max's fiefdom—rivaled the best in the country.

Max expected seventy new kids, mostly incoming ninth graders, to show up for the week of freshman band camp. He always asked upperclassmen to come in before the full camp and volunteer, as well, which usually doubled the group. A few days before, from his vacation condo in Tennessee, he'd called and asked an assistant to set out 150 chairs on the band room's concrete risers. Now, alone in his domain, Max walked each semicircle, smoothing and straightening, thinking ahead.

An hour before the start of band camp, the three drum majors had already seated themselves at a card table in the hallway, behind boxes of name tags and markers. Drum majors didn't play drums. They were the band's student conductors. Their visibility conferred automatic status, and many band members dreamed of being chosen. In many bands, drum majors were the group's strongest leaders or musicians. But at Concord, although he didn't advertise the fact, Max kept his strongest students on the field, where he felt their work was more valuable.

The hallway quickly filled with students who hadn't seen one another since school had let out in May. Its brick walls echoed with greetings and excited chatter. Standing by the entrance before he returned to the band room, Max could hear brief snippets of conversation from the returning students—". . . camp counselor . . . ," ". . . mission trip . . . ," ". . . broke up and now she's going out with. . . ." A few boasted and complained about long hours behind the cash registers at Target or stocking shelves at the grocery store. A girl in line said to a friend, "Remember when I was a freshman and I was, like, 'Wah, where do I go?'" Max could easily pick out the freshmen in the growing crowd. They were the faces he didn't know. They were also the kids who looked anxious or scared, or stood by themselves. If his system worked as it should, the minutes ticking toward the start of band camp would be the last time its newest members would feel so alone.

By eight-thirty, every chair in the band room was taken. Kids lined the walls. Still more students pushed in from the hallway. The room grew hot and stuffy, but also quietly expectant, like a crowded theater before the curtain rises. Max stood in front of them. He carried himself with the ease of a man used to having an audience and used to being obeyed. He made the casual clothes he was wearing—a T-shirt celebrating the previous year's championship, khaki shorts, bright red running shoes— seem like a uniform. But he also smiled widely. He bounced on the balls of his feet as he waited. The anxiety that had wakened him before dawn had become barely contained eagerness.

He raised one hand, and the atmosphere changed instantly. A hundred and fifty chairs scraped the linoleum in unison as their occupants sat up straighter. Even though kids still blocked the hallway, the air seemed immediately less stifling.

"Obviously we underestimated how many would be here today," he told the crowded room. When he had taken attendance, he would learn by just how much: One hundred and ninety-seven students had squeezed into a room built to hold a hundred and twenty. "When we start next Monday with everybody, the number of us on paper is"—he drew out the number as he spoke it—"two hundred and forty-three." Someone whistled appreciatively. Max grinned in the direction of the whistle, and crow's-feet appeared at the edges of his eyes. "Right now it looks like it may be the biggest band of the last twenty years."

Everything Max Jones had worked for in nearly two decades at

Concord was primed to come together in a season of superlatives—biggest, best, strongest, hardest, first. The biggest band he had ever directed. The best-prepared freshman class. The strongest group of senior leaders. The most ambitious combination of music and choreography. All of it pointing toward that greater dynasty.

Max had asked the drum majors to bring the previous year's trophy down from its place of honor in the music office and set it on top of the piano. Its five feet of gold-plated wedding cake towered over him. He let a hand linger on it while he welcomed the new students to the program and all of them to the new marching season. He sought out those faces he hadn't recognized in the hallway; many still looked timid and unsure. He would try to put them at ease—he'd make a point of committing every new student's name and face to memory by the end of the week—but he knew that some would fear him all season, or even for four years. He would ask those teenagers to work harder than they had ever worked before, but even as he did so, he needed to make their first week in band so compelling that they wouldn't let go for anything—not for sports, not for their friends, not for other teachers, not even for their families or churches.

He saw the potential for strong leaders in every section. Amanda Bechtel, officially a senior as of that first day of band camp, sat in the smallest semicircle of chairs, her back straight and her flute upright in her lap. She was the band's best musician, although not necessarily its most gifted. Ever since the sixth grade she had practiced like a professional, and her dedication over time had lifted her higher than those around her. Max looked for saxophone player Cameron Bradley, whose talent rivaled Amanda's. Cameron had been an energetic foil to the previous year's low-key section leader, and Max expected great things from him over the coming year. He was surprised he didn't see the lanky senior in the crowd. He eyed Brent Lehman, the lone fourth-year player among the trombones, and remembered the hotheaded selfishness he'd seen in Brent as a junior.

Nick Stubbs, the new drumline captain, stood at the back of the room with his arms folded, flanked by other drummers. Max liked the slight young man. Nick mowed Max's lawn; Nick's father had been a band director across town in Elkhart. But Max wasn't sure whether Nick could hold together the percussion section, a perennially unstable compound of the band's only musicians selected by audition and its least engaged students.

Grant Longenbaugh sat in the last row, surrounded by new trumpet players. Max had noticed him earlier in the crush of kids out in the hallway, his signature brown cowboy hat pulled down low over his head, but he'd entered the room bareheaded, honoring his director's rule against wearing hats inside the band room. Max had given Grant no title, but he didn't need to. Max thought Grant was one of the most natural leaders he'd ever worked with. He only wished he had more like him.

"We have this little trophy," Max said, patting the gilded hardware. The students laughed. "It's bigger than some people in here. I'm barely taller." More laughter.

"We have a trophy. We have a banner. We have T-shirts that say we are the state champions, which now we are the defending state champions. But the reality is, you now—even though you participated in that—you now are nothing." He emphasized the last words: *You. Now. Are. Nothing.*

The rustling of paper and cloth, the creaking of chairs, even the breathing of 197 teenagers, seemed to stop. The room went completely still. Max stood still. He knew the power of silence. In those four words lay an important truth. The students in front of him were not the previous year's band. They weren't even a band, not yet. They were nothing but a group of individuals, many of them strangers to one another. Only they could determine what they would become.

He let the words, spoken and unspoken, reach inside the seniors, the juniors, the sophomores. He let them reach inside the freshmen, hinting that they had a role to fill in the band, and that what they did counted. The stillness stretched. Then he started talking again, conversationally, as if he hadn't given them their fundamental challenge for the months ahead.

THE NEWEST MEMBERS of the Concord Marching Minutemen stepped out into the hazy brightness of a Midwestern summer day, instruments and notebooks in hand. They found their places on the band's practice field, which, in contrast to the posh indoor facilities, was little more than a scrappy, shadeless patch of pavement on the high school's outermost parking lot. Until they left the band room, the new students might have imagined that Summer Advanced Concert Band, as the class would be listed on their report cards, was only a tougher version of something they already knew. Most had come up through the elementary and junior high concert bands, and some had watched older siblings go through the program. They were already used to competitions, even to winning. The eighth-grade concert band had earned the highest score in Concord history at the statewide middle-school competition. But now the new students stood awkward and uncertain on the pavement, the unfamiliar, bigger buildings of the high school all around them, at the entrance to a new world.

For the next three and a half months, they'd seldom sit to play their instruments. They'd rarely play from the sheet music their director had already handed out for their notebooks. Instead, they'd learn why Max insisted they use plastic page protectors. They'd play the music on those pages in drizzle and in downpour, in heat so searing, it softened the tar in the cracked pavement, and, later, in sleet blowing down from Lake Michigan—and play it from memory. Soon enough, their notebooks would lie in piles against the fences that bordered the practice field, while they marched and moved to the music, sweating even in the freezing temperatures of late October. By the end of marching season, standard concert band, with its seating charts and music stands, would seem far too orderly and boring to some of the students; for others, it would come as a reprieve.

With those steps outside, the freshmen also entered a new academic realm, one far more porous to the community than classes held within school walls. Starting that first day, they would learn and practice and perform mostly in public. Even as the students gathered into sections by instrument—saxophones in the farthest corner of the practice field, along the fence by the soccer fields; clarinets near a concrete concession stand at the entrance to the football field; high brass by a fifty-yard line painted on the asphalt—half a dozen children wearing swimsuits and towels draped over their shoulders hung back at the doors to the school's pool to watch the action. Their mothers pulled them inside after a few minutes, but they were the first of many who would linger and watch.

An even more striking aspect of their open-air classroom was who was doing the teaching. None of the seven Concord band directors taught that first hour, not even Max Jones. The older students in each section took charge, trumpet players teaching other trumpet players, clarinet players working with clarinets, and on through the band's nine instrumental groupings. Earlier Max had outlined what he wanted the older students to teach that first day: standing at attention, horns up and horns down and, if time remained, turning to the right and to the left. But the director himself took his time coming out to the practice field, and once he arrived, he said nothing. Hands behind his back, he floated from group to group, watching.

Grant Longenbaugh, his cowboy hat shading his face, worked with three freshman boys on marching band's basic building block: standing at attention. He started on the ground, kneeling in front of each boy to put his feet in the position Max demanded—heels and toes together, pointed straight ahead—and worked his way up. He looked at them as he taught, speaking to each one in a low voice, and he encouraged every effort. Knees together, he instructed, but not so tight that you teeter. He pantomimed a knock-kneed topple, his arms and trumpet windmilling, and drew short, nervous giggles from the freshmen. On to the stomach, pulled in just so. Chest up, spine straight, straight, as straight as you can make it, but shoulders relaxed and back, not up around your ears. He talked, but watched even more, seeming unhurried—just enjoying a pleasant summer morning hanging out with the guys in the parking lot, practicing good posture. Max Jones, floating nearby, couldn't catch Grant's words, but he caught the younger students' attentiveness and a subtle easing into the task at hand.

All of them wore name tags. Grant had slapped his onto a T-shirt from Cornell, one of the colleges he'd visited the week before. One of the freshmen had written on his tag in yellow marker, making it un-readable in the bright haze. Grant didn't need the tag, though. He'd sat with the junior high students at the all-schools concert in May and met some of the incoming trumpet players then. Earlier that morning, in the band room, he'd committed the other names to memory. He called his group of three by name: David, Mike, Caine.

Two of the freshmen hadn't hit their growth spurts yet. They were, developmentally, still very much boys. Grant towered over them. Even though he stood not quite six feet, his frame had already filled in. At times he was embarrassed by his bulk, by what he called his tree-trunk legs and a wideness in the chest that tended to thickness. But he could use it to varying effect, and did, that morning. He let his back sway and his trumpet sag down. "Don't stick your butt out like J. Lo," he told the boys, wiggling his own for emphasis. Then he pulled himself upright. He threw his chest forward and grasped his horn with bent arms nearly shoulder-high. He looked formidable, almost adult. His eyes burned into a space far above the boys' heads.

That part he'd saved for last. When they stood at attention, he explained, they were to lift their chins until their jawbones ran parallel to the ground. He called his small group to attention and had them hold the pose for several moments. He was teaching the freshmen more than a marching maneuver. He wanted them to understand the level of detail they'd be responsible for. He wanted them to feel the pride that came with the stance, wanted to let that unnatural tilt of the chin give them the courage to be champions.

"Good work," he said.

The nervous freshmen soaked in his gentle words, his encouragement, his confidence, even the name of the university on his T-shirt, all of it nourishing a larger sense of what they might do, and who they might become.

Grant made the task look easy. Max watched other sections working and saw students stumble teaching the same basic skills. Anyone who marched in the band the year before knew how to stand at attention, how to snap an instrument into playing position. But some were unable to translate what they knew into words. Others found it easier to chat than to spend time on details. Some rushed through the process, covering up their anxiety with bluster. Still, everywhere Max looked, he could see young men and women trying—trying to teach, trying to learn.

Versions of Grant's lessons played throughout the other sections. The voices of the older students filled the ears of the freshmen.

"I should be able to look right up your nose."

"No, you can't see your instrument when you have your chin up like that. But it's the Concord way. It's part of what makes us look different out there."

"When Mr. Jones says, 'Atten-hut,' you stand tall and absolutely still and yell out, 'One!' as loud as you can."

Brent Lehman was pleased with the progress of the beginning

trombones, four freshmen and a third-year student new to Concord whose family had picked the school district expressly because of its band program. Brent took seriously the responsibility of leading his group. Just before the end of the school year, his father had been diagnosed with cancer, a rare form of non-Hodgkin's lymphoma. "This is what I'm going to die from," he told the family. Brent had confided only in Mrs. Greene and Grant Longenbaugh. Though his father's newly bald head was a constant reminder of the cancer at home, Brent thought mostly about band. He saw the coming season as a chance for redemption. During the previous season, he'd yelled at classmates he thought weren't working hard enough, sometimes slammed his trombone down in anger, and fought with his section's only senior and leader. Now he occupied the same position in the section, and his first taste of leadership was laced with regret.

Brent saw a freshman shrink from an overbearing upperclassman, and winced inwardly. He watched junior Brandon Schenk, sporting a bright yellow T-shirt with "Fools for Christ" in big block letters across the front, demonstrate to the newcomers how to grasp their trombones by pretending to strangle his. "It's a death grip, not a concert hold!" he yelled. Brent laughed along with the rest, knowing that his feelings would have been tinged by rivalry a year earlier. If the new students learned well because it was Brandon who taught them, Brent was determined not to mind. He'd become painfully aware that the sophomores and juniors didn't trust him. Even if he earned their respect, he couldn't lead the eighteen-person section on his own.

Only the drumline didn't join the other sections on the practice field. The drumline included a single freshman, but counted several rookies who'd moved onto the line from the pit and needed to learn to march with drums strapped to their bodies. A college student working as summer staff was already drilling them. He kept his charges under the only shade trees, several groups of broad pines along the side of the parking lot between the music building and the practice field. The snare drummers wore carriers that fit over their fronts like Roman soldiers' breastplates. They slid their snares onto hooks attached to the carriers, leaving their hands free for their drumsticks. Nick Stubbs stood erect, comfortable under the weight of the drum and the carrier, while the novices on the line fidgeted.

Max called the band to attention from a portable megaphone and announced a twenty-minute break. It wasn't a terribly hot day, but band moms were handing out water at the music-department entrance. No doubt marching band was a strange introduction to high school: a class in which your classmates taught you skills that were otherwise useful only in the army, a class held outside where anyone could watch, a class where your own parents might be hovering over you.

The students started to run across the parking lot to the school. Grant yelled, "Be sure to thank the moms!"

THE DAYS TURNED hot and steamy, with temperatures in the high eighties—normal Hoosier summer days, but hard going for some of the newest members of the Concord Marching Minuteman Band. Max reminded his students about wearing sunscreen and hats, but sunburned shoulders, peeling noses, and red, sweaty faces showed up in every rank.

After the first day, Max took over more of the teaching, working with the band as a whole. He told the students that he was going to push them harder and faster than any band he'd ever taught. He talked them through the fundamentals of marching, showing them how to roll their feet forward from the tips of their heels, and then he taught them to march backward, keeping their legs straight and staying up on their toes. "We never do that on the second day of band camp," he said approvingly. He added music to their movement: "We're going to play that well-known concert piece, the B-flat scale." He ratcheted up the tempo they marched to, introducing them to "our old friend, Dr. Beat," an electronic metronome. Its amplified clucks reverberated across the huge parking lot. They started marching at a tempo of 68, a slow walk, an amble. On the third day, he turned the metronome dial until it ticked out 120 beats a minute, the tempo of a military march. The previous year's band—state champions, as if they needed reminding—gave up at 160, he told them. Before the end of the season, however, they would need to go all the way to 200, to three and a half steps per second.

The seniors and other upperclassmen worked as Max's lieutenants. They drilled their instrument sections in the new fundamentals. They marched in the outer positions in their ranks, the better to look down the lines and fix them. They stepped out to watch beginners or walked beside them to give pointers. Max sometimes called his best marchers—Grant, Brent, Amanda, Cameron among them—out of rank to demonstrate nuances of the Concord style, such as the fierceness of a body snap during a turn or the angle at which heel met pavement to initiate a step.

In those first days, the raggedness of the marching seemed to fit the scrappiness of the surroundings. All around, freshmen turned to the right when Max called out "left face," to the left when he called out "right face," and even collided with one another. The novices were getting a feel for the hard work ahead of them, although they hadn't yet played their music and marched at the same time. The notes some of them played in small groups sounded no better than their marching looked.

Max told his new band members that by the end of the week, he wanted them to march up and down the pavement, between the concession stand on one end and the soccer fields that bordered a subdivision called Green Valley on the other. And he wanted them to play the school song from memory while they did it. He said, "Let that be Green Valley's wake-up call."

"Anchors Aweigh" set fewer than fifty notes to a simple march. It was an odd selection for the school song, a U.S. Navy march appropriated by a landlocked Midwestern high school. But then the entire school identity was a mongrel mix: The district had taken its name from a New England village, but pronounced it "Con-CORD" in the broad and slightly nasal Os of the upper Midwest; and even though its mascot was a Revolutionary War soldier, at some early moment in the school's history, a decision had been made to pair the soldier with a sailor's tune. In spite of its musical simplicity, some of Max's youngest students had trouble mastering their school song. Senior Diana de la Reza noticed a shy freshman named Adilene Corona hesitating before she played some of the notes on her clarinet. "That high D," Diana told her, pointing to the music. "Try this for the fingering." She carefully moved Adilene's fingers into position. The freshman pressed her lips against the mouthpiece and blew. A loud bleat came out of the clarinet's black bell. In other groups, trumpets squawked, trombones belched, flutes screeched.

Every year, band camp revealed the kids who needed the most work. The new freshman class was the most musically talented to enter

Max's program, but it also included students who still struggled with music's basic skills. In band camp, those students couldn't hide behind their more expert classmates. One of the biggest challenges and rewards of any marching season for instructors and upperclassmen was bringing those kids up to a level with the others.

The experienced students listened not only to the notes the band's new members were forming in front of them but also to a sort of ghost music, a felt memory for how the band could sound and feel from the inside. The freshmen dimly sensed that the others heard things they didn't yet, and it made them pliant and more willing. The directors heard it, the best teachers among the students did, and sometimes parents did, too. But the freshmen wouldn't hear it until they'd finally played music in the open, moving along with the melody in precise patterns and time. They needed to join their music and movement to the person on their left and the person on their right, and on down a rank, to feel the beat of a drum rising through their soles, the quick shudder of feet hitting the ground in unison. When they did, those real sounds would lodge in them. Only then could they start to understand the full power of what they were learning.

On the first day of band camp, Max had told the upperclassmen, speaking over the heads of the freshmen, "They can't possibly know, until October, what is even being asked of them. But you still have to teach them."

Max Jones often told the students in the band that seniors taught and freshmen learned. He expected sophomores and juniors to learn how to lead, but in the absence of clear expectations, many students in the middle classes weren't sure of their roles. Grant made it clear in his section that his notion of leadership included sophomores and juniors, and showed them how. On the first day of band camp, Grant had noticed that one of the freshmen, Amanda Himes, hung back from the rest of the trumpets, even during announcements. He also noticed that several of the freshmen boys taunted her almost offhandedly, as if they'd been doing it a long time. Her face contorted into a scowl. He sent Laurie Schalliol, a sophomore, to bring the younger girl back into the fold.

Laurie was thrilled that Grant had asked her to help, even though she'd instant-messaged him in a panic the night before. "Omigod!" she'd typed in her message. "I still feel like a freshman! No way I'm ready to teach!" But she prided herself on being a total-immersion band geek—"Why be popular when you can be the majority?" she quipped—and she considered herself addicted, after one hit, to the rush of winning. She wanted Concord to bring home a championship trophy at the end of the 2004 season, too. She wanted to put to rest once and for all her father's insistence on the superiority of the Giant Concord Marching Band in which he'd been a drum major back in the seventies. And she was willing to let Mr. Jones notice her dedication and name her drum major the following year.

Laurie was pleased to come to the aid of another girl trumpet player. Amanda Himes told Laurie that she stood so far away from everyone else because she refused to sit between two freshmen boys who teased her. Laurie, who'd seen the number of female trumpet players in her own class dwindle to two, commiserated. "You're lucky," she told the younger girl. "There are four of you this year."

She could have traded her own stories about being mistreated by the boys, but instead, she told Amanda that not all the guys in the high-brass section were mean. "Sit next to Grant," she said, and forced a line of first trumpets to slide over for the freshman girl. This broke one of the unwritten rules of the band, that first parts stick together. A lowly third trumpet never sat with the firsts, certainly not next to the section leader, and especially not when that third trumpet has just spent most of the morning glaring at everyone. But Grant grasped Laurie's intent, and he put a stop to the muttering and head-shaking. Amanda seemed to relax ever so slightly, away from the other freshmen. It was a start.

Laurie knew Grant was kind to misfits, because he had been kind to her. In junior high, she'd thought of herself as an outsider, different and dressed to stay that way. She'd come to school in black, chains, the whole Goth wardrobe. In band, the boys had picked on her behind Mr. Spradling's back, but she was the one who got in trouble when she lost her temper. She hadn't wanted to stick with band in high school until Grant came to the junior high, along with several other sophomores in the band, to encourage the eighth graders to sign their commitment forms. He talked to her, and that was all it took. She'd nursed a crush on him all through her freshman year.

Now she had become the band camp's official unofficial greeter, along with another early-arriving girl. Every morning, Laurie and her sidekick held forth from a ledge in the band hallway, cracking band jokes, taking band polls, quoting from band scenes in movies ("This one time? At band camp?"). She was proud that Mr. Jones himself sometimes stopped and asked for the day's poll question.

Grant had invited Laurie into the Concord band and made it feel like home. For an unsure teenager, finding a place to belong could be as elusive and welcome as finding love. Laurie had stayed in the band, and now she wanted to pass Grant's gift on to the new students.

It was unusual for one of Max Jones's seniors to focus so strongly on teaching the younger leaders, but Grant took his notions of leadership from several sources. One came fully with Max's blessing: Tim Lautzenheiser, a former band director and college classmate of Max's. Max invited Lautzenheiser each February to give a leadership workshop at Concord for band students from Concord and nearby towns. "Dr. Tim" was a tall, skinny character who stayed in near-constant motion during his workshops, and whose voice could slide between booming bass and screeching falsetto, both at top volume.

Dr. Tim liked to remind his audiences at Concord that they were the best students in their schools. "Scary, isn't it?" he'd said to the five hundred or so kids at the most recent February session. "Truth is, you are. Statistically, you're in the upper twenty-three percent academically." He reminded them of a fundamental difference between band and their other classes. "You can go to history class and have a bad day and it doesn't have to affect anybody else in that class. You don't want to listen to the teacher talk, you can put your head down on your desk and fake being sick. But in band when you don't do it, who pays the price?"

"Everybody!" the students shouted.

"And that's why we do it over and over and play that music over and over and over. . . . And every band director lies to you." He pretended to talk through a megaphone. "'C'mon, kids, we're only going to do it—'" He paused for audience participation.

They obliged: "'One more time!'"

Grant enjoyed the humor, but also absorbed Dr. Tim's points. He turned one of Dr. Tim's one-liners over in his mind, trying to decide if it fit his experience. "You have to give one hundred and ten percent as a leader to get the people you're leading to give fifty percent back." He wondered, as well, about the workshop leader's assertion that in any group, 10 percent will be positive leaders, 10 percent negative leaders, and the rest followers. Those proportions didn't seem to fit the Concord band, where he guessed that as many as a third of the students were trying to be positive leaders.

Grant also responded to the thread of humility than ran through Dr. Tim's talks. Dr. Tim told them, "Leaders do the stuff nobody else wants to do," like picking up the trash and straightening the chairs. That February, as he did every year, he told them what Grant and others in the band called "the toilet-flushing story." He started by asking, "You ever in the bathroom in school and you open one of the doors and . . . ?" He left to their imaginations, barely, what might be lurking in one of the stalls. "You know what most of us do? We close the door! Like, I'll leave it for the next guy to deal with! We don't go, here's an opportunity to lead." Here he had lifted one foot, pressed it down, and made a loud sucking sound, at the same time throwing both arms up over his head. Onstage, he looked more like a soccer player who'd just kicked a game's winning goal than someone in a bathroom stall. He screeched, "I'm a leader!"

Minus the humor, maybe, much of what Dr. Tim told them was standard fare in leadership seminars around the country. Except that he wasn't talking to business managers; he was talking to teenagers who could immediately put his advice into action. In fact, the Concord band students who attended Dr. Tim's workshops had more opportunities to lead—and more responsibility to, with real rewards and real consequences—than many adults. Grant liked being asked to aspire to an adult level of goodness, even greatness.

But Dr. Tim had said something in the most recent workshop that Grant hadn't remembered from the earlier ones. He'd said, "No fourteen-, fifteen-, sixteen-, seventeen-, eighteen-year-old kid has any business with leadership. Here's the reason: The part of your mind that makes logical, sequential decisions—the part of your mind that says, 'If I do this, it's going to end up looking like this over here'—that part of your mind will not be fully developed until you're about twenty-five years old." And then he said, "Student leadership is probably an oxymoron."

Grant had taken that statement personally—and as a challenge.

When Grant heard Dr. Tim talk, he heard a high-speed takeoff on the Sermon on the Mount, in which Jesus told his followers to take care of the weak and the poor of spirit. At Nappanee Missionary

Church, where Grant had been going to youth group since junior high and Sunday services since he'd earned his driver's license, he regularly heard the pastors exhort him to take his spiritual journey seriously and to find ways to live his faith in the world. Nappanee had given Grant the confidence to act on his beliefs. Whether Dr. Tim had put the verses in his head, or whether the pastors at Nappanee had, or whether Grant had simply been drawn to them in his own study of the Bible, he took the Sermon on the Mount as his text and test of leadership. Drawing on some of the simplest injunctions of the New Testament, he tried, every day, to do what Jesus would have done. Taking to heart the verse in Matthew that said, "whoever would be great among you must be your servant," he tried to lead, selflessly, by word and example. He saw a direct connection between his work in the band and his role as a Christian.

Out on the field, one of Grant's classmates invited all the high-brass players to a pool party to celebrate the end of freshman band camp. Grant asked Amanda Himes if she was going. Her mouth jerked. She said she didn't think her mother would let her.

After practice, Grant walked over to the line of cars waiting outside the music department. He explained about the pool party to Amanda's mother. He promised to drive her to and from the party himself. Amanda had never been in a car without an adult, or alone with a boy, ever. Her mother said yes.

Within the space of a week, Amanda Himes had changed dramatically. Her face, which had been contorted by anger and fear on Monday, had moved a long way toward relaxing. In fact, she was quite pretty, and her smile, which she'd flashed a few times, hinted at mischievousness. She no longer stood by herself, separate from the group. At least in the band, the taunts had nearly disappeared.

Laurie Schalliol, having helped Amanda, and therefore Grant, was smiling, too. She could joke about how unrealistic it had been to pine for Grant the year before—"He's the perfect guy for an impressionable freshman: completely unattainable"—and say that now she only wanted to wear his cowboy hat. But on her personal website, when she wrote about a great and unrequited love, her friends knew exactly who she meant.

Other girls yearned after the gentle trumpet player and more than a few boys idolized him, even though he wasn't terribly charismatic or classically good-looking, or even particularly friendly. He didn't make a point of getting to know the other students. But he listened to them, and the quality of his attention came almost as a shock, especially to the younger students. He never yelled. He seemed to understand even before they did that they were giving their best, and then, somehow, they were. Along with his attention and his ear, he gave them respect and his time. The adoration and love he got in return were part of the burden of leadership, Grant style.

Grant understood the emotional boundaries as few seventeen-year-olds would. But the currents of his own emotions were becoming less clear. Even as he ministered to the band, all he wanted was to spend time with Leandra. At the prom in May, they'd danced only twice—he'd thrilled at the press of Leandra's slight frame against his stocky German body—and they'd talked all night. Grant couldn't believe they'd had to dress up in a tux and a fancy dress to do something so simple. He learned more about the five years that Leandra had spent in eastern Europe while her father installed radio transmitters for Christian-radio broadcasters. "I've never lived outside Indiana," he told her; even though she was American by birth and background, her perspective seemed broader than the Americans he knew. Now that the conversation had started, he didn't want it to stop. But after the end of the school year, life, or maybe God, had kept them apart. Grant had gone with his dad on their annual canoe trip to the Boundary Waters of Minnesota; Leandra had traveled to the Dominican Republic on a mission trip. Leandra had visited friends in New Jersey and spent a week at church camp; Grant had toured colleges with his parents. For the past six weeks, they'd been in town at the same time only two full days.

On one of those days, Grant had invited Leandra to climb the lookout tower in Oxbow Park and exchange their final papers from Mrs. Greene's class. It was a sweet, geeky invitation. Oxbow, a green oval of open space and forest, stretched along a meander of the Elkhart River near the subdivision where Grant lived. The tower rose four sets of stairs above a large meadow at the park's center. He and Leandra settled themselves facing each other on the tower's wooden platform. He read her paper on the life of a missionary kid; she read his on love. Grant felt an ease and a peacefulness that was new, along with a flutter of excitement. When he and Leandra arrived together at youth group that evening, a few minutes late, he heard their friends breathe out an *Oh!* and saw understanding sweep across their faces. Even in his embarrassment, Grant wondered if the others could hear the silent conversation continuing between the two of them.

THREE TOWERS, TWENTY-FOUR feet high and ten yards apart, rose above the parking lot. The directors used them only during marching season, to hear the band's sound and observe students' positions on the pavement. On the last day of freshman band camp, during a break in the students' work on marching fundamentals, Max checked his watch and climbed crisply up the steel rungs on the outside of the center tower. A green travel bag rested against the small of his back. Max always stood on this tower, directly over the fifty-yard line painted on the pavement. No bigger than a dinner table on top, the metal structure swayed in even a light breeze. Some of the other directors, who were a quarter-century younger, hated going up the ladders to the towers, hated the way fear soured their mouths by the time they pulled themselves onto the wobbly platform. Gay Fetters Burton, the best assistant Max had ever worked with, had been so anxious about the ladders and the height that she'd avoided the towers nearly completely during her fourteen years at Concord.

Max pulled "Dr. Beat" out of his bag and plugged it in next to a music stand welded to the platform. He toed the green bag under the stand without pulling any music from it. He didn't need a score for what he'd be doing.

He stood alone on the tower. From his high vantage, Max could tell that most of the students had already gathered on the pavement, instruments in hand, even though their break wouldn't end for several more minutes. Less than two hours of work remained in the week. Thin clouds, like cotton batting pulled to fine strands, streamed overhead. He'd checked three online weather reports before coming out. Somewhere beyond those clouds, a band of heavy rain and lightning was headed their way. All week, they'd dodged the thunderstorms that had been forecast. Tornadoes had been sighted one evening; another night, high winds had toppled trees around town: nothing out of the ordinary. But the weather had held for the Concord band, as it usually did, somehow. Max hoped they could squeeze in one last dry session on the pavement.

The wind came up and clouds scudded past, but the rain held off. Max felt inside his bag for a Windbreaker and pulled it on. He fit a wireless microphone over his head, leaving the sound turned off for the moment. A few blocks away, a freight train rumbled through, giving three long blasts of its whistle. He leaned onto the waist-high railing and looked out.

Concord High School spread in front of him in a low, sprawling mass of brown and yellow brick. Directly across the parking lot rose the flat, featureless wall of the gym. Max lowered his gaze and looked over the pavement. He noticed some students running across the school's main parking lot, another hard rectangle that adjoined the band's practice pavement along one short end. Behind him, just out of sight, one of the district's few remaining cornfields butted up against a football practice field and County Road 24.

From the tower, Max picked out Grant Longenbaugh's brown cowboy hat. He wasn't surprised that the trumpet section leader already had the high brass aligned in rows and looking up to the tower, waiting for cues from their director.

Max shifted his gaze slightly to the right, to the clarinets. It landed briefly on Adilene Corona. He'd been trying all week, but he still couldn't pronounce her name right.

He swung his view to the back of the pavement, to the percussion section, and saw Nick Stubbs standing straight, chest out. That year especially, Max needed a strong drumline captain. Max didn't think Nick had contributed much as a leader during freshman camp—he'd hardly acknowledged the younger students—but standing at the ready, Nick looked the part.

For a moment, Max let his gaze go out of focus. He didn't know for sure what was inside the young people below him. On Monday, the band would expand by almost 60 kids, to its full size of 243, plus the rest of the summer staff and the other directors. He wouldn't know for weeks whether the largest band of his career would rise to the challenge of the most demanding show he had ever assembled, but by then it would be too late to change it. He asked for nothing less than eight minutes of perfection. Sometimes he overreached, wanting more from a group of teenagers than they could deliver. But as the last of the band members hustled to find their places in their sections, he couldn't help but feel excited by the promise in front of him.

Over the next weeks, their show would become the summer's soundtrack. Men would turn off their riding lawn mowers and sit still in the sweet smell of cut grass to savor the show's melodies and commit them to memory. Over pancakes and coffee, band dads would debate the mechanics and materials of the show's props. People who hadn't enrolled a child in the Concord schools for a decade, or more, still knew that the band had played "Peace Variations" when it won the championship in 1992, and "Chaos Theory" when it won in 2003. They would drive out to the school on Wednesday nights to park facing the practice field, windows down, listening and watching. In some confluence of acoustics and community, the band's music would carry farther as the state finals drew nearer. People burning leaves on the other side of the tracks would hear the band working through the show in segments, polishing and refining. They'd hear Max's voice, never yelling but always prodding, asking for more—"One more time, please." "Again, please." "Again"—his insistence on perfection so unyielding that someone hearing it from the security of his own yard might feel it working on him, might feel his own measure being taken and yell out, *Enough! It's good enough!*

Once, after his father had retired as a Methodist minister, the elder Jones had told Max, "I know you didn't go into the ministry. But as a band director, you have ministered to thousands of students and families." Max had grown up in parsonages around Indiana; he'd majored in organ music at Ball State and played the organ for several churches when he first came to Concord. But he kept his faith to himself. The tower was Max Jones's pulpit. Never mind that he couldn't see a single one of the 206 churches in the Elkhart phone book. He couldn't tell which kids, in the sea of teenagers below him, wore T-shirts that proclaimed their personal relationship with Jesus Christ, which kids attended Nappanee Missionary Church or the other evangelical churches that had sprouted faster, even, than the subdivisions. He'd heard the jokes, too—how Max, like God, could control the weather; how already this year, a freshman saxophone player, asked Mr. Jones's first name by his parents, had supposedly replied, "God?"

Whatever would come to pass was ahead of him. In a few moments, he would call his newest band to attention. He would have them march in sets of eight, first without playing, then playing the B-flat concert scale, and finally playing "Anchors Aweigh." He would watch them individually and he would watch them collectively, seeing things that no one else could see. He would listen, and when he spoke, the trio of loudspeakers attached to the metal stilts would magnify his words—correction, challenge, condemnation, praise—and boom them out across the parking lot to echo off the hard walls of the gym, off the performance center, off the long wing of the music department, out over the subdivisions and the fast-disappearing cornfields. From down on the practice field, the voice of God would seem to come from everywhere.

At exactly a quarter to ten on the morning of Friday, July 23, Max Jones switched on the sound from the tower. "Band," he said quietly, "atten-hut."

One hundred and eighty-one teenagers stuck their chins into the air and stood a little taller. In a few seconds, they would hear the command that told the flute players to lift their silver cylinders between lips and chins, out over their right shoulders, parallel to the ground, and trumpet players to raise their horns to the heavens. Now their eyes lifted above the horizon, seeing only sky. Sunlight glinted off brass tubas and trombones. In a single voice, they called out.

"One!"

2 ⋆ Roots

It was called "mandatory camp" for good reason. No matter how gorgeous the summer weather, for the second week of marching season Max expected the entire band to practice together for eight hours each day. For that one Monday through Friday, he insisted that every student work from eight in the morning until four in the afternoon. To many of the teenagers, the forty-hour week carried symbolic weight and lent the work adult heft, which at least made it bearable.

The penalty for missing even part of a day was severe. Max had told the freshmen on their first day in band, "You miss a day next week and we kick you out." He'd given the impression that not even a death in the family could release a student from the obligation. "Not even your own," he'd said, deadpan. "As long as you're still breathing, I expect you to show up."

Max had his reasons. The simple math went like this: After school began in August, the band would formally practice slightly more than an hour each school day. One month of school translated into approximately twenty hours of practice. During that one week of mandatory camp, the band could work as many hours as in two months during the school year. No other week during the marching season gave them such an opportunity to move ahead, and Max needed to make the most of it.

But a more complicated algebra informed Max's thinking. He had a logical, strategic mind, and he'd sorted through many variables before arriving at the hours and requirements for each of the fourteen weeks in the marching season.

The formula that Max had arrived at differed from those of the other elite bands in the state. Other directors introduced the music for their marching-band shows in the winter, and started their summer band camps immediately after the end of the school year. Max delayed the start of marching season so his students could take summer vacations with their families. He devoted much of the early practices to preparing for a purely fun, seemingly unambitious performance at the Indiana State Fair. Max also maintained strict limits on the number of hours his students spent in rehearsal. After school started, he didn't hold extra afternoon practices. He scheduled just one evening practice a week, on Wednesday nights. He wanted his students to have enough hours left in their days to work part-time, go out for a sport, or act in the fall play. Other competitive programs practiced four and five afternoons a week and eight hours on Saturdays, and extended their seasons into November to compete in the Bands of America Grand National Championships. For these bands, marching season could run nearly all year. Max's equation accepted one given: Every other serious band program in the state of Indiana required more hours from its students over time than Concord did.

On the first morning of full camp, Max reminded his students of the difference. "You will never know this," he said, "because you'll only be in the Concord band; but we probably rehearse about half, maybe three-quarters, the hours of most of our competitors."

His strict limits applied to other variables as well. Max spent only a fraction of the more than $100,000 some programs put out for their costumes, drill arranging, music permissions, and props. While directors in wealthier school districts charged their band members additional fees—some nearing $1,000 per student—Max charged students $50 each year for uniforms and $25 to rent instruments, among the lowest fees in the state. And the uniforms they marched in were almost twenty years old.

There was one variable for which Max set no limit. Many elite bands held auditions. Some programs designated a "freshman" or "novice" band. Other directors intentionally wrote drills for fewer students than they had, allowing them to cull the weakest marchers and musicians by naming them alternates and not marching them in competitions. Max opened the Concord program to every kid who wanted to join. On that first day of full camp, he welcomed kids who had never studied music before, and kids who spent their school days in special ed classes. He had marched students with physical disabilities, including students who were blind.

Max was emphatic that marching band was not a sport but an academic class, with grades, stringent requirements, and a heavy workload. However, if you looked at the band as an athletic team, then the Minutemen signed up every kid who wanted to play, even if that kid didn't know the basics of the game. Max fielded no varsity, no JV. No one got cut from the team. Everyone learned all the plays. Every player suited up and was on the field every minute of every game. And, that year, the team roster would run to nearly 250 names.

Max made every student a promise: Show up, work hard, and work together, and you can compete, and excel. And, perhaps just as important to teenagers: You can belong.

The directors whose formulas placed a higher value on winning believed they needed extra intensity to hold their positions on the national stage. Their approach brought marching bands more in line with current competitive practices everywhere, from win-at-all-costs athletics to hardball, bottom-line business. Their bands filled most of the slots in Indiana's Class A finals and dominated the Bands of America competition.

Max took his job just as seriously as they did. But taking home a championship trophy each year was not as important to him as creating champion kids.

All of his math served that goal. The marching season needed to give every student in the Concord band a high-quality educational experience, and it needed to give each student multiple opportunities to learn and practice the basic skills of good character. To Max, marching bands weren't merely a clichéd image of America. They *were* America— or at least a vehicle for creating the kind of citizens and communities that made America great. And yet, he'd learned over the years not to underestimate the transformative power of winning.

Max Jones had created winning Indiana bands for nearly forty years. At Winchester High School in the 1970s and 1980s, his bands had won six of the first eight Class B championships, a dominant run that was still remembered. During his fourteen years in that central Indiana town, Winchester bands placed as low as second only four times. In nineteen years at Concord, during an increasingly competitive era, Max's bands had made eighteen appearances at the marching finals, almost as many at the concert-band finals, and won dozens of jazz competitions.

How he could achieve such success without undercutting his larger goals had become the problem he needed to solve. His solution was elegant in its simplicity, hard in execution. Max Jones simply made better use of time than anyone else.

He planned every aspect of the Concord music program in specific, bulleted, color-coded, timed detail. Every day of the season, he wrote out a by-the-minute schedule and distributed it to his staff. Every schedule gave the date, the weather forecast, and the school and sports activities that day, and listed the four reasons people became members of a group. Max's efficiency was an extension of his personality. In fact, he made little distinction between personal and professional efficiency. He kept his hair cut short, which wasn't remarkable in itself, except that he scheduled a year of appointments all at once, and noted them on the music department calendar. From spring through fall, he paid Concord band students to mow his lawn every other day. He liked order and believed, correctly, that his almost superhuman ability to squeeze the most out of any given minute gave the Concord band an advantage over bands run by mere mortals. For that second week of band camp, he organized the practices around precise five-minute intervals, but soon enough he'd set up schedules with times like 3:29 and 7:12.

He accepted one luxury the first morning of mandatory camp: He repeated himself, for dramatic effect, and for the few dozen kids who hadn't heard him speak the previous week. He had written the attendance from freshman band camp at the top of the double whiteboard at the front of Room 406, the band room: Monday 197, Tuesday 188, Wednesday 185, Thursday 185, Friday 181. The numbers had dropped from Monday to Friday, but every single number on the board had broken all previous attendance records. The numbers themselves weren't nearly as impressive as the unprecedented volunteerism by the upperclassmen that lay behind the numbers.

Max pointed to five rectangles of green felt hanging from the ceiling above the whiteboard, each marked with a year and the words "State Champion" or "State Runner-up." They celebrated the band's "banner years." Max singled out one of the rectangles. "Back in 1992, we had another state champion band. You can see the banner following it. The '93 band has a banner, but it's not a state championship banner. It has state runner-up."

He scanned the room. "I bring that up, because the '93 band didn't think they had to work as hard, once they were state champions. They figured it out about two weeks before state finals. That's when they got really serious about trying to win. But it was too late."

"Here's a visual for you. This is a state championship shirt." He pointed to his shirt. "This is last year's band."

He pulled the shirt off over his head, revealing one beneath it in plain gold. "This is the new year," he said, pointing to the new T-shirt. "There's nothing on it. It's a blank. But you have a golden opportunity."

Luxury over, he moved to the tasks at hand. From now on, with few exceptions, he would measure every word he spoke against the clock.

At precisely 8:50, with 243 students accounted for in the stuffy band room, Max handed out three pieces of music. One of his goals for the week was to introduce every piece of music that they'd play that season. The freshmen had learned the school song and the national anthem the week before. Before the end of the week, they would play through five more pieces.

Four of the compositions would comprise the fall field show, which Max had named "Roots of American Music." The songs took listeners from African-based rhythms through the stylized blues of Dixieland to the jazzy, syncopated beat of swing—a romp through an American musical landscape. The freshmen had started to learn one of the field-show pieces the week before, but Max handed out a new version that morning. He explained that he'd already made changes to the score. "The music is all written," he told them, "but as the upperclassmen can tell the freshmen, just because it's all written doesn't mean diddly. You'll get umpteen versions. We'll play it and I'll say I don't like that, that's not so good. So I rewrite it and rewrite it." To keep track of the changes, Max color-coded the versions. That morning, he handed out orange sheets. By the end of the week, the students would also see a neon green version, along with rewritten versions of three other pieces. Max didn't want the students to lose a moment's opportunity to play the season's music—and he wanted the music to match perfectly with what he heard in his head. Many of the notes would change, and Max expected the students to keep up with him.

One of the compositions would open both the State Fair show and the field show. Max called "Gabriel's Oboe" a ballad, by which he meant that they would perform it at a slow tempo, and in a smooth, legato style. Playing a ballad in a marching-band show was unusual, but starting a show with a slow-moving piece was almost unheard of. And the distinguishing feature of "Gabriel's Oboe" was part of what made the new show possibly the riskiest Max had ever assembled: a two-and-a-half-minute flute solo.

One day the week before, Max had called several seniors into his office to discuss the solos in the upcoming shows. Then he dismissed all of them except Amanda Bechtel. He told her she needed to memorize the long solo for "Gabriel's Oboe" by the start of full camp. "We're basing the whole first part of the show," he said, "on you."

At one time, Amanda might have thrilled at such a challenge and opportunity. The solo would have seemed a reward for years of work, a prize to take home to the father she tried hard to please, a former band director who had transferred his musical ambitions onto Amanda. But her sense of priority, and mission, had changed.

It showed in the silver Star of David she wore around her neck. She'd bought it during her seventeen-day tour of Israel. Everything about the trip had been significant for her. Her father had originally forbidden her to go. But she'd felt so strongly that she was destined to make the trip that she begged him to leave his mind open to God. When her father did change his mind, she called it a miracle from God.

After seventeen hours in the air, she'd stepped into the dry heat of Tel Aviv and wanted to fall to her knees and kiss the ground. She had the persistent feeling, everywhere she traveled, that she had come home. She visited places she knew from the Bible but had never expected to see. There they were: the Sea of Galilee; Capernaum, where Jesus had given the Sermon on the Mount; and the holy city, Jerusalem. Seeing it all made everything she'd been learning real to her: God's covenant with Israel and the Jews; how Jesus would reign from its rebuilt temple; how God's chosen people, the Jews, would have one final chance before Armageddon to accept Jesus Christ as the son of God and their savior.

For the first time in six years, she hadn't practiced her flute. Instead, she talked and prayed, sometimes all night, with the others on the trip. She sensed a new identity emerging, beyond her music. "That's who I am," she confessed in one of the late-night prayer sessions. "Hi, I'm Amanda Bechtel. I play the flute." But everything that mattered most in her life now led her to Israel.

She wore the Star of David as a talisman of her new identity and a reminder of her commitment to return. No one around Concord was likely to mistake her for a Jew—as far as she knew, there wasn't a single Jewish student among the 1,400 students at the high school. Those who noticed her necklace understood it, correctly, as a symbol of her devotion to bringing about a Christian heaven on earth.

Amanda received the news of the solo without excitement. "No pressure," she said dryly.

She had started working on the piece right away, responsible as ever. At a flute party at the end of freshman camp, Amanda watched the movie *The Mission*, for which the song had been composed, to get a better understanding of it. From the music Max had handed her, Amanda imagined the movie would be uplifting. But the film, based on the brutal history of Jesuit missionaries in South America, began so violently that the girls turned it off. Amanda was sure her parents wouldn't have approved. She had memorized the entire piece by the start of mandatory camp.

Now Max introduced the song to the rest of the band. He told the group that he'd seen a video of another band performing the piece, seen a young woman play an expressive oboe solo, and said to himself, "We have one of those." He played that video for them, plus recorded versions of the song from Ennio Morricone's score. In one version, the melody was accompanied, or, more accurately, punctuated, by timpani drums that sounded like thunder, or the boom of cannons. In the other, voices overlaid the melody as in sacred music, but percussive, hinting at the native rhythms below the liturgical chorale. Max wanted that contrapuntal sound for the opener of the show. He needed the thunder underneath the hymn.

———

ON THE PRACTICE field, Max continued to drill his students in marching fundamentals. He quickened the pace, changed directions on them, taught them to slide side to side. They played the B-flat concert scale while they marched, then "Anchors Aweigh." Max explained how to play to the box—how they should lift their faces and instruments to the judges' section—and how to rotate their torsos while playing and marching. Max did most of his teaching from the tower, the seniors led from within their ranks, and, until school started, additional summer staff for every section along with all the assistant directors taught on the ground. The new students could barely move without bumping into someone ready to teach them and drill them. By the end of the week, Max told them, they would play "Gabriel's Oboe" by memory while they marched nine sets of eight steps. To many of the freshmen, meeting such a goal would require a miracle.

Part of Max's success—and his efficiency—lay in the pipeline he had built between Concord's elementary, junior high, and senior high schools. The pipeline was on display everywhere during full band camp. His assistants, four full-time directors and a part-time percussion instructor, who had been teaching the incoming sixth graders in beginning band camp, now switched those classes to evenings and joined Max at the high school, along with the color-guard instructor. A dozen college students, most of them former Concord band members, served as summer staff. Acronyms and shorthand and cryptic references drifted in and out of the instruction, and everyone knew what it all meant, even the newest members of the band. Posture, technique, approach, philosophy, priorities—everyone involved with the Concord band was on the same page in more ways than one. The value of such continuity was impossible to measure precisely, but it was hard to overestimate.

Max and his staff functioned much like a family business, or even a family, with Max the patriarch and his assistants in the role of sibling children. Max had been Scott Spradling's band director at Winchester starting in seventh grade, and his boss at Concord for seventeen years. He'd been Steve Peterson's director at Concord. Both Scott and Steve had mowed his lawn. As a high school student at nearby Elkhart Memorial, Bryan Golden used to stand on Concord's sidelines just to watch Max's band practices. He later did his student teaching under Max. All three men had struggled, initially, to call Max anything other than "Mr. Jones." Golden, the youngest, still felt intimidated around Max, while Scott Spradling and Steve Peterson jockeyed for his attention and praise.

The 2004 season would be a landmark for both Peterson and Golden. For the first time, every student in their sections had come up under them. Max had hired them to replace another former Winchester-student-turned-assistant, Gay Burton, who had left Concord seven years earlier to start a family. (Max liked to point out that it now took two men to do the work of that one woman.) If the three male assistants were Max's "sons," Gay Burton was his favorite daughter, the one in whom Max most saw himself. He still missed her.

April Duffey was the one director on Max's senior staff who hadn't grown up under Max or his legend. (Amy Davis, the percussion instructor, and the young woman who taught the color guard, also came from outside the Winchester-Concord nexus.) She had played clarinet, baritone, and violin at Richmond High School in central Indiana, had earned double degrees in biology and music in college. She was versatile, hard-working, and sensible. But, drifting outside the sibling eddies of the other directors, she sometimes also found herself outside the staff's main currents as well.

The shared history and long tenures of Max's senior assistants gave them an intimate knowledge of his program and the values that underpinned it. They'd lived it. And they did, still, putting in long hours not always associated with schoolteachers, and bringing the same focus and creativity to their work that actors brought to theater. They knew all the students, and each year they started a new generation on its way up.

On the practice field, Scott Spradling took the high brass and Bryan Golden the low brass. Steve Peterson and April Duffey split the woodwind section. Though teaching within the same system, each brought a different personality to the work. Golden appeared more tentative, more earnest, more nerdy alongside the Spradling and Peterson show, and younger. When he stood in front of the 140-student pep band during basketball season, he looked barely older than the students he was directing—and just as gung-ho. (Concord's boys' team hadn't lost a home game in almost three seasons, a run that people chalked up to Concord's trifecta: the team, the fans, the band.) Golden cared deeply about his kids in the low brass, cared about their lives and concerns, and the kids responded. The young director made a special point during that week's eight-hour days to encourage a couple of severely overweight boys who struggled with band camp's physical demands. He walked beside them as they marched, told them that he knew they had it in them, that it would get easier, and let the boys decide how broadly to define "it." Golden was a fine musician in his own right, a trombone player, but he was beloved by the kids because of his heart.

Peterson was freckled, funny, patient, easygoing. He wore a straw hat and sunglasses when he worked, hugged his students, and quoted from kids' movies he'd watched with his three-year-old son. During the woodwind warm-ups that week, he found apropos lines from *Finding Nemo*—"Shark bait, hoo-ha-ha," "Watch out for the ring of fire!" and "He's just a *boy*!" the last word shouted at a high pitch. His wit could be sharp. But he delivered it with such charm that his victims hardly felt the slice. Working that week with Cameron Bradley and another senior on their saxophone duet for the State Fair show, he said, "You're playing it like it's #27 in *Accent on Achievement*," referring to a lesson in the beginning instruction book used by the sixth graders. Like Max, he'd developed crow's-feet from smiling into the sun. He held his musicians to a less exacting standard than Scott Spradling did his, but his section was cohesive and happy playing for him. He seemed fully vested in the success of the marching band—unless you watched him teaching the top jazz band later in the year and saw how passionate he could truly be. Jazz brought him fully alive. The energy he brought to *that* teaching was off the charts, and the results carried over to his jazz students who marched in the band.

Spradling was intense, demanding, sardonic. He leavened his hard-driving approach to teaching with colorful images and sophomoric humor that played well in the younger grades and was tolerated by the older students. (When he heard one of his trumpets playing flat, he quipped, to groans, "Why B-flat when you can be sharp?" Every student who'd ever played under him knew that whenever they played Beethoven, they also had to endure Spradling's joke, "You know Beethoven composed this piece of music, right? He's not composing anymore. He's de-composing.") He led the band in stretching exercises to a dumb camp song by the name of "Baby Shark," in which a swimmer progressively lost body parts to a shark attack and went to heaven, accompanied by the motions of playing a harp—or maybe not, to fingers held like devil's horns. He masked his intensity less than Steve Peterson did and was the most likely of Max's assistants to call out students by name when they made mistakes and the most willing to tease and needle them. As a result, students complained more about Spradling than any other director, but they respected the quality of work he got from them. Year in and year out, the high brass was the strongest and most polished of Concord's instrument sections. Trumpet solos, trios, and fanfares were a staple of Concord marching-band shows for a reason.

Alongside "Gabriel's Oboe," Spradling focused his section's attention that week on "Lucretia MacEvil," a rock-and-roll tune they'd play only at State Fair. "Lucretia MacEvil" had been a Top 40 hit for Blood, Sweat & Tears during a time when a niche existed for rock bands with big-brass sections. "Lucretia" was a classic example of what Spradling called the "higher, faster, louder" school of trumpet playing. The song was meant to be played loud, going to louder; its rapid pace and off-beat staccatos and accents supplied its musical interest; and the first and second trumpet parts eventually reached above high C, the holy grail of young trumpet players.

Spradling told them, "You need to start looking at something other than the notes. Look at the accents, the staccato. The accents on the 'and'—as in one-*and*-two-and—are what make the song funky." He worked with them on articulation, their lack of it, especially in the younger students. For one particularly difficult passage, he had them sing the rhythm—*Do-di-di-dah!-dahhhh-dahhhh-dah!-dah!-dah!-dah!*— then finger the notes on their horns while they sang. Five times he had them play the passage. Five times he offered pointed, wise-cracking feedback: "If you were working at the drive-through, we couldn't understand anything you were saying." "Thanks for playing nice, friendly notes, just like all of you. Now play them how they're written." Finally he called out, "Horns down," and let them shake out their arms and give their lips and mouths a break. They were moving much more quickly than they had the week before.

He drilled the group on trouble spots in the last two measures of the song, where a series of sharp staccato notes walked up the scale all the way to the D above high C. From within the ranks, Grant heard the younger students miss and crack the high notes. Even though the composition was their "fun" song, for State Fair, the music was technical, difficult. Grant himself—the best trumpet player in the band—couldn't hit every note every time.

Grant wasn't someone who picked up a trumpet and effortlessly produced notes on it. Fellow senior Craig Searer had more ability; even sophomore Laurie Schalliol had more raw talent. But Grant had made the most of what he had. When he was younger, he'd wanted to be a "wah-wah boy," someone who could lay back and send out a stream of notes. (His sister had dated one, who'd gone on to play with the Cavaliers drum corps, which was like making it to the Olympics. Grant had been inspired.) He'd taken private lessons outside of school. He'd done endless exercises to strengthen his lip and mouth. In spite of the lessons and his diligence, though, he still wasn't able to blow his horn the way he'd once imagined doing. He controlled his air, not by breathing, but by "muscling" his horn, pushing it into his teeth. He knew he played with a heavy hand, that his technique would ultimately limit how well he could play, that it already had. He no longer practiced as much as he had in junior high. For a time, he'd even dropped the private lessons. He wasn't willing to take time away from his other interests for increasingly diminishing improvements. Music was one of the few places where talent, intelligence, and sustained effort hadn't led Grant as far as he wanted.

Still, he had fun playing the trumpet, and he had made it to the first chair in the first concert band and been given a solo part in the field show. (And Spradling, who'd been a "wah-wah boy" himself in high school and later in drum corps, thought that Grant was a better teacher because music and rhythm hadn't come easily to him.) Grant wouldn't stand in the top ranks of all the trumpet players who'd ever walked the halls at Concord, but he was the best that year, and he was proud of his lineage.

Grant's section of the band displayed a certain swagger, possibly as a reflection of Scott Spradling's competitive personality, or maybe it came with the higher, faster, and louder territory. The high brass was the only instrument section with its own cheer. All the trumpets, flügelhorns, and mellophones huddled together after every practice. Their cheer was nothing special, just "Go!" and "High brass!" repeated in an ever-faster, ever-louder call-and-response. In previous years, the section leader first spoke a few words in the huddle, but that year Grant had suggested that the honor rotate among all the seniors. In any case, some of the other trumpet players were constitutionally better suited to such displays. Craig Searer—tall, good-looking, his brown hair tipped with blond—looked the part. He was widely liked, and likable. Hard-working Jared Nymeyer sported an earring and moussed hair. Grant had gone to school with Craig and Jared since elementary school. They'd started band together, taken lessons from the same teacher, had jockeyed for concert-band chairs and solos. That spring, in jazz band, Mr. Peterson had started calling them the "three amigos." The silly name, perhaps inadvertently, acknowledged that the top three trumpets were likely to have three of the biggest egos in the high-brass section, maybe the entire band.

With ego came competition. Grant had felt the thrust and parry of the others' jealousy, mixed in with their camaraderie. He'd made it into the top jazz band from junior high and all the way to symphonic band as a freshman, ahead of both his classmates. He'd been given a small solo in the State Fair show as a sophomore. There were other re-minders of Grant's elevated position: best leader in the band by accla-mation their junior year; the only trumpet solo in their final marching season. Grant hoped the "three amigos" fun would cut across that groove, and that if the *dos amigos* were going to feel competitive with him, it'd be over who was the best leader. *That* kind of competition could only help the band.

Grant's faith required him to practice humility. And by nature, he preferred to blend in with the crowd. Yet his success in the band and everywhere else had informed his sense of himself as above the crowd. At least he'd managed to beat his ego into less obnoxious forms than most seventeen-year-olds with all the world before them.

By midweek during full camp, he was one of the few who climbed all the way to the top of Lucretia's steep stairs.

ON FRIDAY MORNING, drizzle slicked the pavement. An unsea-sonably cold wind swept down from Lake Michigan, thirty-some miles to the northwest. But long habit prevailed, so even though the day was chill and overcast, each instrumental section made its way to its pre-ferred cool spot. The high brass huddled under shade trees by the ju-nior high, which was a short walk across Minuteman Way, down a steep hill and across a narrow footbridge. The rain kept up through the work in their sections and then their work back on the practice field for marching fundamentals. The students splashed through puddles, soaking their jeans above the ankles, some all the way to the knees. Right before noon the rain tapered off and stopped. The air turned heavy, and the temperature on the high school's reader board jumped ten degrees. Right before lunch, Max brought his bedraggled band together on the junior high track.

Though the students had gone through at least parts of every song in their sections that week, Max had not yet worked on "Gabriel's Oboe" with the full band. On the last day of the forty-hour work week, he prepared them to play through the entire ballad. He stood at the top of a small grassy rise along the oval track, which elevated him above the group as he conducted. Trees on the other side of the track provided naturally good acoustics. All of this put him in his element. Anyone who didn't understand what Max Jones was all about simply needed to watch him work over the next thirty minutes.

They got no further than five beats into the song, the bass clarinets playing a low F, when Max cut them off. "Again," he said. Then, turning to Steve Peterson, below him on the hill, he asked, "Did the bass clarinets play?"

Peterson answered, "There was a mosquito in my ear, so I couldn't hear the basses that time." The bass clarinets got the message, but after three more too-soft attempts at the song's first notes, Max was still cutting them off.

On the fifth try, they made it all the way through. Amanda played the solo for the first time in front of the full band. Parents watching off to the side clapped when she finished. Max moved directly into a critique. "What I am not getting is enough of the low sound to balance against the soprano voices. If you talk about the pyramid of sound, the high instruments are up at the top, the low instruments are down at the bottom. It takes a lot of you at the bottom to balance that little peak at the top."

Bryan Golden shouted out, "Tubas, that's thirty to one!"

"Again," Max said.

The band played again, and again.

"If you listened to the recording, you'd never hear them tongue, even though they are. It's gotta be so legato. There's no slipping and sliding, but there's also no gaps."

"Again."

"That was definitely a half note followed by another half note."

"Again, please."

"I still do not get the volume it's gonna take to support all the rest of the band. You need to take it up. If you call that *forte*, you need to take it up to *fortissimo*. If you're calling that *mezzo forte*, take it up to *forte*."

After a few more tries, Max gave a sigh. "Look at your music, please," he said. He walked them through the ending, note by note. The last half of the piece was a series of crescendos building off long, sustained notes. Four measures from the end, short, powerful accented notes marked the final drive. Max said, "That should give you more ammunition to power it up. Every beat gets strong stronger stronger"—Max's voice increased in volume and forcefulness with each repetition of *stronger*—"until the *fortepiano* one measure before the end," bringing the volume back down before a final grand crescendo.

"Everyone, please," he said, raising his arms. "We're running out of time."

The difference in sound, in phrasing, in dynamics, from just a half hour earlier was astonishing. And it would pale in comparison to what they would sound like in October. It would need to. Max gave them one last criticism before he dismissed them to lunch. He said, almost to himself, "For the size of band you are, you're being very conservative in giving us your upper end."

As the long week drew to a close, Max was pleased with the positive signs he saw all around him. Some were small. Their playing that week proved the high score of the junior high band in their statewide contest hadn't been a fluke. He noted that once again, and only for the second time in his teaching career, every student who had signed up for marching band had attended mandatory camp. He liked how far the full band had moved in one week. But he knew it would take more than good indicators to repeat as state champions. He couldn't quite compare that year's full camp with the previous year's, because a change in the State Fair schedule had meant that he couldn't work first on the State Fair show and then turn to the field show. He'd needed to overlap work on both shows, which had led to confusion. Not all the teaching had gone well, but overall, it was a small bobble in a great week.

If Max's algebra had a weakness, it was that one of its key variables was beyond his control. Two hundred and forty-three kids could not be taught by seven adults and a dozen part-time summer staff. His system relied on, depended on, the older students leading and teaching. The variable had to be solved for anew every year.

Despite the limits Max put around the band's official practices, the older students knew that winning—and showing they wanted to win—required putting in extra time once school started. In fact, it was possible that Max's system asked the Concord students to work the same hours as the other intense programs from which Max liked to set himself apart. As he saw it, however, there was a crucial difference. He didn't demand the hours. He let the students choose them.

He left them to decide, as a group, what their goals would be and how hard they wanted to work. Each year he told them that they would determine how well they would do. Each year he could see that most didn't believe him, or in their collective ability. And then he tried to let them either surprise themselves or meet their own collective consequences.

EARLY SATURDAY MORNING, two buses carrying Concord seniors and band directors left the school for the shores of Lake Michigan. The air smelled like rain and the sky ran dull gray, not a day that shouted, *Go to the beach!* Nonetheless, Max was in a good mood. The number of students who stayed in the band all four years had been increasing in recent years. A good sign, in Max's view. He knew the reverse was happening in some of the hardcore programs, which he thought were burning out too many musicians, too young. All but three of the forty-five seniors in the band had signed up for the trip, more than the year before, enough that he'd needed to hire another bus. Another good sign.

Max had taken seniors on trips with him throughout his teaching career. He and his wife, Dianne, had traveled all over the country to watch other high school bands in the years before their son Gavin was born, often taking students along with them. Many summers, they'd driven to Wisconsin to watch his favorite bands practice, back when Bands of America had been a shoestring operation and its big contest was held in the summer. He'd traveled to watch drum corps as well, the all-brass, all-star, and, until recently, all-male bands that had for many years been a major source of innovation in the marching-band world. Their curvilinear drills and sophisticated choreography had pushed the boundaries of what spectacle could be achieved on a football field. Max was acknowledged as the first among his peers to borrow from the drum corps, surprising judges with the simple, now almost laughable, innovation of giving differently colored flags, a rainbow of colors, to the Winchester color guard. He had long since dropped the traditional "chicken-scratch" knee-high step in favor of a low-to-the-ground step that allowed his bands to break free of straight lines, to quicken their pace. It was now the accepted step, and called "corps style."

At Concord, he'd institutionalized the idea of a drum-corps trip for the entire senior class. In recent years the flow of new ideas from drum corps had slowed, but the drum-corps championships remained the ultimate model for marching bands. Seeing those shows was still a large part of the trip's appeal for him, and the kids. That year, he'd scheduled them for an afternoon practice of the Cavaliers, a corps based in suburban Chicago, and later that night, for the last competition before the world championships in Denver. The seniors would stay overnight in Chicago. Max knew that most of the seventeen- and eighteen-year-olds had not traveled widely, and that at least a few had never made the two-hour drive to the third-largest city in the country. He wanted them to experience its pulse and rhythm, too. It was part of the education.

First, though, they made a stop closer to home, at the Indiana Dunes National Lakeshore, a park that ran along the southern shore of Lake Michigan. To get to the water's edge, the group hiked a short trail across wetlands and through a small chunk of woods. The bogs they crossed held an unusual assortment of flowering and meat-eating plants, from arctic bearberry to prickly pear cactus. The park's botanical profusion was the result of the same glacial melting that had created the great lake itself, and was considered one of the country's best examples of biological diversity. But the main attraction for most people, and for the Concord group as well, was the park's sand dunes, which rose dramatically one and two hundred feet above the lake, changing with the winds, season to season, from year to year. Mt. Baldy, their destination, was a "live" dune—active, like a volcano, backing away from the beach at the rate of five feet a year, burying forests and wetlands as it went.

From the top of Mt. Baldy, Lake Michigan stretched below the students toward the horizon like the inland ocean early explorers believed it to be. Chicago lay fifty miles along the shore to their west. Closer, the tall stacks of Gary's decaying steel mills remained hidden from view by low, rolling hills. The gray hourglass of the coal-burning power plant in Michigan City dominated the shoreline to their north. Residents of a nearby town had filed lawsuits against the public utility that operated the power plant, alleging that high levels of boron, manganese, molybdenum, and arsenic had leached into their drinking water from more than a million tons of land-filled coal ash. The black ash, the same consistency as the dunes' windblown sand, had also been implicated in northern Indiana's high rates of asthma. The visitors from Elkhart could have recognized the shoreline as a vivid illustration of modern-day economic flora in addition to the story it told of Ice Age ecology.

The weather remained unsettled, and even though it was the middle of a Saturday morning, the seniors had the dunes to themselves. A few of them scouted around for the best jumping-off points. Others had already made their first exploratory leaps off the dune's steep sides. Max let them roam a few minutes before he called them together under a small grove of cottonwood trees at the top of the dune. As soon as they'd gathered in a circle, some sitting, some standing, he started talking. He'd joked during the previous week about the dunes being an "energy center," but he truly hoped that the conversation they were about to have would fuel the rest of the season. He said, "We're sitting among the roots of trees, beginning the roots of American music.

"This is the best opportunity you have as a class," he continued, getting right to business, "to get your thoughts together about the year. In my book you're a stronger class than last year's seniors. What happened last year . . ." He paused, because he wasn't entirely sure what had happened the year before, or the season before that. He had an intuition that the solemn-faced group circling him had a plan he wasn't entirely privy to—that underneath him and the other directors, they were directing something, as well. He picked up his thought. "What happened last year was, somehow that class enlisted you into leadership."

Over the years, Max had seen just about every approach teenagers could take to leadership. At Winchester, he'd seen one of his juniors—a young Scott Spradling—lead a mutiny that overthrew that year's seniors. He thought that Concord's Class of 2005 had had reason to mutiny, as well, during their sophomore season. Max had half-hoped they would. He felt the seniors that year had been lazy. Several students had been kicked out for hanky-panky under blankets in the back seat of one of the buses. The night before state finals, a senior and two freshmen were discovered with alcohol in their hotel room. The next morning, the band had marched its biggest show of the year with three holes. Concord had placed second nonetheless, but in the plaza afterward, Max had refused to lift the runner-up trophy sitting next to him. He'd told them later, "This was not a banner year. This was not a champion band."

But the Class of 2005, as sophomores, had not taken on the seniors in a battle for power. In Max's mind, the class had shown remarkable maturity in choosing to work with the weak group of seniors. The next year, Max saw them join forces, now as juniors, with seniors who were talented but inconsistent. He especially admired the way they'd channeled the energy of senior trumpet player Evan Jarvis, whose charisma rallied the entire band, but whose double standards and disregard for the band's rules set an equally powerful negative example. Together, the two classes had created a championship season. Max had been hearing about the Class of 2005 for years from Dianne, who had taught music to many of them in elementary school. But for him, the reputation of the class had started two years earlier and had only grown since then.

Max wrapped up his remarks: "When I'm talking about state, let me be clear. I'm not talking about trophies. I'm talking about 'How I grew as a championship person.' About you saying, 'When I graduate from high school at the end of the year, I'm ready to tackle anything in my life.'" He reminded them of the time and of the train they had to catch at one-thirty, and then stopped, ready for them to start.

Nick Stubbs spoke first. "This is my last year in band." He shook his head in disbelief. "My freshmen year was not the greatest. Sophomore year there were a lot of problems. Last year something came together. The band just cared for the first time. I'd like to care again. Not whether we win or lose. Well, OK. Being the last person to march off the field at the RCA Dome . . ." His voice trailed off and he shook his head again. Then he looked around the group and grinned. "I *would* like to do that again."

The senior drum major spoke next. Pat Doherty's father would be picking him up after the meeting on the dunes to drive him to an American Legion baseball tournament in southern Indiana that weekend. Pat, who was batting almost .500 that season, hoped baseball would be his ticket to a college scholarship; his father counted on it. Only a few of Pat's classmates knew how much pressure he'd come under from his coaches and teammates to skip the senior trip, or the trouble he'd gone to—and had asked his father to go to—so he could sit under the cottonwoods that morning. Instead he joked around a little, said he hoped they'd win again, and ended by saying, "I just want everyone to get along." On the edge of the group, Bryan Golden and Steve Peterson exchanged glances. Earlier, they had bet each other how long it would take the group to utter one of the standard senior phrases: I just want everyone to have fun; I just want everyone to get along, or be friends. Two kids in, and the wager was over. And sure enough, many of the comments that followed came down to one of those statements.

It took some time for forty-two seniors to tell their individual stories. Attention drifted. Cell phones rang, and were answered. Around noon, other visitors began spilling onto the dune and spreading out over the sand. Kids ran close to the group gathered in the grove, trailing kites and yelling. Max reminded the remaining seniors to speak up so everyone could hear.

Amanda Bechtel was brief. She felt sick to her stomach when she spoke in front of groups. "I've always looked ahead," she said. "Now, I'm thinking about what I'll be leaving behind." Looking back at her own history in the band, however, meant touching some sore spots. Those who thought of Amanda primarily as the band's best musician would have been surprised to know that she almost hadn't signed up for band to begin with, because the Wednesday evening practices conflicted with the youth group at Nappanee. Her father, the former band

director, had insisted. He'd told her, "Then make band your mission."
But he hadn't insisted that she play her flute, so her first year in the
band, Amanda instead tried out for the color guard. She loved dancing,
twirling a flag, even spinning a rifle. When auditions for concert band
came around, late in the fall, the mousy freshman seemed to come out
of nowhere ("nowhere" being where some of the musicians thought
the girls in the guard belonged), and earned the third seat in the symphonic band. Throughout the rest of that year and into the next, the
older girls in the section alternately snubbed and hazed Amanda. She
felt the cattiness even in her junior year, when the competition for first
chair went into the audition equivalent of double-overtime. She vowed
never to stoop to such behavior when her time came to lead.

And, two weeks into the 2004 season, she hadn't. She knew that
gossip and bickering continued in the section, but accepted it as the inevitable result of so many girls working closely together. (Only two
boys had breached the flute ramparts that year.) She stayed out of the
emotional dramas and kept her focus on the work in front of them.
The directors already treated her more like summer staff than as a student. She didn't consider herself a natural leader, but years of music
lessons had given her confidence that with practice, new, even scary,
skills would eventually feel like second nature. Still, she was glad when
her turn speaking in front of the group had passed.

While the others talked, Brent Lehman piled up sand under his
championship ring. When his turn came, he patted the ground around
the display. "Last year, the climax of the year wasn't state." He couldn't
bring himself to tell the others the shame he'd felt along with the pride
in winning. He knew he'd acted badly in the band, without really
knowing how not to. Despite the values of tolerance and nonviolence
in his Mennonite faith, he'd developed the habit of responding to frustration with anger. He'd come up in the band seeing the upperclassmen—
including an older brother he idolized—lead by intimidation. He had
only recently started noticing role models who did it differently.

Earlier that summer, while lifeguarding at a Mennonite church
camp in Michigan, he saw a pastor work with a difficult kid who
pushed back at everything Brent had asked him to do. The pastor
listened to the kid complain for a while and then, with a huge smile,
asked, *You want to pick up big rocks?* For the rest of the week, the
troublemaker and the pastor hoisted rocks onto ever-larger piles. At

the final gathering, the beaming kid picked up a huge rock, practically a boulder, to shouts and whistles. For Brent, watching that process had been a revelation. He realized how quickly he'd jumped to conclusions, how little he'd taken the boy himself into consideration. A framed picture of the kid cradling the huge rock now sat on top of his dresser at home.

But as a senior trying to do things differently, he had two things working against him. He had to overcome his history in the band. And he had to overcome the ways in which his isolation kept him from connecting to those around him. In the circle, he said only, with an extra pat on the ground for emphasis, "My climax for this year will be the chance to touch people's lives."

Grant's turn to speak came near the end of the long circle of seniors. He'd listened with his head down, also smoothing the sand in front of him, noting Max's reference to what they all called "the sophomore meeting." He knew it had become the creation myth of his leadership role in the band, the moment that the light came down from the heavens and anointed him.

He and tuba player Keith Yoder had called for sophomores to stay after practice one day right before the Concord Invitational, an important milestone every season. Keith had called the meeting to order. Nick had given a rim shot on his snare that had left everyone's ears ringing. Grant and Keith, together, laid out the issues: the lack of initiative on the part of the seniors, their double standard, their lack of interest in winning. Others jumped in with examples. Someone yelled, "Let's mutiny!" The call was met by cheers. Grant felt the energy of the group swirling, gaining force. He raised his voice over the noise of the crowd and talked about giving respect to the seniors, even if they hadn't earned it. Students who had been there would remember the phrase "Act as if they're the leaders we want them to be." Another phrase became attached to Grant and was passed down to new students coming up; in this retelling, Grant had asked, "What would Jesus do?"

Grant didn't remember putting it that way. If anyone had called out such a question, it would have been Keith. He noticed that people didn't even remember Keith being up there. He knew that the idea and its philosophical foundation had been something he and Keith had come to together. But Keith, who had transferred to a boarding academy for gifted students, wasn't in the circle that day on the dunes.

There in the circle, Grant stayed determinedly low-key. He talked about approaching Mr. Spradling and asking if it was OK that the high brass had more than one section leader. He urged everyone to stay connected to the freshmen. "We don't want them to shut down," he said. "They're moving so fast. We're all moving so fast."

As he talked, he began building shapes in the sand, oblongs connected to circles, an Easter Island primitive. He stopped, looked up and around the circle. In a lighter tone, he said, "Know what my favorite memory from last year is? Wednesday night practices, when we were working on 'Chiaroscuro,'" the 2003 show's hardest piece of music. Others murmured at the name. Grant seemed to change, as if banked embers had flickered, then flared into flame. He continued. "Doing everything twenty-five times, everybody so exhausted, remember? And we'd yell up to the tower, 'Please, Mr. Jones, may we have another?'" Grant didn't mention the role he'd played the previous year, as the shadow leader who'd softened Evan Jarvis's edges and let the other trumpet player claim the spotlight. All around the circle, people nodded and smiled, and seemed to gain energy from the memory, as well. "What crazed, insane enthusiasm we had!"

That's what he wanted again.

The other directors took their turns after the students. The drizzle that had dogged their practices all week began to fall, darkening the sand. People on the circle's outer edges moved in closer to get under the cover of the trees. Steve Peterson said, "Some of you were my first class in beginning band. I have the pictures in my office to prove it. I don't know how it happens, but you guys have grown up.

"Seniors, a lot of what we do is really similar. I don't relate to being a student as well as I used to, since I've been away five years now." Students laughed, generous with their youth and willing to grant one of their directors visiting privileges. "Part of your growing up, you really start to look at yourself less, in the name of serving others. That's a pretty special thing."

People stood up and stretched after the long round of sharing and trickled away in groups of two and three. They had an hour to get back to the buses. The next afternoon they'd board buses again and spend a blistering afternoon in Naperville watching the Cavaliers. The show that year was called "007," a takeoff on James Bond movies involving a briefcase, male dancers in tight-fitting tuxedo leotards, chase scenes, and an improbable escape by the hero. The Concord students would be able to tell it was a stupendous show; it would go on to win the drum-corps world championship a few days later. Brent Lehman and others watched and dreamed of possibly marching in the Cavaliers themselves someday. All of them couldn't help comparing what they saw with their show, their program, themselves. They checked watches, counted beats, did the math, realized that the tan, muscular, sweat-drenched college-age musicians on the field below them were basically running through their ten-minute show without stopping. A tempo of 220! When a voice from behind them called down to the young men on the field, "Turn to page 184," a buzz went up in the Concord group. The show wasn't close to over. How many pages of movement and chore-ography did those guys have to learn? Concord's complicated champi-onship show from the year before had required seventy-five drill pages.

They would gradually realize that what they were seeing in that sta-dium, from the accomplished athlete-musicians, was something like what Max Jones was asking of them. He'd been right: The freshmen couldn't possibly know it yet, but suddenly those veterans of the Con-cord band did know it. They ran the calculations again, this time for themselves. All but the first two minutes of their fall show would run at a tempo higher than anything they'd ever marched; they'd march the last two-plus minutes at a tempo of 200, just below what the Cavaliers were sweating through on the field below them. And they'd be asked to perform, to tell a story that went deeper than anything they'd ever tried before. The talk in the stands on Sunday afternoon would betray an anxiety in the seniors that none had admitted to Saturday morning be-neath the cottonwoods.

If the seniors had known what was in Max Jones's mind that same weekend, their anxiety would have turned to panic. He was preparing to leave Concord. He'd been asked to help run the Purdue University "All-American" marching band starting the following fall. Right now, only his wife and a few close friends outside the band knew. Some details remained. He needed to tell his staff what he was thinking—that this was his own golden opportunity, and potentially theirs. He was excited beyond words. He had no idea how much his decision would rock the family.

Now, though, in their final moments on the dunes, the sun came out, bringing warmth that would grow back into summer's heat. Seniors left the shelter of the cottonwood grove to jump out over the steep sides of the dune. Amanda Bechtel talked a couple of the girls into running with her off the lip to a sandy landing below; each time, she came up laughing. Grant and Brent and several other boys traded turns springboarding from one another's backs to gain more air. Brent, who knew how to dive from being on the swim team, landed a couple of flips. The fine, creamy sand sifted around their feet and streamed over their fingers as they clambered up on all fours, only to take another running leap out beyond the edge.

Behind them, Max and the other directors watched from the cottonwoods. The trees whose trunks the group leaned against were possibly as tall as fifty feet, even though they appeared to be only a few feet taller than the directors. Like icebergs, most of their height lay submerged. Any limbs that were buried had set out roots. If the wind carried enough sand inland that the roots were bared, they'd revert to being limbs and sprout leaves.

Brent and a couple of guys ran back to the cottonwood grove and captured Max, dragged him to the top of the dune, and tossed him down the other side. Digging around in the sand for his glasses, Max muttered, "I'm too old for this."

Grant, Amanda, and some of the others trudged back to the top of the shifting sand. The sun felt warm on their skin. The sparkling blue of Lake Michigan stretched to the horizon. A soft breeze came up off the water and ruffled the leaves of the cottonwood. The question of their senior year hung over them. Would their own roots hold them back, sustain them, grow in new directions?

One, then another, and another, laughing, whooping, they jumped.

3 ★ Middletown

The calendar turned to August. Life around Concord became suspended under a haze of brightness, and it seemed possible that summer might go on indefinitely. Neighborhoods re-tuned at the higher pitch of children squealing as they ran through sprinklers, the concentrated chatter of swimming pools, the snap and *sproing* of a diving board. Max moved band practices to the evenings, acknowledging the heat and the circadian rhythms of the teenagers in the band, whose bodies were primed by hormones to get up late and stay up later.

On the first Monday of the new schedule, while afternoon heat still baked the pavement, nine women gathered at the music department. Shadows hadn't yet lengthened enough to offer much relief from the sun, and the first hint of coolness wouldn't come until after sunset, if it came at all. Some of the women rolled clothing racks out the door of the storage room behind Laurie Schalliol's greeter's ledge, single file down the hallway. The others followed behind, carrying clipboards and sewing boxes neatly arranged with straight pins, safety pins, needles, thread, and extra buttons. The procession shared a family resemblance with fairy-tale illustrations of tailors and seamstresses preparing to fit royalty.

The mothers expertly maneuvered the racks into a small, stiflingly hot concrete-block room. For the rest of the week, the little room would serve as the band's fitting area, filled with one suit of clothes, the Concord Marching Minuteman Band uniform, repeated nearly 250 times. Over five days, the mothers would try to match every student in the band with a uniform that fit. The little room, which already possessed the dimensions of a steam bath, quickly started functioning like one as well. By the time the first student arrived—Amanda Bechtel, punctual as usual—the room was full of red, sweaty, still-smiling faces.

Even in the heat, the moms knew that this was their easy day. For the most part, they were fitting seniors. Every match they made reduced their chances of making subsequent matches, which was why the fittings were structured strictly by seniority. No matter how hard the moms tried, some freshman always got stuck with a mummy-wrap cummerbund, or pants that needed a six-inch hem, or a jacket with sleeves too short.

When Amanda didn't remember the number of her uniform from the previous year, one mom found it on a clipboard and called it over to another, who pulled two hangers from the racks and carried them to Amanda. On one hanger hung a dark green jacket made from a material that looked like wool but was actually heavy-duty polyester. The weave and weight of the fabric marked the jacket as decades old, as well as old-fashioned. Six double lines of thin gold braid rose up its front. Small loops of the same braid decorated either side of its high collar, and shiny gold buttons studded the front. The braid and buttons together made the front of the uniform look almost like an instrument itself, a sort of fabric glockenspiel. Amanda's pants and a pleated cummerbund, both in the same thick material as the jacket, but cream-colored, were folded over the second hanger. The cummerbund had been stored "sweaty side up" after the previous year's championship, so it could dry completely. With younger students, one of the mothers would go over all the details of folding and hanging the different parts of the uniform. But with the seniors, and especially with a student as responsible as Amanda, there was no need. She shrugged the jacket on over her T-shirt and tugged the pants up over her shorts. The overall effect was military, classic, just what anyone who'd ever watched *The Music Man* would expect a band uniform to look like.

She turned around in place while two moms studied her critically. One tugged at the front of the uniform. "It pulls a bit here," she said, showing Amanda where the fabric tightened slightly across her chest. "It's looser here," Amanda said, grinning, hitching up her jacket to show them the space between the pants and her waist. But the decision was quickly made: The set would do just fine for another season. "I've now had the same uniform every year," Amanda announced with satisfaction. She'd worn the uniform only a few minutes, but her hairline glistened with sweat after she'd stripped back down to T-shirt and shorts and handed the hangers back to the attending mothers.

The moms were part of an elaborate volunteer network of parents who helped Max and the directors run the marching band. They rode buses as chaperones, drove the band's trucks and semi-trailers, loaded and unloaded instruments. They built props for the shows. Before competitions, moms helped pin up students' hair so it didn't show under their tall hats, and performed on-the-spot shaves for young men who hadn't heeded Max's dictum about being clean-shaven. A handful of them with nursing degrees oversaw the band's medicine chest, giving out pain relievers and cough medicine and, on long trips, prescription medication to kids who needed it. Parents took pictures and video and produced an impressive multimedia annual yearbook. They ran concession stands at football and basketball games to raise money for the band. They held a barbecue in the fall and a "pie-and-cry" banquet before graduation. All of which gave the band moms and dads an intimate view of teenagers' lives, lives often hidden from other adults. Max sometimes told other directors that he had more parent involvement than he knew what to do with, but he knew that the difference between a good band and a very good band, a champion band, included thousands of volunteer hours. And who would do that, if not parents?

Parents joined with different motivations. Some wanted to help the band win, others to relive a part of their own high school years. Some appreciated the opportunity to observe good teachers at work, or good music being made. But collectively, the more than three hundred mothers and fathers who had signed up that year to be band parents shared a willingness to spend long hours with a big group of teenagers, working mostly behind the scenes to support the student's goals. Part of what repaid the parents' labor was the chance to be in the orbit of their own children, to observe them among their friends and engrossed in their own work. But many were also drawn to the chance to be involved in the lives of other young men and women. At some level the parents understood that a crucial task of the community involved ceding center stage to its youth, in a necessary preparation for their entrance into adulthood. The parents' role was to remain in the wings, stepping in only when needed. In the Concord band, teenagers were given independence and support, both, and time in the spotlight.

Like the other moms, Candy Yoder had known several of the students even before they joined the band. She was the mother of Kim, a sophomore flute player, and Keith, who had run the legendary sophomore meeting with Grant. One of the students she'd known a long time was Cameron Bradley, who'd undergone a dramatic transformation over four years. In his freshman year, Cameron had stood five foot three and weighed 160 pounds. Now, in the uniform room, Yoder and the other moms watched as he pulled on the jacket he'd worn the previous season. They saw right away that it was too small. He'd grown at least another two inches, was probably a foot taller than he'd been four years earlier, and weighed less. The size 32 cummerbund he'd worn the previous year now wrapped too far around his waist. He no longer looked like a boy but like a tall, boyishly handsome young man. Candy Yoder could still picture him as a chubby kid who clowned around for attention.

She didn't need to know students, though, to reach out to them. Like the other band moms, she watched out for kids on the periphery, kids left out, or kids who were struggling. She sometimes discreetly slipped lunch money to students who had none. She didn't necessarily know if a student in the band was struggling at home or at school or if other troubles might be lurking in a teenager's life. But as with all the band moms, her maternal radar never stopped turning.

Mark Tack, the head of the band dads, felt a similar sense of duty. He looked for men who were involved with their own children and were willing to reach out to those of others. So many fathers wanted to be involved in the time-intensive process of building props that he could handpick the group. He told the dads, as his wife told the moms, that once they became band parents, every kid was their kid.

Brandon Schenk rushed in, red-faced and sweaty. Brandon noticed Jordan Parker, the new student from Nebraska whose parents had picked Concord because of the band program. "You're a Marching Minuteman now!" he exclaimed. He praised the new student to the band moms who were meeting Jordan for the first time: "You should see this character snap a horn. He's dangerous!" he prattled along. "It's so hot!" he announced to his audience, pulling a sweaty T-shirt away from his body. "Look at me! I'm *lactating*."

Most of the moms had experienced his exuberance before and had received his bear hugs or heard him call out, "Hello, darling!" as he breezed by. Brandon was gleeful that he could fit into the same pants from the year before. "I've been eating like a wild pig, but they still fit. Isn't that amazing?" The moms laughed, responding to his humor and ease. Brandon was picked on outside of band, parried bullying questions in the school hallways—but these things existed beyond the reach of the moms' radar. They fussed over him, finished fitting him, and hugged him back.

Teenagers who wouldn't listen to their own parents, or who might shrug off a mother's touch, were far more likely to take in what some other adult said, or receive their ministrations. Around the moms, kids fat or skinny or pimple-faced could forget, at least for a while, that they hated the way they looked or the way other kids looked at them. Within the band, adults held the teenagers up, paid close attention to them, touched them. It could feel like love.

WHILE THE UNIFORM moms tucked and fitted at the high school, other parents were making their own preparations for the upcoming marching season. Chris and Jeff Longenbaugh had decided to renovate their basement in advance of Grant's last year of high school. For the past two marching seasons, their house—specifically, their basement— had served as the band's unofficial gathering place after competitions. First it was Grant's friends who'd come over to snack on food that Chris prepared and to watch videos that Jeff took of their performances. Grant didn't explicitly invite anyone, but by the end of his junior marching season, Chris sometimes counted three dozen teenagers in her house at a time. Despite Grant's worries about the expense and burden, Chris and Jeff both encouraged him to widen the net as far as he wanted. Other parents started coming, too, bringing more food and staying on for their own gathering upstairs. The parties had felt like celebrations.

Thinking ahead to Grant's senior year, Chris took a hard look at the basement: The carpet was threadbare; the old sofa and recliner hadn't held up under the onslaught of so many teenagers; the space seemed too small and dingy for the joyful gatherings they anticipated. So they decided to renovate, starting with a new leather couch and chairs, including three recliners that Grant picked out.

Anne came home from Purdue, where she was working for the summer, to help pull up the old carpet and take down the drywall. Once they got going, they also tore out a dividing wall to open up the space even further. All of them took turns with sledgehammers and crowbars.

Talking to her elderly mother on the phone later, Chris admitted that her back still hadn't recovered from the physical labor. Her mother pressed her: Why make all that effort when Grant will be gone in a year and it'll be only you and Jeff in the house? But Chris loved how all four of them had worked together. She could still feel the surprise of breaking through what had seemed solid, how unexpectedly easy it had been to create a new space out of the old; she could still see the white haze that had stuck to their clothes and hair. She tried to answer her mother's question with her own: "And what are we going to be doing this time next year?" She and Jeff had one last year with a child at home, and they were determined to make the most of it. The memory of the work buoyed her, in spite of the ache in her middle-aged back.

The Longenbaughs understood the larger lessons of band, even though they were among the minority of Concord parents who hadn't been in band themselves. At a high school like Concord, where the music tradition went back more than forty years, the bloodlines in the band were especially strong. It was common for students to take up a parent's instrument. The newspaper ran an article about a boy on the drumline who was the third generation in his family to march in the Concord band. Dick Lehman, first-chair trombone in the same class at Elkhart High School as Chris Longenbaugh, had seen both of his sons learn his instrument.

The continuity colored and defined Concord. Through families such as the Longenbaughs and the Lehmans, you could trace the history of the place, its sense of identity, and how it conferred identity as well.

THERE IS NO town of Concord around Concord Community High School, and never has been. Concord has no town government, no police department, not even a post office. What it has is its schools.

In the 1960s, when the parents of Grant Longenbaugh, Brent Lehman, and many other Concord students were growing up in the area, Concord was known as a country school, drawing mostly from farms in the open, gently rolling countryside, plus a few trailer parks and small housing tracts scattered around the unincorporated township. Much of the land was worked by descendants of German-speaking Amish and Mennonites who'd arrived a century earlier from settlements in Ohio and Pennsylvania in search of cheap, fertile land. Maps still identified the area around the high school as "Dunlap," but Dunlap was little more than a whistle stop on the New York Central Railroad, midway between Elkhart, the manufacturing town immediately north of the school, and Goshen, the agricultural county seat, five miles south down the tracks.

The double railroad tracks angled between Elkhart and Goshen there, following the Elkhart River. In those days, the rumble of train wheels provided a steady accompaniment to transactions in the small cluster of businesses near the train stop, and loud, multitoned whistles interrupted conversations several blocks away. Highway 33, a state road that carried mostly local traffic, and not much of it, paralleled the train tracks. Farther north, the new interstate toll road between Ohio and Chicago gave Elkhart its own exit; two miles above that was the Michigan state line.

Most of the roads, though, were numbered county roads. Early surveyors had laid them over the landscape along the four points of the compass, even-numbered roads east and west, odd-numbered north and south. All of them ran straight, intersecting at right angles. Horse-drawn buggies traveled along the shoulders, carrying bearded men and bonneted women. The plain numbers suited their plain style.

You could say that Concord first became aware of itself as a community in 1963, when the district finished construction on a new high school big enough to hold a thousand students, almost twice the current number of graduates. A year after the new high school opened, the Concord district hired Jeff Longenbaugh's father as its principal.

The Longenbaughs moved to a house on County Road 26, about a mile south of the high school. Across the road, bulldozers were busy turning farmland into a new subdivision. Like the farm families before them, those moving in were drawn by cheap land and their own dreams, which apparently included a brand-new ranch house on an acre of lawn. By rural standards, the houses were close together. But the subdivisions themselves were widely scattered. There was no village green or main street where people met and talked. The new streets curved and turned in on themselves, and no sidewalks edged them.

Without the shared history and concerns of farming, without the social infrastructure of an established town, the new residents looked for a point of connection and identity, and it started with the new high school.

Realtors started advertising homes in "the Concord school district." More curling roads and subdivisions started filling in the patchwork squares of cornfields and pasture. More students enrolled in the schools. People began saying they were from Concord, as if naming a town.

After three years at Concord, Jeff's father took the principal's job at Elkhart High School, a step up to a better job at a bigger school. The family moved across the township line into Elkhart proper, into a larger home in an older neighborhood.

Unlike Concord, Elkhart had a definable history as a town. It had been a river-barge stop, a railroad center, and bit player in the country's early automobile industry. Elkhart was located on a direct line between the factories of Detroit, Michigan, and the steel mills of Gary and Hammond, Indiana. Like those towns, it had made its mark in manufacturing, but its citizens held Elkhart above towns that traded in heavy industry and hard labor. What made Elkhart special was a combination of old-world craftsmanship and a skillful use of new manufacturing methods. What Elkhart made, and what had made Elkhart famous, was musical instruments. Band instruments.

Charles Gerard Conn, a brawler, businessman, and bandleader, had been making rubber stamps in Elkhart in 1875 when he experimented with adding rubber to his trumpet mouthpiece. An Elkhart native who had fought in the Civil War and seen for himself that the country was mad for brass bands, Conn moved quickly from producing mouthpieces to manufacturing brass instruments in brick buildings along the St. Joseph River.

Within a short time, Conn had built the first of several factories that turned out cornets and trumpets, trombones, mellophones and euphoniums, and eventually, under the direction of John Philip Sousa himself, the world's first sousaphones. Conn added woodwinds to the line, and brought in skilled European artisans to produce flutes and clarinets and the first American-made saxophones. Before long, several dozen instrument-related companies had set up shop in Elkhart, attracted by the current of energy and the supply of talent. The people who came to work in the factories were English, French, Italian, German. Musicians mentioned Elkhart, Indiana, along with Paris, France, and other European centers of craftsmanship.

Conn's high-grade American salesmanship soon made the Elkhart name synonymous with the most popular band instruments in the country. Conn paid Sousa to outfit his world-famous touring band with the company's instruments and spread their reputation; Sousa's most accomplished musicians tested instruments for Conn; Sousa routed his band's tours through Elkhart, where they performed for packed audiences in the town's opera house. In speeches and in print, the two men trumpeted the belief that bands brought people from all parts of society together and fostered community, a necessary condition for democracy. Together, they made "striking up the band" an act of American patriotism.

Conn broadly defined his role as a businessman and community leader. He supported labor rights, welcomed unions into the company's workshops, and instituted a profit-sharing plan. He started a newspaper, which he named *The Elkhart Truth*, and variously served Elkhart as mayor, state legislator, and U.S. congressman. He set a tone that would be followed by later captains of Elkhart industries, including the owners of Miles Laboratories, the makers of Alka-Seltzer. The band-instrument manufacturers, along with other town leaders, hired architects to build Italianate, Queen Anne, and classical revival edifices along Elkhart's Main Street. They encouraged the town's cultural aspirations, supporting a symphony and several grand theaters.

In 1915, Conn sold the instrument business to an even shrewder businessman. C. D. Greenleaf fought the company's unions, but improved the factories and kept the Conn name. By the time the United States entered the First World War, C. G. Conn Ltd. manufactured some ten thousand brass instruments and five thousand woodwinds every year, and Elkhart was known as the Band Instrument Capital of the World.

The market for musical instruments shifted after the Great War. Bands, which had been touted as a healthy, moralizing force for adults, increasingly dispensed their civic medicine in the schools. During the Depression, while factories elsewhere shut their doors, Elkhart's music manufacturers scrambled to keep pace with the orders for student instruments. The good times rolled through the postwar era.

When Jeff Longenbaugh and his family moved to Elkhart in 1967, Conn had recently produced its millionth instrument. The Longenbaughs settled into their new neighborhood not far from the St. Joseph River. Many of the music industry's corporate leaders had built homes of brick or stone along its banks; terraced lawns stepped down to the river. Jeff went to school with their sons and daughters, and grew up with a view of the world shaped by that almost-unique moment in the country's history: a time when a medium-size town could be a player on the national and international stage; a time when a town like Elkhart, Indiana, could seem to exist in a worldly context and yet remain a complete, almost closed world unto itself. You could grow up in Elkhart and feel, quite appropriately, that it held all one could ask for in life, without having to leave for New York or Boston or San Francisco, or even Chicago.

In many respects, Elkhart mirrored "Middletown," the name that two sociologists, Robert Lynd and Helen Merrell Lynd, coined for the central Indiana town of Muncie when they set out in the 1920s to study a town "as an anthropologist does a primitive tribe." Their report established the real-life Muncie as an example of "Middle America," a composite but useful illustration of the nation's typical, mainstream life. In studies over several decades, the manufacturing town was portrayed as a proud, self-sufficient, even self-satisfied place. In Middletown, as was true for Elkhart and hundreds of similar towns, a broad range of work provided incomes and opportunity. The studies described its citizens as hard-working and practical, patriotic and optimistic, but ambivalent about change. Residents of Middletown, researchers found, easily tried and accepted new material things (cars, washing machines), new pleasures (movies, television), and new jobs. But their beliefs about the truth of the Bible, the primacy of the family, the importance of fitting in, and the rightness of America changed very little over the same time.

An uneasy equipoise existed between Middletown and cosmopolitan America. Middletown, the Lynds learned, suspected big-city America of thinking it was backward and unsophisticated, but its residents prided themselves on their town's role as an essential contributor to the country's well-being and as a repository of America's heartland values. The people of Middletown believed in progress, but also in absolute truths. They generally assumed that everyone should believe in one great nation, under one great God. Except in their hopes for their children, for whom they wished even easier and happier lives than their own, the citizens of Middletown preferred that the bedrock of their world remain unchanged.

Such was the kind of town the Longenbaughs moved into when Floyd Longenbaugh took over as principal of Elkhart High School. The high school reflected the town's prosperity. At nearly four thousand students in three grades, it was one of the largest high schools in the state. Sophomores occupied their own buildings on a sprawling campus close to downtown. Elkhart was the state champion in football during Jeff's sophomore year, and runner-up in boys' basketball the following year. When the football or basketball team won a post-season game, the school canceled classes for the following Monday. Nearly ten thousand fans packed the North Side gym for home basketball games. Jeff, the student manager of the basketball team, sat on the bench with the players. Student cheer blocks, separated by gender, filled the stands under each basket. Jeff's girlfriend, Chris Lohman, a tall girl who lived a few houses down from him, sat in the girls' cheer block. She wore white gloves and a bib, blue in front, white in back, and blended in with the other girls to create letters and pictures.

Chris's father, an executive with General Telephone, moved the family from Westchester County, New York, to run the company's Midwest office around the same time that the Logenbaughs moved to Concord. Chris and Jeff, good students without being grinds, popular without being "popular," buffered by comfort and small-town privilege, floated in and out of several layers of social pecking order at the high school seemingly without concern.

But tensions intruded on their idyll. The day after Chris's senior prom, a group of white thugs, some of them Elkhart students, ambushed a group of black teens on the Indiana Dunes. The school instantly polarized. In the days that followed, groups of whites and blacks roamed the neighborhoods around the high school, looking for a fight. Riots closed down the high school for four days. The remaining weeks of her senior year, Chris didn't dare go to the bathroom at the high school; she avoided downtown, afraid to walk its streets.

Though few knew it at the time, the racial tensions foreshadowed larger social forces that would change Elkhart forever. By the mid-1960s, school-music programs had entered a long decline. Learning to play a trumpet or clarinet was no longer associated, in the minds of teachers or parents, with patriotism and civic duty; instead, it was increasingly lumped with drawing and drama in an expendable part of the curriculum called "the arts." That change, along with new musical tastes, siphoned away the fuel of Elkhart's chief economic engine. In 1969, a second-generation Greenleaf sold the Conn instrument business to a publishing company, which first moved production to cheaper parts of the country—Abilene, Texas; Nogales, Arizona—and other countries, and then sold off the pieces altogether. For three decades, no instruments would be manufactured under the Conn name in Elkhart.

Dick Lehman bought one of the last trombones made in Elkhart before the move. It was an 88H symphonic model with a rose-brass bell; engraved on the top of the bell were the words "Made by C. G. Conn Ltd., in Elkhart, Indiana." Dick, the son of a Fuller Brush salesman who was known around town as "the whistler" for his method of alerting potential customers to his presence, knew his parents had spent money they couldn't afford to buy him the instrument. But he loved to play, and he had a talent for it. He found his home in the Elkhart High School band.

And in church. Dick Lehman was a Mennonite. His roots in the area stretched back several generations on both sides of his family. Mennonites shared the same religious ancestry as the Amish, the same persecutions from the state churches of sixteenth-century Europe, and the same persecutions from those churches' reformers. Amish and Mennonites shared the same basic beliefs, as well, stressing a separation between church and state, "nonconformity" to the world, and following Jesus' example in a daily practice of faith. Some Mennonites looked and acted much like traditional Amish, who shunned electricity, telephones, automobiles, and many of the trappings of modern society. Others, including Dick's family, were indistinguishable from "the English" in what they wore and where they lived. Dick grew up learning the differences among the various orders, as they were called, some of whom allowed modern technology, with varying degrees of restriction, and even cars—as long as the bright chrome was painted a humble black—but sometimes had trouble keeping track of the schisms.

All of the orders shared what was called a "peace tradition." Mennonite and Amish children alike were taught the story of Dirk Willems, who in the sixteenth century was pursued across a frozen river by a

Dutch sheriff trying to arrest him because of his faith. When the sheriff broke through the ice, Willems turned back to save his pursuer's life, was captured for his trouble, and burned at the stake. The story gave a gruesome but unforgettable twist to the biblical injunction to love thy neighbor: Bring no harm to others, even if it kills you.

During the Vietnam War, that pacifism translated into a refusal to bear arms. Dick spent his last years at high school worried about the draft. He couldn't be assured that the local draft board would grant him conscientious objector status. Classmates taunted him, telling him that "C.O." meant "chicken-out." From within the Mennonite community, he heard warnings about the kinds of questions the draft board would likely ask: A robber has a knife to your mother's throat. There's a gun in a drawer. Would you use it? Dick thought that was a dumb question: He was a Mennonite. He wouldn't have a gun in a drawer.

There was another shared belief among the orders: the responsibility to the greater community, which was a matter of survival among the farm families and among all Mennonites a matter of faith and social conscience. Dick grew up feeling part of a large network of Mennonite families, spread across many states and countries, and expecting that service and mission work would be part of his life as an adult. His view of the world, compared with that of most of his contemporaries at Elkhart High School, was local and global. His sense of community—of identity—didn't depend on town centers or village greens, or on sidewalks that connected neighbors.

AGAINST THE FOREBODING backdrop of the war and race riots and the collapsing music-instrument industry in Elkhart, a new era was beginning across the township line in Concord. In his first year as principal at Concord, Floyd Longenbaugh had hired a local boy fresh out of Indiana University to run the school's music program. Joe Beickman had a flair for fashion, cars, music, and promotion. Long before the concept became ubiquitous, he'd branded Concord, creating a niche that Concord uniquely filled. The "Giant Concord Marching Band," which marched as many as 350 students, appeared in the country's major parades—Rose Bowl, Macy's, Fiesta Bowl, Orange Bowl. Beickman used a showman's tricks to make his bands seem larger, truly "Giant." He spread out the lines of marchers so outside guides walked only inches from the curbs; he padded the ranks with honor guards, flag girls, pom-pom girls, twirlers of different types, even junior high students. Jolene Bontrager, who six years later would marry Dick Lehman, played French horn and marched at the Indianapolis Speedway in the spring of her eighth-grade year at Concord, tucked into the middle of a row so her squawks couldn't be heard.

The fault lines of race and class that existed in Elkhart were almost totally absent at Concord. The high school had continued to grow, adding more buildings as its population reached, and then exceeded, a thousand students. The district remained a place apart, not fully formed, but it was discovering a new identity. Residents who dared hope for football or basketball victories over Elkhart would be disappointed every year. But the Giant Concord Marching Band bowed to no one.

When Joe Beickman died of cancer in the first month of 1985, at not yet age forty, so many people wanted to attend his viewing that it was held in the new auditorium. The auditorium seated only a thousand, but 1,500 people filed past the band director's open casket as a trumpet trio played hymns from the upper balcony. That same day, the superintendent announced that henceforth the new performing arts center would bear Beickman's name.

Max Jones was just finishing his second year of teaching at Southport High School, outside of Indianapolis, where he'd been hired as a sort of music-program turnaround artist. The school of two thousand students seemed enormous after rural Winchester, where the enrollment had fallen to five hundred students by the time he left. Indianapolis's south side was booming then—the Dome had just been built—and Max relished the feel of a place that was busting out all over. Everything about his new life energized him: the bustle of the big school, the closeness and culture of the city, the pride he felt in his colleagues and the pleasure he took in their company, the challenge of teaching students so different from himself. Some of his best students were black kids who rode buses an hour each way from their neighborhoods north of the city center. He and Dianne now had Gavin, a toddler. They joked about being poor as church mice. They'd been unable to sell their house in Winchester, so they were church mice with two houses and a mortgage payment at 18 percent interest. They walked a lot, and their social life revolved around the music staff at Southport. Max often talked his colleagues into strolling over to a nearby White Castle for dinner. The church mouse in him appreciated its 40-cent hamburgers; in spite of the others' teasing, he even claimed to like the way they tasted. Max was so happy at Southport that he talked about staying for the rest of his career.

So when their former minister called and urged Max to apply for the opening at Concord, Max was hardly interested in the job. But one seemingly trivial thing intrigued him: Joe Beickman had been known for having absolutely the best office of any band director in the state. Max thought he wouldn't mind seeing that office if he had the chance. He wrote out one sentence on a piece of paper and mailed it off. He figured he and Dianne would drive up to Elkhart, he'd sit for a few moments in the famous office, they'd visit their friends, and then they'd return to Indianapolis.

Nearly a hundred applications from directors hoping to be the next Joe Beickman had arrived at the office of Concord's then-principal, George Dyer. Dyer understood the importance of the music program to the Concord community, and he took the search for the new director seriously. He didn't rely on applications alone. He called people around the state and asked who they would recommend for the job, whether that person might be interested or not. In this way, Dyer heard about directors who had created strong programs, or had won championships, or had worked miracles under various constraints. Among several names that came up repeatedly, one stood out: Max Jones. Invariably, Dyer's respondent would continue, ". . . but you'll never get Max Jones to move to Concord."

The more Dyer heard, the more sure he became that Max Jones was the director he wanted and Concord needed. Even though other well-known directors had already shown interest in the job, and even though he kept being told that Max would never come, Dyer told his wife that he was going to hire Max Jones as Concord's next director of music.

The night before the interview, Max had second thoughts about the next day's joyride. He knew he wasn't going to take a job at Concord. He called Concord's superintendent and apologized for his one-sentence application and the reason behind it. Coming up would be a waste of everyone's time. It's OK, the superintendent said. Come up anyway.

The office did not disappoint. It was the centerpiece of a suite of offices that looked to Max like they belonged in a big corporation. Joe Beickman's, in particular, looked every bit a CEO's space. It occupied a corner on the second floor, with big windows on two sides, and plenty of wall space left over for artwork and awards. A conference table and chairs fit comfortably across from a large desk. The space was nothing like Max's inside-hallway cubby at Southport, and was better than the office of any band director he knew in any high school or even in any university. Max wasn't sure he'd even seen an athletic director's office that substantial. He couldn't help imagining what it would be like to be treated even better than an athletic director.

What he'd thought would be a perfunctory interview with Dyer lasted five hours. When it was over, Max thought, *Boy, I sure would like to work for George Dyer.* Before heading home, Max and Dianne drove around the area, not quite sure where Elkhart ended and Concord started. They took in the river and the railroads, which they liked; and the deadness at the center of Elkhart and the isolated neighborhoods, which they didn't. During the long drive back to Indianapolis, they talked about moving to Concord.

Back in Southport, however, Max had misgivings, and when Dyer followed up, Max said he was staying put. The principal asked if he could call again. In one of their conversations, Max made Dyer a proposition he didn't think Concord could accept. He told Dyer, "I want to build the best overall music program in the state of Indiana." (He thought it redundant to say "the best in the country." As far as he was concerned, the best program in Indiana meant the best in the country.) Max figured that would put an end to his conversations with George Dyer, but he was wrong. Dyer said Max's lofty goal sounded perfect. The day before Southport won third place in the state concert-band competition, an achievement that would add to Max Jones's legend around the state, Max Jones sat in his tiny office with George Dyer and signed on as Concord's next music director.

Max and Dianne bought a house in a Concord cul-de-sac, grateful to have only one home and one mortgage, at a reasonable rate. Max moved into his new office on the first of June, less than six months after the emotional memorial service for Joe Beickman.

Though Max was careful not to compare his own achievements to Joe Beickman's, he quickly realized that he'd seriously underestimated the strength of the community's attachment to his predecessor. The Giant Concord Marching Band had given the local residents a national presence, however ephemeral, and an identity they did not want to lose. For several years, Max had to deal with students and parents who were mad at him simply because he wasn't Joe Beickman. He would grumble later, "When you die, you become a saint."

Many in the community feared that Max Jones would dismantle what Beickman had built over the previous twenty years, and that's exactly what he did. He got rid of the honor guard, the pom-pom girls, and the rifle twirlers. He made replacing the band's existing uniforms a condition of taking the job. The jackets were a bright Kelly green, with a big "C" sewn to their fronts. That look had worked fine for a parade band, but the Concord band was no longer a parade band. And it was no longer "Giant": Max's first year at Concord, the number of students in the marching band dropped to a modest 160; two years later, participation fell to 116.

Max discovered that his students had been taught to play music by rote, not by learning musical concepts and applying them. He made allowances for his predecessor's illness, but not for the staff who remained. When one of the assistants left, he hired someone who already knew his approach: Gay Fetters, a former student of his at Winchester, who had done her student teaching with Max in Indianapolis. He asked the district to allow private teachers to use practice rooms during the day, and then urged students to take lessons. In every way he could, he raised the musical bar.

One of the things Max wanted to keep, and part of his calculation in taking the job, was Concord's strong community support of its music program. But the intense involvement cut two ways. Parents filled his spacious new office to complain and to give him orders. The first year, parents told Max he was to buy new cymbals. *Like hell I'm going to buy new cymbals!* he thought. They took their disapproval to the principal, to the superintendent, and to the school board. When students swore at him in class, Max had the feeling they were expressing sentiments they'd heard at home.

George Dyer could help Max very little day to day. Hiring the new band director was one of the last things he'd done as principal before moving over to the superintendent's office. He confided in Max that he'd felt he had two options for filling the position. He could have brought in a sacrificial lamb and then hired a real replacement after the slaughter was over. Or he could hire someone strong enough to survive the transition. He had chosen the latter. In his new role, Dyer could oversee the funding, staffing, and support he'd promised to help fulfill Max's dream. Surviving the transition would be up to Max.

The battles of Max's first years as director branded him as an outsider in the minds of many in the town, even though Dianne became the music teacher for East Side Elementary School, where Gavin started in kindergarten, and even though Max played the organ at the church they attended. Max worked long hours, and the Joneses' lives revolved around the music department and its demanding cycle of competitions and performances. Max and Diane became good friends with George Dyer and his wife, Shirley, who became the music department secretary. But the intimidating director made few other friends inside the community.

As an outsider, Max was more able than others to recognize changes in his new community. Over time, the families seemed less well off, the parents' jobs less likely to be professional or part of a national company. At the same time, he sensed the community becoming more conservative, especially in its religion.

Max had grown up in churches around the state. He had never felt pressure from his minister father to adhere to a particular creed, or even to profess one. He'd come to see his father's acceptance of people as a measure both of his faith in God and of his faith in humanity. Increasingly, though, Max saw people around Concord drawing lines and putting themselves, and God, on the only right side of those lines. He disliked their need to know where others stood on matters that Max thought best kept between oneself and God. He didn't want to hear people proclaim that they'd been saved, or that they'd given their lives to Jesus. He was uncomfortable when band parents told him he was a fine Christian. When his own church elders told him they no longer needed him to play the organ at the main service, because the music would now be provided by a praise band, Max continued to attend the services. But the tuneless melodies and insipid lyrics offended his faith in music, and in time he started taking his church services on early-morning television, where he could appreciate the close-ups of the massive pipe organ at the Crystal Cathedral in Los Angeles.

He saw religion changing the school as well. In the mid-90s, Concord hired a principal who made no secret of his evangelical beliefs. Max saw how the students responded to the principal's insistence that their souls mattered more than their grades. But Max thought he saw a darker side. He noticed that the principal frequently hired the graduates of nearby Bible colleges. Grace and Bethel Colleges and Taylor and Indiana Wesleyan Universities advertised themselves as evangelical Christian schools and outlined their doctrinal positions and "lifestyle expectations" in their school materials. Bethel College required its faculty and staff to recommit in writing every year to a "covenant" that stated that the Old and New Testaments were "the very Word of God, verbally inspired in all parts and therefore wholly without error as originally given of God, altogether sufficient in themselves as our only infallible rule of faith and practice." Some of Concord's hires from those schools were fine teachers, just as some of the teachers from non-church-affiliated universities were not. Concord had never been what Max would have called intellectual; but now he detected among his colleagues a growing aversion to striving for excellence in things they considered "worldly." To Max, it seemed a way for people to cloak mediocrity in heavenly garb, and mediocrity of any type ran counter to his own beliefs.

But he kept those thoughts to himself. Doggedly, he worked on his dream of creating one of the best music departments in the country, and by any measure he had succeeded. Still, after nearly twenty years at Concord, Max knew some people still called him "the new band director." Despite his success, despite enlarging and deepening the reputation Joe Beickman's bands had brought to the community, Max Jones still felt like an outsider.

CHRIS AND JEFF Longenbaugh hadn't particularly planned to return to the place they'd been raised. They married after Chris graduated from Purdue; Jeff had just turned twenty-one. They stayed on at Purdue for Jeff's veterinary training, Chris supporting them as a speech pathologist. The young couple talked about leaving Indiana, exploring other parts of the country. Jeff had developed an interest in nature photography and was drawn to wilder places. But after Anne was born, being close to both sets of grandparents and their extended families took on new importance. In 1988, when Jeff was offered the chance to manage a new veterinary clinic in Goshen, they had no second thoughts about coming back home.

But they didn't move back to their old hometown. Elkhart was in decline, its stores closing and its businesses changing. Miles Laboratories had been purchased by Bayer, the German pharmaceutical company, and most of its corporate managers relocated. Elkhart's storied music industry existed only in withered form without the company that had nourished and defined it. Selmer, a flute manufacturer that had managed to stay in Elkhart even as its ownership passed from one conglomerate to another like a low-value playing card, continued to occupy some of the former Conn buildings; the main Conn plant, however, now belonged to Coachmen Industries, which used it to make recreational vehicles. Fine brick and terra cotta buildings still lined Main Street, but Main Street was dying.

The place to shop, now, was the Concord Mall. It drew shoppers from across northern Indiana and had touched off a chain reaction of development along both sides of Highway 33. Chris and Jeff found an affordable tri-level house in one of Concord's older subdivisions, unintentionally joining the white flight out of Elkhart that had begun when they were still students at Elkhart High School, and which had accelerated after the race riots that some delicately referred to as the "troubles." Many of the families had moved only a short distance, into the newly bulldozed neighborhoods to the south, and by the time Jeff and Chris moved in, the town-that-wasn't-a-town had sprouted ranch houses and split-levels in a maze of new developments with names like Wildwood, Pinecrest, River Manor, and Green Valley. In the time they'd been away, Concord had grown to resemble thousands of suburban communities across the country, in its homogenized similarities becoming a new sort of Middletown, a stand-in for Middle America.

The Longenbaughs saw their subdivision as a safe place to raise children. All of the fathers in the neighborhood worked hard, but their focus was on family, not career. None bragged about the hours he worked. Jeff's commute took less than fifteen minutes, its only irritation the chance crossing of one of the 125 trains that rumbled through Elkhart every day. Like Chris, most of the moms had worked—some, like Chris, in jobs they loved—but stopped when they had children. The neighborhood came ready-made with playmates for both Anne and Grant, and companionship for Chris. When Anne started first grade, twelve other children from the subdivision joined her at East Side, as well as Gavin Jones from a neighboring enclave.

Anne was their sunshine child, always in the middle of a group of friends. She put on concerts in their backyard, using broomsticks as microphones; she turned family reunions into casting calls and organized the many cousins into elaborate plays. They worried less about her happiness than Grant's. Grant was quiet, cried easily, liked being alone. He spent hours in the sandbox and with LEGOs, rattling the bins as he looked for some particular small piece. During the family reunions that so energized Anne, Grant would retreat to his bedroom. But he liked being at the edges of Anne's bright light.

Chris, whose degree in audiology included courses in early childhood literacy, realized that at age three, Grant was reading along with her as she read books to him. When he started kindergarten, Grant's language comprehension tested at a sixth-grade level.

Over time, Chris also realized that, just like other parents of "special needs" children, she had to fight to get Grant what he needed, to force even a good school system like Concord to think creatively enough to keep her son interested and engaged. She was aware of other parents dealing with similar issues at other Concord elementary schools: Lynn Bradley, whose son, Cameron, was at the top of his class at Oxbow; and Candy Yoder, whose son, Keith, was eating up teachers and spitting them out at West Side.

Jolene Lehman, meanwhile, was dealing with other issues of difference. When Brent and Scott, Brent's older brother by two years, came home wanting the same ninja or warrior toys as their friends, Jolene explained to them why she wouldn't buy toys that promoted violence. She knew that both of her boys felt the sting of being different from the other kids, and she knew the irony of feeling like outsiders in an area where their Mennonite roots ran so deep. She and Dick were part of the small progressive wing of the Mennonite church. They belonged to a congregation whose stance that sexual orientation was a non-issue for church membership had cost them their voting rights, for a time, in the church conference. Rather than living in Goshen, they had chosen to live in Concord, where Mennonites were almost as rare as liberals. But their world also extended in many directions. She and Dick had both gone to Goshen College, where Dick had studied for the ministry. He quit the seminary in his last semester, however, and became a potter whose work would be internationally recognized. They had frequent visitors—Mennonites, artists, friends made through Dick's work and the couple's travels—and Brent and Scott grew up more like artists' children than like other Concord children.

Brent and Scott also grew up accepting juxtapositions that would seem bizarre almost anywhere else: horses and buggies tied up to hitching posts outside the Wal-Mart; a large family of Old Order Mennonites sitting down to eat at a fast-food restaurant, divided by gender at separate tables; dark-suited, bearded men pedaling recumbent bicycles along the shoulders of a county road. Jolene would have preferred her kids to feel completely accepted by their peers. But she and Dick were determined to raise Brent and Scott with the values of their faith, and to feel comfortable with its principle of nonconformity, whether that difference was immediately obvious or more subtle. If their children didn't fit in, that was a price the Lehmans were willing to pay.

Chris, too, worried how Grant fit in, especially as he tried to find his way in the groups that inevitably developed during junior high. She wanted Grant to be happy and worried about his difference. She and Jeff both saw how extra expectations developed around Grant, and tried to help him bear the burden. They wanted the best for their son, and understood that in many ways he represented the best of Concord. But they worried what that meant in a place like Concord, if being the best made you different from everyone else.

As a high school student, Anne started going to Beulah Missionary Church, an evangelical church at the edge of town. Until then, the family had attended one of the Catholic churches in Elkhart, following Chris's upbringing. Grant had been an altar boy at St. Vincent's. But both children disliked the musty youth groups, and Jeff and Chris had become disenchanted with the church hierarchy. "Let's cut out the middleman, Mom!" Anne finally said to her mother. Grant followed his sister in exploring a version of Christianity that was so different from the rituals of Catholicism that it sometimes seemed another religion entirely. In seventh grade, he started going with Cameron to youth group at Beulah's sister church, in Nappanee.

Chris and Jeff were taken aback by the growing seriousness with which their children, and their children's friends, took religion. It wasn't that they didn't take their own religious faith seriously: Chris had taught both of her children to pray, and the family often prayed together before bedtime. But the way religious faith had permeated their children's lives was foreign to their own experiences. Chris and Jeff could think back to their years at Elkhart High School and recall the "Michigan lunches"—forays across the state line, only a few miles north of the high school, that took advantage of the twin circumstances of a drinking age of eighteen in Michigan and an open campus in Elkhart—and the thinly veiled drug use and cigarette smoking, and the winking acceptance by adults. Now their children were reading the Bible every day, attending Christian youth groups one or two nights a week, and praying before school with their friends. The new faith may have kept Anne out of some trouble, for which Jeff and Chris were grateful. But they'd noticed a change in Grant since he'd joined the many kids who went to Nappanee Missionary Church. They'd gone with him a few times, and the Sunday services had seemed harmless enough, if very different from what they were used to. But in recent months, the sermons had seemed to put Grant in a dark mood for the entire day, and take part of the week to recover from. Chris wondered whether the message Grant heard at Nappanee somehow amplified his own perfectionism. She and Jeff started to think of Nappanee as a Pied Piper, and worried about where the music was taking their son.

Chris and Jeff looked for every chance to make Grant's last year in high school fulfill the promise of his earlier years—and maybe help him lighten up and enjoy it along the way. That was partly why they'd torn into their basement, with Anne there, too, getting the place ready to party.

THE NIGHT BEFORE State Fair, the band ran through the show twice on the football field, under the lights. The grass was lush, full, green. Parents filled two sections of the wooden stands and spilled into a third. Max spoke briefly. It was a culmination and a kickoff.

Max's focus during the week heading into State Fair had been on teaching the band's newest students how to have fun, onstage, in front of an audience. Compared to what they'd soon be learning for the field show, the State Fair routines were little more than loose improv; the idea was that the students could concentrate on performing, and have fun doing it. The year before, students had flipped onto their backs like overturned beetles and kicked their feet in the air while they played.

That evening, in front of the parents, while the woodwinds played "Gabriel's Oboe," the brass sections "performed" their warm-up exercises, miming the motions to the "Shark Attack" song and "Head, shoulders, knees, and toes (knees and toes)," without the usual loudly shouted lyrics. The surreal combination, surprisingly, was quite watchable.

Max had cribbed a few touches from the Cavaliers' drum-corps show. At the end of "Gabriel's Oboe," the band members brushed one shoulder with the fingertips of the other hand, as if they were James Bonds dusting off their tuxes after having dispatched a few villains. For the end of "Lucretia," they borrowed a one-handed swipe across a hat brim that Max liked for its cockiness, to which he'd added a sound— *sploosh.* Then, just for the fun of it, he'd decided to precede the gesture with the words "mercy, mercy, mercy." "Get Southern," he'd commanded in his best Dixie drawl.

The Dixieland ensemble, led by Grant on trumpet, played a snippet from their field-show piece to give the rest of the band time to form itself into the State Fair finale: seven letters, spelling C-O-N-C-O-R-D. Creating words on the field had long been out of fashion in the band world. But Max had wanted to do it for years. Still, all the focus on performing, on fun, didn't lower his standards or his expectations.

After the parents left, the band returned to the parking lot for more work. The summer evening had stayed warm. Beetles and stinging gnats swarmed around the lights at the edges of the practice field. The night smelled of insect repellent and cut grass and carried the mournful dissonance of train whistles and the long clatter of wheels on the railroad tracks. An Amish buggy had driven by earlier, carrying a stern-faced couple dressed in black.

Max focused on just eight counts—the transition between "Gabriel's Oboe" and "Lucretia MacEvil." Their rendition of the Blood, Sweat & Tears song started with the shouted words, "Whatchu gonna do?" After a week of reminding them to cut loose, Max still didn't like their diction, their energy and, most especially, their self-consciousness. He told them to growl the words; he swung his hips between firmly planted feet and pumped his fist. When they laughed, he cut them off: "You're not letting yourself go. You're not conveying rock and roll. It's not fun." He emphasized the last word. *Fun.* The chatter below continued. He looked down from on high, seeing that many of the students below him were looking at one another instead of up at him, almost desperate in their attempts not to stick out from the herd.

Frustrated and irritated, he said: "I will say, last year's band, they could do it. We also had a vocalist who could really get the crowd going," referring to Evan Jarvis. In the silence that followed, you could almost hear a gauntlet hitting the ground.

THE PARENTS WHO sat in the stands that evening might have been thinking about more than a checkpoint on the road to state finals. Of course they wanted their children to perform well. State Fair was a performance, after all, in front of ten thousand people.

But they were aware of troubling signs, both on the field and off, that went beyond marching band and competing. The band moms who'd spent so many hours fitting uniforms saw that more students than ever before were obese, requiring uniforms in a size 50, or larger—sizes they hadn't even ordered eighteen years before. And the band moms were disheartened by what seemed a minor problem in the decreasing number of mothers who could hem a pair of pants or sew on a button. The band moms had seen hems held in place by masking tape or safety pins, or simply sent back untouched. They didn't like what those sad hems suggested about a parent's attention to detail: the details of basic living, the details of children's lives, details of time and energy that responsible maintenance required. On the first day of fittings, senior trumpet player Keith McCrorey had told the moms that he just couldn't ask his mother to hem his pants for him. You could almost see another mark being added to the "going to hell in a handbasket" side of the band mom ledger, until he asked to borrow a needle and thread to do the work himself. A murmur of approval had followed him out the door.

If Concord sometimes felt like an island of wholesome tradition amid changing times, it was an island reached by bridges. Divorce numbers, even among the churchgoing families, mirrored those for the rest of America. Teenage pregnancy had crept into the school—even, occasionally, into the band. The band moms in charge of the first-aid kit saw that more and more students were taking prescription medication, for attention-deficit disorder, hyperactivity, asthma, diabetes, depression. Elkhart and Goshen school districts had recently reported gang activity, and some parents worried it was only a matter of time before it spread to Concord. Local authorities were struggling to stamp out the methamphetamine labs blighting what remained of the region's agricultural roots.

And the economic future of the area, which Elkhart's music-instrument industry had once assured, by now seemed anything but certain. Selmer, the flute manufacturer, had landed in the portfolio of an investment firm and merged with Steinway, known for its pianos. In 2000, the new company brought the old pieces of the Conn business back together in Elkhart. For a fleeting moment, some imagined that signs at Elkhart's city boundaries would once again proclaim its place in the music world. But the world now included facilities in China and Korea that produced instruments using cheap labor and less refined—but steadily improving—processes. Two years after re-establishing production in Elkhart, Steinway sent production of saxophones overseas. On the first day of April in 2004, the remaining Conn-Selmer plants locked their doors on the last of their unions. In the Selmer plant, only 15 of 120 employees returned a month later when the plants reopened under new wage and work structures. In Elkhart as a whole, where thousands of workers had formed wood and metal into music-making instruments, only a few hundred remained.

Earlier that summer, a laid-off worker had written in a letter to *The Elkhart Truth* that he could see how paying overseas workers 45 cents an hour could entice owners. But he protested the timing and placement of a twenty-foot-tall abstract sculpture of a trumpet at a major intersection. "Who is Elkhart saluting?" he wrote. "Must be the out-of-state investors, certainly not the craftsmen who no longer have jobs. So if you think Elkhart is the band capital of the world, you are wrong. It is Beijing."

What American consumers now knew Elkhart for were the recreational vehicles produced by more than a dozen RV companies clustered in the area, along with their less splashy younger sibling, the manufactured home industry. These engines of Elkhart's new economy paid good money to their managers and owners, but their production did not require craftsman labor, and paid accordingly. Signs leading into Elkhart now proclaimed it the "Recreational Vehicle and Manufactured Home Capital of the World," but the old stability had gone.

The city was becoming a place of small, persistent crime as more of its neighborhoods teetered on the edge of urban decay. The biggest presence downtown, now, was a charity mission, proclaiming its message on the faded marquee of what had been a movie theater. The Elkhart mayor was best known regionally for his ongoing battle to hang the Ten Commandments on his office wall and for his scheme to build an Amish theme park called "American Countryside" on the city's outskirts.

There was some energy in the city: Notably, investor groups were trying to put together a riverfront park near downtown. But the leaders of Elkhart's new industries didn't demonstrate the same philanthropic and civic-minded priorities as their predecessors. And the people who lived in Concord didn't go to the Concord Mall. Instead, they drove to the shiny new malls twenty miles away in Mishawaka, which made Concord's look shabby by comparison.

By 2004, Concord may have seemed an incomplete suburb, but it had done a suburb's dark job of starving off the city of Elkhart. Still, it felt one significant change when the RV industry moved in: The new factories attracted Hispanic workers from the South and West, and enough of those immigrants had settled inside the boundaries of the Concord school district to change its lily-white composition, probably forever. The fit was surprisingly good for a community born of white flight. St. Vincent's had added a priest who spoke Spanish, and planned for another. Concord teachers appreciated the newcomers' focus on education. But they also noticed that some of the new parents struggled financially, and that few had gone to college and not many more to high school. Test scores in every Concord elementary school had already fallen.

The students in the band still thought of Concord as the preppy school, and described themselves as rich kids. But Concord looked well-to-do only in comparison with its nearest neighbor, and it looked a little less well-off every year.

If the job shift continued, Concord's new crop of high school seniors wouldn't be able to return home after college and find good jobs in the area. The parents who'd watched the band perform on the deep green of the varsity football field couldn't assume that their children's lives would be as easy as their lives had been.

The researchers and academics who continued to study "Middletown" had detected biases that may have miscolored the Lynds' earlier reports. The Lynds, firm believers in progress themselves, had assumed that becoming aware of larger social forces in the world would make the people of Middletown more comfortable with change, less afraid of difference. But the new research suggested another response. Those who felt their most deeply held values threatened often responded not with optimism or acceptance, but by retreating. They'd stay with other like-minded souls in like-minded institutions, holding tight to their belief in what had been true before and surely would be again. And let the rest of the country go to hell.

In Concord and all the other new Middletowns, parents worried not only about the future of their children, but also the future of their values.

Except when it came to Max Jones, the marching band, and the music program. The parents saw the lessons Max was teaching their children as going against the general drift of the country. There were the basic life instructions: take hats off indoors, hold the door for others, say *please* and *thank you,* pick up after yourselves. The Concord parents thought these courtesies were not well-taught elsewhere, and believed their children would gain certain advantages in the years to come over children whose manners hadn't been so carefully tended. There were the instructions about excellence and achievement: Give your best at all times; break down large tasks into individual components; build on past achievement; and, most of all, do the work, do it again, do it until it's perfect.

There were the instructions in leadership: Learn everyone's name; take care of one another, especially the ones having trouble; teach what you know; come early, stay late, and pick up the garbage.

And there were the subtler, more complex lessons involving what it means to feel joy, to feel pride, to care. If it didn't sound preachy or feel subversive, it was because all of Max's lessons were in service to one goal: performing the show of their lives.

That was what the band parents at Concord strove for. "The show" wasn't State Fair, or any of the field-show competitions, not even state finals at the RCA Dome. "The show of their lives" was literally that. The parents were helping Max put on one of the biggest, most spectacular, longest-running—and most challenging—shows on earth: raising children.

4 ★ Perfect

When Grant Longenbaugh started kindergarten at Concord's East Side Elementary School already reading chapter books, and soon was writing his own cliffhanger stories, that was just something he did, unremarkably, the same way he cried easily and walked pigeon-toed. Nick Stubbs drew elaborate weapons. Brent Lehman meticulously straightened the seams on his socks. They were simply themselves, and Grant was one of them.

They had the same teacher for second and third grade, an energetic young woman who had recently led the school's gifted and talented program. Mrs. Holland told them they were an incredible group—the best class she'd ever taught. All the kids believed her. Except by the end of those two years, some of Mrs. Holland's students believed something else as well: If it weren't for Grant, away in some remote, nearly adult aisle of the library while the rest of them clustered in the early readers section; Grant, the first kid in East Side history to answer every question correctly on the statewide third-grade assessment; if it weren't for Grant, they wouldn't be special. The feeling spread among those classmates, a belief they shared but rarely acknowledged, like a family secret, which in a way it was.

It was only a matter of time before the growing awareness of the differences between them led to internal rankings. In Little League, Grant was the catcher; big enough, but slow. Pat Doherty, a West Side boy they sometimes played against, was fast and light on his feet, but hated losing. From Oxbow, Cameron Bradley played timid at third base, better at second, and got angry when coaches insisted on having their way. The boys would remember these things about one another and file them away, and even joke about them years later in the band. No parent, no teacher or coach, not even the kids themselves could stop the judging and sorting.

And so something shifted in how Grant's classmates saw him. Maybe not every kid in the class, but enough. He was no longer one of them, but separate from them, above them. A saying developed, and stuck. Repeated enough times, in the right singsong tone, it could feel like a taunt: "Grant's perfect. Grant's perfect. Grant's perfect."

To the Longenbaughs, the teachers who followed Mrs. Holland were not all as skilled at challenging their son. (One teacher later confessed that her own son had asked her, "What are you going to do with the smartest kid in the school?") Grant's first great friend, Tommy, a boy across the side-yard fence with whom Grant had constructed LEGO kingdoms and who had, with Grant, forced the library to create a super-champion category in its summer reading contest, moved away. In fourth grade, feeling alone, the smartest kid in the school started coping.

He turned his facility with language into deflecting humor. Even better, he discovered a knack for physical comedy. He'd always had unusually elastic skin, and had long entertained his family by blowing air into his cheeks and lips. He worked out a repertoire of silly faces that he learned to deploy with the offhand skill of a balloon-man at a birthday party. Over time, he acquired a reputation for making people laugh. He thought he'd rather be called goofy than perfect.

School sometimes bored him now. Done early with his assignments, and looking for a way to pass the time, Grant started helping other kids with their work. He began quietly in elementary school and continued into junior high, even when subject teachers made classes more fun again. He cared how the other kids felt. He noticed the body language of anxiety and hopelessness, its hunched shoulders and darting or hooded expressions. Once he knew he could help, he felt he should. What he started out of impatience and frustration he continued out of duty, yet even his negative motives created a positive impression. The adults praised his selflessness and set him above his classmates once again, and so his specialness and separateness grew more tightly bound.

Like his father thirty years earlier, Grant hung out with athletes. He was in the popular crowd without precisely being of it. The status gave him cover for getting straight As and spending his Saturday mornings in private art lessons, drawing birds' nests and fruit. He cultivated a talent for blending in, even as he continued, quietly, to try to be the best at whatever he did.

In junior high, he noticed that every grade he'd ever received was an A and started working to maintain the run. He became conscientious about his homework, even when it seemed like make-work, and he took note of the other smart kids, especially Cameron Bradley and Keith Yoder. Cameron invited him to youth group at Nappanee, and Grant liked the energy he found there—the games, the music, the speakers, even the bright rooms they met in. But Grant also tried to fit into the junior high cliques. He'd moved on from the elementary-school friendships with kids like Brent Lehman and had found a place with the popular kids. He didn't want to blow it by joining the nerdy Christian group.

At the end of junior high, something shifted again. Achievement and its hierarchies would become harder to hide at the high school. Grant had a decision to make. How much was he willing to stick out? How different did he want to be? Without precisely calibrating, he nonetheless picked and chose. He would continue to strive for his best in his classes, but he would also maintain his place among the jocks, going out for baseball. And he would continue to mask both his effort and his successes.

Grant had watched his sister play saxophone in the high school's best jazz band, and he envisioned himself being a part of it. He auditioned as an eighth grader. Anne came back from her first year at Purdue to coach him in jazz techniques. He made it into Jazz I, the top jazz band, as an incoming freshman. So did Keith Yoder, on piano, the two of them along with several others creating an unusual concentration of incoming freshmen. Jared Nymeyer and Craig Searer, the other top trumpets in the class—the dos amigos—made the second jazz band, still a remarkable achievement for students who weren't even in high school yet. But the old jealousies flared again, and so did the taunt.

That same year, Grant painted a picture of Elkhart's music heritage. An ink rendering of his trumpet, representing all the band instruments manufactured in Elkhart, anchored the painting. In a blue-and-purple watercolor wash along its left edge, he brushed in the Concord jazz band—his sister playing saxophone, Gavin Jones on trumpet—and next to them, a restored ELCO Theatre marquee promoting the Elkhart Jazz Festival. He carefully copied the sheet music from "It Don't Mean a Thing (If It Ain't Got That Swing)" and "Anchors Aweigh" and marched three ranks of musicians wearing Concord's colors in from the bottom right—Grant and his class, about to join the tradition. It was the most complicated composition he had ever attempted, and it won him an award. Max Jones asked if Grant would let the music department hang the painting in the lobby of the performing arts center. Against the high school's broader canvas, though, Grant tried to become less visible day to day. An injury kept him from trying out for the baseball team. He purposely held back from class discussions and slouched in his chair. He kept a similar low profile in the hallways, in the lunchroom, in the school's gathering places.

The tension Grant felt between fitting in and excelling eased during his sophomore year, and it happened in the band. School had started, competitions had started, and Max, frustrated with the level of effort he saw, told his students they were failing him and themselves. One night, when the youth of America were at their computers sending instant messages and talking in chat rooms, Grant and Keith started an online conversation about what Keith termed "Mr. Jones's horrible little pep talks." They didn't disagree with the harsh assessment of the band: The seniors weren't leading; too many students weren't working hard and didn't seem to care how well the band did. But Grant and Keith did care. Not only that, as they talked online, they started to believe they had a solution to the band's problems.

The two sophomores had discovered a flaw in Max's system, in its emphasis on seniors as the band's leaders and freshmen as the band's learners. The hierarchy gave little or no direction to the other two classes. Yet their experience had already taught them that if the sophomores and juniors didn't follow the seniors' lead, the freshmen wouldn't follow, either. The seniors couldn't lead alone, and the freshmen couldn't follow alone.

Typing back and forth, late into the night, the two sophomores grew bold. They felt they were more dedicated, more motivated, and smarter than the seniors who were supposed to be leading them. "They" meant the sophomores; "they" meant Keith and Grant. Grant would never have spoken such an arrogant thought out loud, and he would have been annoyed if Keith had. But sharing it, they pushed onto new ground. They asked each other, What can we do?

Their faith underpinned their answer. Earlier that night, Keith had copied down several passages from 1 Corinthians in the Bible, Paul's first letter to the Christians and Corinth. All of the verses spoke directly to the question. One of the passages said, "I appeal to you, brothers, in the name of our Lord Jesus Christ, that all of you agree with one another so that there may be no divisions among you and that you may be perfectly united in mind and thought." Keith and Grant were perfectly united in how they could apply the spirit of the passages to the band.

They decided not to be divisive, not to fight the seniors. They arrived, instead, at the notion of leading from below: "Let's pretend they're leading us the way we want to be led and follow that." They e-mailed others, bringing them in. They borrowed language from the ministers at Nappanee for their private battle cry, "Be blameless," adding another of their own devising: "Take it hard." They would give no less than their very best at all times, be unflagging in both energy and effort.

At the sophomore meeting at the far edge of the practice field, Keith, who had a loud, grating voice that forced people to listen, called their classmates to order. Nick gave that rim shot. Grant and Keith hadn't mapped out exactly what they would say. As Grant listened to Keith speak and then spoke himself, he heard echoes of their exchanges, and the class responded.

For the rest of the season, Grant and Keith continued their "lead from below" campaign. Students in other classes noticed the energy coming from the sophomores and joined in. Some evenings Grant and Keith shared the keyboard at the computer in Grant's basement, typing out encouragement to an ever-widening group. The two teenagers had figured out how to motivate a large number of people, and in doing so, had learned how to change a community. It was the most exciting thing Grant had ever done, more interesting than making art, more exciting than getting straight As. Leading from below had the added advantage of letting Grant stay in the background, camouflaged. In fact, Grant's years of keeping himself reined in, going through his days at Concord partially obscured, had probably helped. Otherwise, his classmates might not have followed him so readily.

Later, as the legend of the sophomore meeting grew, Keith would be scrubbed out of most retellings. But for Grant, Keith being there was the best part: the two of them driving for excellence; sharing the leadership, the planning, the risk—and all of it on display. Even though they had markedly different personalities, the relationship had been a gift to both of them. Keith would later say that he'd been waiting for someone he could really talk to, and Grant had been the first to listen that deeply. In their silences, he said, the deep parts talked.

The band—turned around by the sophomores—was named state runner-up that year, and Grant gave in fully to being a geek. He remained friendly with the baseball and tennis players. But being popular simply stopped mattering. His parents gave him a truck for his sixteenth birthday. He slapped a Concord Band oval on a back window and drove it, increasingly, to Nappanee for Sunday morning services, Sunday evening youth groups, and during the summer months, Wednesday evening "Spirit and Truth" sessions for young adults, often picking up Keith or Cameron along the way.

Keith talked him into joining a couple of the school's academic teams, and Grant became a state champion for the second time later that year, with much less fanfare, when Concord's English academic team won the Indiana title. On the same day, he and Keith and a senior girl, Laura Koester, lost a tiebreaker and finished second in the Fine Arts contest.

After the school year ended, four of the academic team members—adding in Kate Housman, another senior girl who'd been on the math team with Keith and Laura—stopped studying together but continued talking. The friends did nerdy smart-kid stuff. They played chess. They listened to classical music. Grant and Keith taught themselves Elvish from *The Lord of the Rings* trilogy. Grant, suddenly, had found peers, plural. For the first time in his life, he could stretch his mind fully without having to worry about putting someone off.

He and Keith, along with Keith's sister and father, drove twenty-four hours straight to New Mexico, spent three days as cowhands at a ranch, and drove twenty-four hours straight back. The rest of the summer, the four friends practiced the roping skills Grant and Keith had learned, and "roping" one another and one another's cars became an inside joke and a signature. Past midnight one night, they tested the elasticity of Grant's mouth. The final count: seventy-two grapes, or thirty-eight marshmallows.

The friends hung out in the philosophy section of a new Barnes & Noble bookstore in Mishawaka. If someone asked what they read in that aisle, they'd answer: Kierkegaard. They did read a little Kierkegaard that summer (and Spinoza, Locke, and Kant), but "Kierkegaard" was more a metaphor for their real purpose. They were thinking about Life's Great Questions, and the roll of "Kierkegaard" off their tongues was like a metaphysical drumroll, calling their minds to attention.

For them, the Great Questions revolved around God. What was God? What relation should they have to God? How involved was God in human lives? They started from different places: Keith was staunchly evangelical and fundamentalist in his beliefs; Kate, raised Catholic, had become a vehement nonbeliever; Laura believed that God was whatever people wanted Him-Her-It to be. Grant, raised Catholic and drawn to Nappanee, listened more than he talked. But they all shared a desire to make sense of their lives in the largest possible context.

They wrestled briefly with the tangled question of God's existence. But even Kate, who called herself an atheist, found the idea that God might not exist too horrible to contemplate for long. Keith, whose belief in logic still fit neatly within his fundamentalism, used the Law of Non-Contradiction to satisfy them: If there is no God, then that is an absolute truth. But if there are absolutes, there must be a God. They tried to understand God's will. Do we need to do specific things? they wondered. Or is following God's will a more general prescription? Their conversations flowed around that central core without needing resolution, the process itself offering pleasure.

Keith and Kate dominated the discussions. Grant wasn't as invested in finding his way through logic, argument, and persuasion. He felt himself more attuned to the transcendentalists, searching for and wanting to find God in everything. The questions and the company energized him. He felt engaged, alive. He was allowed to be who he was, silly, quiet, subtle, even indirect. The other three were sensitive to his cues. When they were at Grant's house and he was ready for them to go, they didn't make him say so. They just knew, and left. There was something in their time together that felt like grace.

Grant's parents were less enthusiastic about how Grant was spending his time that spring. One school night, he called to say he wasn't going to make his ten o'clock curfew. He was talking with his friends in a parking lot, he told them, the four of them sitting in the back of his truck, and he wasn't ready to come home. Chris and Jeff eased the curfew, giving him an extra hour to come home. "I'm not doing that," he said, pleasantly but firmly, and hung up, leaving his parents openmouthed at their end of the line. Grant didn't tell his parents that he simply couldn't bear to leave. Even later, days after his return well after midnight and the inevitable rehash with his parents, he kept the details to himself: the softness of the night air, the forced pauses in their conversations when trains rattled by, the sweetness of the quiet after each train had passed, and the pleasure of starting to talk again. The tang of metal and oil mixed with the smell of green growing things and their own scents, and their voices formed a four-part harmony of belief and dreams and love and hope. Theirs was a confluence, rare in a lifetime, of like-minded spirits. As they came to phrase it, they were "taking part in eternity."

As their season together drew to a close, Kate decided she was a Christian, too, and Keith and Laura fell in love, although they weren't quite ready to admit it. The gang stayed together, but Keith often talked, now, with his head in Laura's lap, while she scratched or massaged it. Grant watched them with a sharp longing. The talk turned to love: love between a man and a woman, love between humans and God.

Band started, but Grant was the only one of the four who needed to make time for it. The two girls had graduated and were waiting to head off to their respective universities—University of Chicago for Laura, Brandeis for Kate. Even though Keith, like Grant, was only a junior, he was going away also, to an academy for high-achieving high school students run by Ball State University. Beginning in band camp, Grant, on his own now, used all the skills he'd learned from the year before. More confident as a leader, working from only one class below, he brought along two classes behind him. The four friends continued their late-night conversations, outside the band. But Kate and Keith left after State Fair, at the start of the new school year. Laura stayed on until mid-September, but eventually she left, too.

Before they parted ways, the four friends started a logbook, a shared journal of ideas and ruminations. Laura wrote the first entry and passed it to Keith, who gave it to Grant just before leaving for Ball State, who wrote an entry and sent it to Kate in Boston. They talked online together most nights, sometimes until two or three in the morning. All of them felt lonely, but Grant felt left behind. In October, when the journal came back around, he held on to it. It would be several months before he was ready to pass it on.

The crash came after the band had won the championship, after the banquet back at Concord in which Grant collected two awards, both times to loud, sustained applause. If there had been an award for the best leader in the band, Grant would have won that, too. After that, there were only classes that weren't challenging enough and people with whom he couldn't fully be himself. Grant slid into depression. By the time Mrs. Greene decided to tear apart her lesson plans for him, the smartest, highest-achieving student at Concord Community High School was taking Wellbutrin each day for anxiety and seeing a therapist. He faced the winter alone.

GRANT HAD TAKEN his faith seriously for several years by then. After his friends' departures, he yoked himself to it.

He continued attending youth group at Nappanee, but now he also made a point of coming to the third morning services on Sundays. He sat with Cameron in the front pews, along with several hundred teenagers. The boys sat on one side, girls on the other, self-segregating to concentrate more fully on their worship. During the praise music that started every service, Grant often caught Cameron marking time with his feet, a band member's Pavlovian response to the songs' simple one-two beat. Cameron complained about their repetitive lyrics and simple chord structures, too. (Amanda Bechtel said it felt like singing straight B-flat for fifteen minutes.) But Grant liked the songs for that same simplicity and steady beat. Songs such as "God of Wonders," which regularly scrolled down Nappanee's giant overhead screens, with its refrain "God of wonders beyond our galaxy / You are holy, holy," gave voice to Grant's own yearnings. He was intellectually curious, but he came to Nappanee to be pried open, lifted up, moved beyond himself.

In the first months after Keith, Laura, and Kate left, Grant drew new strength from the sermons. Pastor Dave Engbrecht, the man who had built Nappanee Missionary Church, was direct and charismatic. He didn't play the Holy Roller or sprinkle his sermons with erudite quotations or conduct one-sided theological debates. What he did, and did extremely well, was give a self-help topspin to Christianity. Several times a year, he took his congregation through directed study guides on "fulfilling God's calling."

Grant appreciated Pastor Dave's unapologetic way of asking the people in his congregation to commit time, money, and themselves to the practice of their faith. If his sermons ran light on intellect and heavy on motivational aphorisms, that didn't bother Grant. Sometimes he and Cameron made gentle fun of the guides inserted in the church bulletins, filling in the blanks ahead of time with answers designed to make the other snort out loud. But usually they listened to Pastor Dave's sermons, rapt, pencils poised above the sheets of paper for the correct answer. When it came, the *scritch-scritch* of their pencils joined with the hundreds around them, filling the cavernous sanctuary with an odd sound of devotion.

Pastor Dave challenged them on two fronts: Discipline yourself to serve God. Surrender control of your life to God. On the face of it, those were contradictory goals, but Grant understood them as part of a ceaseless striving toward God and perfect faith. Pastor Dave frequently asked his congregation to remember that Jesus had sacrificed his life for them, and that God the father had sacrificed his only son. Engbrecht asked the people in the pews what they were willing to sacrifice in order to gain eternal life. The task felt big enough to Grant to absorb all his energy, intelligence, and ambition. In its programs for teenagers and young adults, Nappanee promised that it would mold them into "a generation of champions" for Christ. Grant didn't particularly care for the phrase—it reminded him of the football players in the youth group who claimed that God had a direct hand in their wins—but he had no problem taking what he heard at church and putting it into direct action.

Grant was already used to practicing his faith at home, through prayer and other small actions. His mother had started a "thanks" book during her treatment for breast cancer. Six years later, Grant regularly added lines to the book on her bedside table. Now, however, he lengthened his checklist of devotions. He prayed before school and before every meal and at moments of decision. When he received a token of achievement—an A on a test, a teacher's compliment—he offered it up to God in thanks. He did the extra reading suggested in the study guides and in the youth groups. He read the Bible every day. He had several copies, but his favorite was an English Standard Version that his sister had given him for his sixteenth birthday. It was bound in green leather and just the right size to stick into a back pocket.

By the time he was reading about heaven and hell in Mrs. Greene's class, Grant's friendship with Cameron was deepening. He was still lonely sometimes, but he felt free from sin. He heard plenty about sin at Nappanee. He understood from Pastor Dave's sermons that every decision he made, every act, was an opportunity to fail and to fall away from God. He understood from the sermons and from his friends that Satan was as ever-present as God, always lurking, tempting. All of their souls were in peril every instant. But he didn't feel in peril. As he devoted himself more and more to his faith, he felt perfectly aligned with God's plan for him. He began hearing the voice in his head, *DA*, like thunder.

ON THE SUNDAY before band camp started, Grant, just back from college visits, drove alone to Nappanee. Except for the greeters stationed at the doors, and the boxes of Krispy Kreme doughnuts waiting on round tables, Nappanee's vast, air-conditioned lobby was empty by the time he arrived. The sugary scent of the doughnuts followed him into the crowded sanctuary. He slipped into the seat Cameron had saved for him down front. He could sense Leandra sitting with the other girls at the far end of the row, but resisted the temptation to catch her eye.

All summer, he'd anticipated the day that he and Leandra would be back in town together. He hadn't expected that he would feel so anxious. In the spring, he'd eagerly looked ahead to senior year, to applying to college, and to leading the band to another state title. The first couple of times he had taken Leandra to Oxbow Park, he'd felt that he was praying *right there*, he felt so full of love and close to God. But one night Cameron came over to spend the night and helped Grant strip wallpaper down in the basement. As they often did, they talked about their prayer lives. Cameron had said to Grant, "What I hate is when you're hoping for a *Yes* and it's a *No.*" At that moment, Grant had realized that he wasn't prepared to hear a *No* from God about Leandra. But what if God said *No?* Those questions had lodged in him and grown, generating still more questions, until they were tangled into everything. Months later, he would remember that innocent statement of Cameron's and think of it as the moment his crisis began.

The added weight of the new marching season, now only a day away, exhausted him already. It hung over him like a promise he couldn't keep. Nothing seemed right. He had come to Nappanee that morning looking for a sign from God.

Pastor Dave paced back and forth in front of a pale wooden cross on the red-carpeted stage, his voice amplified by a headset. "God has a calling on your life," he told them. "God has expectations. He has gifted you, positioned you." As usual, Grant took the sermon as if it were directed personally to him. He'd heard these thoughts many times before, wrapped in different folksy stories and Bible verses. For much of the past year, he'd thrilled to the thought of rising to meet God's expectations. But when his minister ended the sermon with a series of pointed questions, it felt to Grant as if the big man in the neatly pressed khakis had collared him and looked right into his soul. "In order to fulfill our calling," Pastor Dave said, "we must place our will over our emotions. You have a choice. You come to a crossroads. What are you going to follow?" Pastor Dave spoke faster, letting some words run together, coming down harder on others. "If you're gonna fulfill your *calling* and you're gonna do that which *God* wants you to do, and if you're gonna leave a *destiny* and a *legacy* and a *heritage*, you *gotta go against your feelings.*"

He seemed to stare directly at Grant, who looked up, afraid not to. The pastor's words burned into him.

Grant drove home in turmoil, his mind churning through painful choices. The morning's sermon had given him his sign. He understood: He was being tested. If he wanted to do God's will, he had to give up Leandra. *He had to go against his feelings.* He tried on the idea. She was just a girl; they were only teenagers. Why should she—or his feelings for her, some of which he couldn't even acknowledge in their lack of purity, or their focus on her face, her hair, her skin, her body—stand in the way of his higher calling and God's chosen path for him?

He couldn't do it. He wanted to please God, but when he imagined himself telling Leandra he couldn't see her anymore, he felt his heart break.

But it broke again when he thought that by not giving her up, he was turning away from God. He turned the question again, and again. Every way he looked at it, the issues seemed starkly clear: *Either I love God with all my heart, or I don't. Either I'm willing to give everything to God, or I'm not.* He felt himself at a crossroads.

The approving voice in his head had disappeared. In its place came a different voice, rebuking him.

That night Grant had a nightmare vision of demons coming for him. He had to ask himself if the scenes were more signs—signs, perhaps, of how much his soul was in peril, or how far he'd already strayed from God. He got up from the waking dream and tried to sketch their shapes, to take away some of their power. But when he picked up a pencil, he felt a jolt of something he could only call evil. He managed to outline a couple of forms before his fear overwhelmed him. He started crying uncontrollably.

One morning during freshman band camp, his parents brought him to a psychiatrist, who added Zoloft to the Wellbutrin, and then upped the dosages when Grant's crying continued. He read in the little green Bible his sister had given him. He remembered a phrase and found it in Psalms: "My tears have been my food day and night, while men say to me continually, Where is your God?"

He read the next verse as well: "These things I remember, as I pour out my soul: how I went with the throng, and led them in procession to the house of God, with glad shouts of thanksgiving, a multitude keeping festival." They had shouted and jumped on the floor of the RCA Dome the previous fall, even Mr. Jones had, when they knew they had won. But that feeling of joy, the pride he'd felt about his role in the band: It all seemed to belong to another life, another person. He could remember his dream from the spring of leaving a legacy of leadership, but that, too, had been drained of meaning.

The Psalmist asked, "Why are you cast down, O my soul, and why are you in turmoil within me?" The new voice told him, *You are nothing.* He couldn't tell whether the voice he was hearing came from God or from Satan.

He kept going to Nappanee, but after every service, the struggle started up again. The sermons, or his guilt, ripped off whatever psychic bandage he'd managed to get in place during the previous week. He was desperate for relief from the constant questioning, the voice in his head telling him he needed to give up Leandra to prove his commitment to God.

At first he told no one, not even Keith or Cameron. He told Leandra he was struggling with what God wanted for him in their relationship. She accepted this. She was a Christian, too. But to her, God wasn't standing in the way. Grant asked her, "Am I freaking you out?"

"No," she answered reflexively, then answered again. "Sort of."

One night at Nappanee's "Spirit and Truth," a Bethel College intern at the church read from *The Ragamuffin Gospel*. He told the group of high school and college students that God's love for them was always at 100 percent. Grant started crying again, but this time in relief. Unsure, Leandra gave him a hug for the first time. Keith Yoder handed him a pencil and told him to stick it crosswise in his mouth. "It tricks your brain into thinking you're smiling," he told Grant. So there they stood, Grant crying, a pencil in his mouth.

He turned to Cameron for help, as well. Driving to youth group on another day, Grant told his friend, "I need another sign from God." "What would be a sign?" Cameron asked. Grant thought of Leandra's birthday, October 28, and said, "28s." They prayed, "Lord, show Grant 28s." The whole next block of mailboxes they passed contained 28s. At youth group, the Bible verse was Romans 8:28: "And we know that God works in all things for the good, for those who are called according to his purpose." Grant's spirits lifted slightly. He'd needed a small miracle, and it seemed to him that God had sent one.

Another reprieve came four days before State Fair, when Grant attended St. Thomas Catholic Church with his family. It was the last day of the annual Lohman family reunion: fifty-some people descending on Elkhart to see his mother's aging parents and one another. Grant and Anne were the youngest of the grandchildren, as their mother was the youngest of her family. (Chris saw Anne, about to graduate from Purdue, surrounded by children, laughing. Thinking of Anne as a mother, she thought, *Her time will be coming soon.*) Chris had grown up attending St. Thomas; she and Jeff had married there. But now they came only on such occasions as this one, the big family reunions. Chris's father liked having his whole brood there, and who was going to deny a ninety-year-old man that pleasure?

The choir sang one of Chris Longenbaugh's favorite hymns, "On Eagle's Wings." The song, a reworking of the 91st Psalm, had been written for funerals, but people had liked the uplifting tune and inspirational lyrics so much that it had become a standard year-round, in Protestant churches as well as Catholic masses. The song had buoyed Chris during cancer treatments and still carried that mixture of hope and mortality for all of them. The choir sang:

> You need not fear the terror of the night
> Nor the arrow that flies by day.
>
> And he will raise you up on eagle's wings,
> Bear you on the breath of dawn.

Grant rushed out of the church before the song ended. Anne followed after him and found him crying on the steps of the church. He tried to explain that he wasn't upset, though of course he was. Listening to the song had released him for a moment from his questions. The words, the music, the choir—all of it had reminded him of God's goodness. He had told his sister a little bit, here and there, about Leandra. Anne knew that his mind had been occupied with thoughts of Leandra all during the demolition in the basement. She knew he worried that he was letting God down. She put her arms around Grant. You can be as much in love with God as you ever were and still be in love with Leandra, she told him. Grant breathed out, relieved. But the voice returned, and kept after him.

Three days later, the day of the final State Fair practice, Grant and Leandra walked into the center of Oxbow Park, to a tree at the edge of the big meadow. They'd been coming to the park off and on to read *Middlemarch*, one of the books that their AP English teacher had assigned them for the summer. Miss Dorothea Brooke's marriage proposals and her quaint strivings for truth and meaning, along with all of *Middlemarch*, bored Grant profoundly. The description of the novel on the back of his book began, "The quintessential Victorian novel . . . ." The first time he and Leandra had sat under the tree to read the book, Grant said to her, nodding up at the tree, "The quintessential tree." It was a jibe at George Eliot's story of provincial England and her ponderous language. But the tree *was* quintessential. Its straight trunk widened at the base into rounded knobs that connected it solidly to the earth. Its branches started above their heads, sturdy limbs that would easily have supported their weight if they'd been able to reach them, and spread widely all around them.

The day before State Fair was a weekday, and the park was quiet, almost deserted. Leandra had been wondering how they were going to identify themselves once school started the following week. Were they boyfriend and girlfriend? She hated the terms. They seemed so, well, high school. And she didn't at all like the connotation that came with them, the expectation below the surface that either you were having some form of sex or you were resisting having some form of sex. Leandra was clear that she would not even kiss someone she was not serious about. Why would she want to do that? She turned the questions of their relationship over in her mind, but she wasn't quite ready to ask it out loud.

Grant wanted simply to be with Leandra.

They agreed to read at least one chapter before they talked or got up and walked around. They stretched out on the freshly mown meadow. They read for a while on their bellies, blades of grass tickling their cheeks. But then, their hands touched and clasped together for the first time. Grant could feel the smallness of Leandra's hand inside his own; he could sense how close his fingertips came to touching her wrist. After a while, he turned onto his back, and Leandra did, too, but their hands and the bed of grass held them in place. The tree threw its leafy shade over them like a blanket. They held hands for several hours, barely talking. For the first time in weeks, Grant felt peace settle inside him.

Later that evening, Grant went to band practice. They played the State Fair show twice in front of families on the football field. Grant's parents sat midway up the stands, close to the fifty-yard line. During the practice on the pavement after the previews for the parents, Grant high-stepped into position at the base of the N in C-O-N-C-O-R-D after his short solo. He looked like a drum major from the era of spelling words in halftime shows. Max commented from the tower, "When Grant goes back, he's quite entertaining. The rest of you are just running back to your spots. Try to be more entertaining, please."

Even that morning, Grant had been worried about the solo. He'd had bad experiences with solos in concert-band competitions, had bungled, he thought, a short State Fair solo his sophomore year. He thought he should be able to play it perfectly every time, the way Amanda Bechtel played her solo. But that evening, he thought of little else beyond the feel of Leandra's hand in his. The next day at the fairgrounds, his solo would seem to bubble up out of him. Both times, he played it jazzy, happy. Even when he heard the judges caution him on tape about playing the blues with too much bounce, he wouldn't care. He still heard himself holding hands with Leandra.

After band practice, Grant drove Leandra back to his house. He wanted to show her a poem by John Donne. He felt the need to explain away the title, "The Ecstasy," and assured her that certain words in it, like "pregnant" and "sex," led to unexpected destinations. "Our hands were firmly cemented," Donne wrote. "All the day the same our postures were / And we said nothing all the day." Leandra wasn't quite sure how the poetry, or even their hand-holding, translated to high school. It took her several more days to talk to Grant. They decided that if people asked, they'd say they were boyfriend and girlfriend, even though the terms seemed far too slight to bear the weight of their true feelings.

Back in the spring, in Mrs. Greene's honors class, Grant had thrilled to Milton's idea of "angel sex"—a connection of soul to soul that completely bypassed the body and its messy human imperfections. Now, unexpectedly, Grant was wondering if the human body and all its sensations might be more than an encumbrance and a vehicle for damnation. Maybe his human attachments—not just to Leandra, but also to Cameron and Keith and the band and the whole physical world, quintessential tree and all—could even be the alloy to his soul, as John Donne had said, strengthening it instead of weakening it. The voice in his head, for the moment, was quiet.

5 ★ State Fair

Adilene Corona stared out the bus window, barely registering the landscape sliding past. The caravan of eight buses rolled south toward Indianapolis on Highway 31, a straight if slow shot into the city. The group from Concord would spend four hours on the road that morning, covering nearly two hundred miles. No other band competing in the State Fair Band Day traveled as far as the Marching Minutemen, and no other band filled so many buses. Adilene's bus, the clarinet bus—in the Concord band, students were usually identified by the instruments they played—traveled in the fourth slot, in the middle of the Concord herd.

The ride down was quiet. Adilene napped, folding her pillow in half and pressing it against the window, a trick she'd learned during the long car trips between California and Indiana, before her family had finally settled in Concord. She'd gotten home past ten the night before, after putting her clarinet on the instrument trailer and paying the money she owed on the band shoes she'd wear the first time that day. She'd still had to pack for the twenty-hour trip—not just the items of clothing and costume she'd use in the performances, but also things a teenage girl might find useful over a day and a night. Into a small pack went a brush, extra elastics to tie back her hair, two pairs of earrings, candy bars and bags of chips, a change of clothes, the pillow with the Looney Tunes slipcase, her CD player, the current favorite from her collection of stuffed animals, and a twenty-dollar bill her mother had given her to spend at the fair. Even after she lay in bed, trying to sleep, she'd packed and unpacked in her mind, wondering what she might have forgotten. It had been easier to dwell on that than on the mistakes she'd made during the evening's run-throughs in front of her family and a thousand strangers.

Twice, she'd turned the wrong direction, a left face instead of a right face, or maybe the other way around. After her first error, nothing else had come easily. Each of the songs had seemed to last forever. Later, guessing that Adilene might be upset, one of the older girls tried to re-assure her. Don't worry, she said. State Fair doesn't really matter. Adilene didn't understand. Weren't they coming to Indianapolis to perform in front of people from all over the state? Wouldn't judges mark off for mistakes? How could she not worry?

Inside the city limits, Highway 31 turned into Meridian Street, a broad avenue that took the buses past some of the town's fanciest turn-of-the-century homes. Adilene noticed the houses as the bus slowed. She thought her father probably knew the names of the flowers that decorated their yards, and that she identified only as splashes of color.

The bus swung widely to pass through high wrought-iron gates and stopped, idling. Girls half-rose in their seats to get a better look at the fairgrounds, the energy and noise level inside the bus rising with them. Indianapolis had built these fairgrounds on farmland in the late nine-teenth century, when cows still grazed freely along Meridian Street. Now, neighborhoods completely enclosed the fairgrounds, turning them into a city attraction. One of the girls pointed to the Coliseum, a tiered brick building the color of a yellow cake, its abutments looking as if they'd been iced with buttercream frosting. Adilene could barely see the top of a Ferris wheel above the bus in front of them. It was al-most noon, but the midway, like the rest of the fair on its opening day, hadn't come fully alive yet. The bus bumped along slowly, and the wooden grandstand came into view, its cantilevered roof casting shade over the seats below. Someone slid down one of the bus windows. They could hear a band playing. Adilene heard applause over the music. She smelled hamburgers and fried dough and grease, and recognized the tang of manure and the mingling smells of animals. Dozens of buses had already parked in a grassy infield facing the grandstand. Band dads waved Adilene's bus into a space by the equipment trailers. Everywhere she looked, in a kaleidoscope of uniforms and costumes, she saw other band kids. Like her, she guessed, except she couldn't imagine that any of them were as scared as she was.

Adilene didn't want to be there that day. She hadn't even wanted to be in the Concord marching band.

It wasn't that she didn't like music. Back in California, in Watsonville, she'd taken music whenever it was offered: recorder in third grade, guitar lessons her mother had driven her an hour each way for, one month with loaned instruments in fifth grade. She'd tried the trumpet, liked it, practiced it in the living room in front of everyone. But the month up, the horn had gone back to the school. That same year, a sixth-grade girl slashed another girl's face with a knife, and once again, Adilene's mother, Camelia Corona, talked about moving.

Until then, Adilene's life had been grounded in the agricultural, heavily Hispanic communities of the Pajaro Valley, which were bounded by the Pacific Ocean on one side and California's coast range on the other. She'd been born in Santa Cruz, but had lived most of her life in Watsonville. Her cousins and four aunts and two uncles lived there—all her mother's siblings—and her mother's parents as well. Their landscape was dominated by endless strawberry fields, blueberry bushes, and long, green rows of lettuce, the stooped-back picking of which had brought Camelia's father to the United States in the fifties, and had eventually brought the bracero's daughter a green card. In the spring, pale pinks dotted the hillsides, stringing party lights through the orchards. For years, from April to October, Adilene's father, Juan Corona, drove a forklift for Driscoll's Strawberries, usually night shift, making good money. At least, it was good money if you didn't want to buy a house in one of the country's most expensive housing markets.

In Watsonville, Adilene and her parents and her little brother shared three bedrooms and one bathroom in a house with five other relatives. Adilene's family slept in one bedroom. Camelia's decision to leave was a complicated mixture involving the desire to live in her own home, anxiety about her children's safety, and her sense that better opportunities lay elsewhere. But for Adilene, life in the Pajaro Valley had felt warm and comfortable, spiced by regular trips to Mexico to visit her relatives in Guadalajara and Michoacán.

Sometimes Adilene blamed her mother for the loneliness she occasionally felt now. Her mother's ambitions had driven them out of that fertile valley. When Adilene was nine years old, Camelia Corona had started working toward a degree in early childhood development at Cabrillo College in Watsonville, and had become the first college graduate on either side of Adilene's family. Camelia's aspirations for herself and her children put her in tension with other members of her extended family, most particularly her father, whose own desire for a better life had brought them to the United States in the first place. Camelia wanted Adilene and her younger brother, Esau, to go to college, too. She frequently told Adilene, referring to college, "It's not an option," meaning, *It's not optional*. Once Camelia decided they should move, nothing could stand in her way—not their family ties, not the beautiful California coast, and certainly not Adilene.

They came to northern Indiana for the first time to visit a childhood friend of Adilene's father. Juan Corona and Asael Mujica had grown up together in Guadalajara and worked together in California. Mujica had left the Pacific for the Great Lakes several years earlier and sent word back that Concord was a good place to live and to raise children. The Coronas visited at the end of December vacation during Adilene's sixth-grade year. Camelia liked what she saw so much that she enrolled her children in Oxbow Elementary School on the second day of their visit. When she learned that less than a hundred thousand dollars could buy a house that would cost more than half a million in Watsonville, it was only a matter of time before they moved to Indiana themselves.

Adilene spent the next year bouncing between the coast and the heartland. She finished sixth grade at Oxbow, sharing one bedroom with her family in the Mujica house. Through Asael, her father found work at a greenhouse in town, but for less than half his previous hourly wage. Combined with the money Camelia brought in working in a day-care center, however, they could make an offer on a brick ranch house with three bedrooms and a generous backyard. The bank didn't require any money down. Their mortgage payment each month would be only two hundred dollars more than the amount they'd paid to share one bedroom in California. They closed on the house in June. It sat one block from the Goshen school district, but Camelia had made sure it was on the Concord side of the line.

After a final strawberry season in Watsonville, the family drove

Interstate 80 one last time out of California on a January morning, their red van packed with any possessions they hadn't already sent ahead. Camelia quickly found work in the Elkhart schools using her college degree and her fluency in two languages, and Juan returned to the greenhouse full-time at better pay. In the new house, for the first time in her life, Adilene slept in her own room. Her mother enrolled her at Concord Junior High, Adilene's fourth school in two years.

Adilene wanted to take band, and wanted to play a sleek, dark clarinet. Steve Peterson placed her in his beginning group, where nearly all the students were sixth graders who rode an early bus to the junior high for band before returning to their elementary schools for the start of their school days. The sixth graders, though younger than Adilene, had benefited from a summer of intensive instruction, plus half a year of daily classes. Adilene lacked that hothouse start. She hadn't learned to sing the first bars of "My Country 'Tis of Thee" as she twisted her clarinet's upper joint into its lower, or to murmur "Tip tip . . . tight snug" while she assembled her mouthpiece. Peterson watched her struggle with fingerings and reading notes, and recommended individual lessons to learn the basics. Adilene met with a young woman at the school once a week for lessons, and she practiced at home, but all of it came hard: new instrument, new town, new school, fewer kids who looked like her. Adilene stopped thinking about playing music and simply tried to mimic the students on either side of her. She became very quiet at school, even though she did well enough to enroll in Indiana's 21st Century Scholar program, which offered financial incentives for college on top of her mother's emotional ones. In band, she tried to be invisible.

But Adilene wasn't invisible. Steve Peterson noticed the way her eyes strayed to the students on either side of her instead of staying on her music. After having her in his band for five months, he also realized that he had no idea what her voice sounded like: He'd never heard her speak. At the end of the year, he didn't jump her ahead to eighth-grade band. He thought she needed another year of catching up. But starting behind, she fell further behind. The Coronas stopped the private lessons; the twelve dollars each week seemed too much on top of the house payments. Adilene started to think of band as something she did to kill time between her other classes.

Going into high school, Adilene wanted to drop band altogether.

She'd heard how hard marching was, how much more difficult the music was, and even how much more demanding the directors became. Mr. Spradling, who taught the brass players and led the eighth-grade band, was adored at the junior high for his sick humor, his headless Barbie collection, and the fact that he was married to beautiful Ms. Amador, the art teacher and one of the few Hispanic teachers in the school district. At the high school, so the word went, he turned into a hard-nosed drill sergeant. Adilene had seen how Mr. Peterson greeted his students with endearments like "sweetie" and "sunshine" and appended "because I love you" to his requests. She'd been on the receiving end of his sideways hugs. Would that change, too, once she was in high school?

But Camelia Corona—who had come to understand the power of music in the community—insisted that Adilene sign her commitment form and join the Concord Marching Minuteman Band. "It's not an option," she told Adilene, and Adilene understood that the matter was closed.

And so Adilene found herself at the center of the Concord community. During band camp, though, Adilene felt even more like an outsider, and even more lost. In one of the best music programs in the country, she didn't know how to play all the notes written on her sheet music. She thrust her foot out too tentatively when she turned, and was often confused about which foot went out for which turn. She marched flat-footed, without the upward-pointing toes that Max Jones insisted on, and especially, she marched out of time. Unfortunately for Adilene, she was easy to pick out. Too frequently, she heard Mr. Jones mispronounce her name from the tower. She and her family had already established a support network inside the area's Hispanic community, but they knew hardly any other families in the band.

Adilene had missed the first night of evening band practice. The red van hadn't started. They tried calling the one band family they knew, but no one answered. In the back seat, Adilene began to cry. Her father wouldn't get home with the other car until late. "Mr. Peterson will be so mad if I miss a practice," Adilene sobbed. She couldn't admit to her mother just how much she struggled in band, so she didn't also say, I'm already so far behind, and now I'll be even more so.

The next evening, still dealing with car problems, Camelia had dropped Adilene off at practice ten minutes late. Adilene rushed onto the practice field, scared that Mr. Peterson would be angry. Instead, Steve Peterson put an arm around her shoulder and walked off to the side with her. He stooped to bring his face close to hers and asked gently what had happened the night before. She tried to tell him about the van and the phone calls, but started crying instead. Maybe she cried because of how hard everything had been, or because Mr. Peterson hadn't yelled at her, or maybe because she wanted to belong in the band after all.

Now Adilene stood in a field filled with teenagers, every one of them in a marching band. If the energy level inside the clarinet bus had seemed high, it ratcheted even higher on the wide, grassy field, and spiked further every time a cheer erupted from the grandstand. Adilene could feel it in the air, the nervous sensation of something big about to happen, something happening already. And she was a part of it.

The bands, like opposing armies milling around before battle, girded by their instruments, were easily identified both in and out of their colorful uniforms. Muncie Southside, in red and black, warmed up next to Concord; girls in their color guard spun rifles 360 degrees a hundred times with their right hands, then a hundred more times with their left. Beneath their uniforms, the Southside band wore T-shirts emblazoned with the band's philosophy: *Competition is a by-product of productive work, not its goal. A successful man is motivated by the desire to achieve, not to beat others.* Adilene had seen the Jay County Patriot Band T-shirts in red, white, and blue, printed with The Pledge of Allegiance. The Jay County students had changed into military-style uniforms. They marched past her, now, staring straight ahead, on their way to the dirt track below the grandstand for their preliminary performance. Like most of the bands gathered in the infield, Jay County had been working all summer on their State Fair show. Band Day was the culmination of their marching season. Taking first place at State Fair was the prize they sought. Adilene could see the seriousness on their faces.

The students in the Concord band looked goofy in comparison. They wore black shorts and tie-dyed T-shirts in orange, red, and yellow. They weren't going to change into their official uniforms for their performance later that afternoon. They would accessorize, however. A few minutes before starting her warm-ups, Adilene put on a tall, clownish, oversize hat covered in green sequins. The Kelly green color gave it the feel of a leprechaun hat, but without the distinctive bowler shape. The hat sat low on her head, almost covering her eyes. She pulled the elastic strap under her chin. Next, she strapped a plastic watch around her small wrist. (Max delighted in calling them "designer watches." Maybe designer time was the only time they kept; Adilene's hadn't worked from the beginning.) She wasn't sure what to do with her plastic battery-operated fan. Max's idea had been to ostentatiously "cool off" while waiting on the track, in front of the serious bands sweltering in their heavy wool uniforms. The light T-shirts and comfortable shorts were normally another small Max Jones advantage in the heat of a typical August day. But that day was cool, and a bite sharpened the breeze. Adilene, who usually wore sweatpants even on the hottest days, felt chilled standing around and held her plastic fan awkwardly.

Students from other bands, as curious about Concord as Adilene was about them, watched from the periphery. The Concord band—by reputation and in appearance—occupied a unique position at State Fair. Its size dwarfed many of the other bands there, some of which totaled only 30 or 40 students to Concord's 240. The Monroe Central band marched a lone clarinet; Adilene's section contained 41 clarinet players, 8 of whom played bass clarinet. Most of the bands came from within a sixty-mile radius of Indianapolis, from midsize towns such as Muncie, Anderson, Richmond; and especially from small towns of several thousand, like Portland, the biggest community in Jay County. All of them looked toward State Fair as the crowning achievement of their year. Each fall, while they performed halftime shows at home-team football games, they could follow the march of the higher-caliber field-show contests in the *Indianapolis Star*, Concord's name prominent in many of the write-ups. In those same articles they could also read about the inter-suburban rivalries of the large, lavishly funded bands around Indianapolis—all of them conspicuously absent at State Fair. When Concord and its eight buses and assorted trucks and semis came down to State Fair, the defending state champion from the fancy field-show contests, it was understandable that some of the bands might feel that one of the rich kids had crashed the gravel-pit party.

And then on top of that to see the Concord kids dressed in silly getups and not even pretending to march proper drills—some were quick to think that Concord was making fun of State Fair and them.

Max had heard from his mother, who lived near Muncie, where the State Fair contest was broadcast live every year, that a radio announcer commonly accused Concord of "slumming" at State Fair, and claimed that Max Jones brought his band to Indianapolis only for the money. (There was prize money, plus transportation money based on distance traveled and number of buses. It rankled some of the smaller bands that Concord always left the fair with the biggest travel allowance.) Ten or fifteen years back, in fact, people had booed Concord when it came onto the track and again as it left.

The drum majors led them toward the grandstand, four across, in nearly sixty rows. From the middle of the rows, Adilene looked ahead into what seemed to be a sea of green hats. The Ferris wheel circled over the midway, to her right. On the roof of the main building, Adilene saw the sign INDIANA STATE FAIR, white letters bordered in red; below it, in italics, *Pepsi Coliseum*. Between the Coliseum and the grandstand, out of sight, other fairgoers traveled the main thoroughfare, checking out the Berkshire and Duroc barrows in the Swine Barn, sitting in on the "Bennie the Bean" Super Soybean Quiz Show, lining up for funnel cakes, fried corn on the cob, deep-fried Snickers bars.

The band turned left, and reached the track. The dirt felt soft underfoot. Adilene could see the grandstand now, right up ahead, in profile. The stands looked full to her, though they weren't nearly as full as they'd be for the night show. Southmont, one of the smaller bands, performed Celtic music in front of burlap-wrapped towers set in a circle to resemble Stonehenge. The hats bobbing in front of her blocked her view of the performance, but she could see the size of the crowd. Her fear rushed back, even stronger now.

Adilene heard the announcer's booming voice over the loudspeaker: "Thank you, Southmont. Stonehenge never looked so good." She heard Mr. Jones give the command to move up to the starting line. Still in the middle of a row, Adilene held her clarinet tightly in front of her. To her left, a shoulder-high concrete wall hemmed in the marchers. Now she understood why Mr. Jones had warned them that the eighty-foot-wide track would feel narrow, even constricted. She tried to glance to the left and to the right without turning her head and keep in step as the lines moved forward, like a twinkling green dragon in a Chinese New Year parade.

Senior Diana de la Reza had moved in beside her in the wider rank. Adilene's fear ebbed slightly in Diana's calming presence. All during summer band camp, Diana had been Adilene's guide, going over fundamentals with her, teaching her fingerings, calling out directions, sometimes even pushing or pulling her into position. The upperclassmen had a phrase for that kind of rough guidance: Diana had "shopping-carted" Adilene. But Adilene hadn't felt pushed around. She'd felt grateful for so much attention from a senior, and such a kind one at that.

She heard Mr. Jones say, "Band. Atten-hut." She called out, "One!" And before she could have another thought, she was in it. A right face. Step-turn-together. At least she put the right, or rather, her left foot out. They walked forward, filling the track in front of the grandstand. Then they were standing at attention, waiting for the drum majors to lift their hands and start the music. After a few counts, Amanda's flute solo rose into the crowd. Behind the rolling drumcart where Amanda stood, trombones silently mimed touching their heads, their shoulders, their knees, their toes, wiggling as they went. In front of the far side of the grandstand, flutes did the Australian crawl, were attacked by sharks, lost limbs, and died, also completely silently. The slapstick brought some laughter from the crowd. Anyone who'd ever seen Concord there knew to expect something crazy. Adilene knew she was supposed to know what to do on what counts, but instead, she watched and turned when the others did, just a little behind. She followed the long clarinet line in toward the center. The wind tugged at her hat, its elastic pulling against her chin.

Now it was time for her to join the music. She brought her mouthpiece to her lips and wet the reed. Just as she was to start, she closed her eyes and uttered a short prayer. When she opened them, she was already behind. She tried to point her shoulders forward and lift her eyes to the box. For the past few weeks, ever since she'd heard about the box, she'd thought of it as Mr. Jones on the tower. Now a huge wall of people towered many feet above her. She didn't know where the magical box might be in that crowd, but as she tried to catch up, she also tried to lift her bell up and play to it.

"The box," in this case, was the six judging stations, up high in the grandstand and cordoned off from the rest of the crowd. The judges— two each for music, visuals, and general effect categories—talked into small tape recorders, which they refilled for each performance from a box of pre-labeled tapes. They also wrote numbers and brief comments on scoring sheets. These were professional, certified judges, who spoke a specialized judging language, in which "clean" complimented a band's marching precision, and "GE" stood for "general effect" and referred to how well the show grabbed and held its audience. In their critiques, judges tended toward a universal first-person. As "Gabriel's Oboe" built toward its haunting finish, one of the music judges encouraged Concord on tape—"That's it! Come on! Let's bring it. Yeah! Nice control, big sound"—but expressed disappointment with the final crescendo. "We want to finish that out, guys. There's a big break in articulation right here. Finish our statement."

Though Adilene had been thinking about it all day, she still turned the wrong way at the end of the song. She didn't see Amanda Bechtel twist and jump down from the drumcart, or hear the crowd applaud the solo. Then she was into the swirl of "Lucretia MacEvil," trying to remember her moves: circling the platform where Cameron Bradley and another saxophone stood and squawked; stabbing her clarinet toward the ground like a spear; holding her clarinet with both hands above her head and jumping sideways. Trying to be crazy and fun. Things she needed to remember hurtled through her brain, some of them too fast to catch. Everyone in the band swarmed together at the end of "Lucretia" for one last long blast. "Mercy, mercy, mercy!" she yelled, as loud as she could, in her best Southern accent.

A fake drumroll signaled the Dixieland quartet to play one chorus of "When the Saints Go Marching In" while the rest of the band scattered. Adilene ran back down the track to her place next to Diana in the tail of the R in C-O-N-C-O-R-D. And then there was the real roll-off, and she was bringing her clarinet to her lips, playing "Anchors Aweigh," and marching—seriously now—down the track, leaving the grandstand behind. She crossed the last white line marked in the dirt just as she reached the song's final notes. She called out "Con-cord and down," and was swept laughing into the stampede as the kids in letters C-O-N-C, and O raced to get off the track, too, before their allotted six minutes ran out. She heard applause and the announcer's voice: "There's nothing like it, the quiet, unassuming Marching Minutemen of Concord High School. Always entertaining." She couldn't believe it was over so quickly.

MAX HAD WATCHED the performance from the track, behind the drum major platforms. He had stood still, the same green travel bag he carried to the top of the tower every practice slung over the top of the megaphone, observing. He'd seen many students out of step, lines that started off crooked, and though he'd been on the ground, not in the stands, he bet that at least a few of the letters in C-O-N-C-O-R-D would be unreadable—more like ΣΟΠΣΟΡΔ, perhaps. He'd been disappointed by the saxophone duet between Cameron Bradley and the other senior. He'd expected the two to do more than wail at each other. But overall, he was pleased. Even students who'd been out of time had tried hard to play and to communicate.

Max used State Fair as a secret weapon in his arsenal of educational tools. As a tool, it functioned quite simply: If Concord placed 18th or better in the prelims, his students won the chance to perform in front of big audiences twice in one day, without worrying how they placed. It was nearly perfect as a strategy: a state-championship contest without the pressure. The goal wasn't to win; it was to learn to *perform*.

Max's strategy worked best, however, only if Concord got to perform twice. Then his students could be nervous the first time out, realize that, and come back and go further, give much more, in the second performance. No matter how many times they ran through the show back at home, even on the varsity football field in front of parents and the community, they didn't learn as much about performing as they did at State Fair.

Like so much of Max's approach, this strategy required a wily form of efficiency. He lost time having his kids learn two shows in a season, when most of his fall-season competitors started earlier and worked more hours to begin with. Time was a precious, hoarded element in the Concord system. But Max gave up time early in the season for a bigger gain at the end. Concord's State Fair show was a hybrid, with its pop tunes and fun-house silliness, but also one piece that reappeared in the fall show. This allowed a sort of time-delayed response to State Fair to occur, especially among the freshmen. At first, the lessons from State Fair wouldn't seem to transfer. But by the end of the season, as if the one song in both shows was the contagion factor, they'd take what they'd learned, and move the show to a higher level. *That* was what made State Fair feel like a secret weapon.

Now it was up to the judges to decide whether Concord would perform again that evening.

Ten, fifteen years earlier, Max wouldn't have wondered. Of course Concord would make the finals. In those days, they often placed in the top ten, even with just a few weeks' preparation.

Concord was the only band in the state to routinely make the finals in both the State Fair and Indiana State School Music Association, or ISSMA, contests. Concord also held the second-longest record at State Fair for making it into the night show—every year since Max had started bringing his band down, nineteen years in a row. But all that history meant nothing to the judges bent over their scoring sheets. A recent change in the scoring had given marching and music equal weight; since then, Concord had just barely squeaked into the evening contest—the year before, by one-tenth of a point.

In 2004, Band Day at the Indiana State Fair was in its fifty-eighth year, making it arguably the longest-running high school marching band contest in the country. Arguably, because other contests made similar claims. The "Contest of Champions," held for forty-three years in Murfreesboro, Tennessee, called itself the longest-running high school band contest, as did contests in Texas and Ohio. The State Fair folks didn't make much of their contest's pedigree, and neither did most of the band directors who brought their bands to the fair, or the communities who came out in force to support those bands. It was accepted that the people of Indiana had been crazy about marching bands for a very long time, and Band Day at State Fair had been a showcase for as long as anyone could remember.

State Fair was a living history. Bands had played at the fair from its beginnings. The first high school band contest at the fair had been held in 1926, during the decade when thousands of schools nationwide added music to their curriculums. Students performed seated and were judged entirely on their musicianship. It wasn't until after the Second World War that fair organizers and fairgoers settled on the current winning combination. In 1947, twenty-five bands had marched on a harness-racing track past a grandstand. Even though the bands could only march forward, limiting their performances to the two or three minutes it took to pass by the grandstand, the contest quickly took off.

In the 1950s, band directors introduced college-band maneuvers into their performances. Odon-Madison Township made a right and then a left flank in front of the grandstand to earn first place. The following year, Noblesville marched backward to clinch a win. A standard format developed: Bands played and marched off the starting line, then set up in formation in front of the grandstand while baton twirlers, and later pom-pom girls, dancers, and flag and rifle twirlers, performed for the crowd. Other than the start and the finish, no lines were laid down on the track; the judging took into account how well the band members guided left to right and down diagonals. All the maneuvers worked in units of forty-five degrees.

The year before young Max Jones started high school in Princeton, a farming community in the rolling hills of southern Indiana, the Princeton Tiger band placed second at State Fair. Nearly a hundred bands competed in Band Day by then, drawn from every corner of the state, from the Mount Vernon Marching Wildcats in its southwest corner, where the Ohio River met the Wabash, to Hammond High School, one exit from Chicago and surrounded by steel mills and refineries that lit up the night sky. The annual Band Day capped the end of State Fair and the summer, coming right before Labor Day and the start of school.

State Fair, then, was a one-size-fits-all contest. As with "Hoosier hysteria," the state's fabled high school basketball tournament, any school of any size could attempt to win the undisputed state championship; although, just as in the basketball finals, the biggest schools nearly always wore the crowns at the end. Ben Davis, a four-thousand-student high school from Indianapolis, marched nearly three hundred students at State Fair all through the 1960s, and often battled for first place with a trio of powerhouse bands from Anderson, an Indiana city so closely identified with the automotive industry that it was nicknamed GMville. Unlike the basketball tournament, which eventually moved to a class system, the Band Day contest remained a place where small schools could still pull off underdog upsets. Monroe Central, the band marching a lone clarinet that afternoon, had won State Fair in 1991.

Max almost didn't go to State Fair his freshman year. He was small—"not much bigger than my tenor sax," he'd say later—and slow to learn to march. What he had, in abundance, was a deep interest in bands. Even as a child, when his father gave him the choice between watching the high school marching band practice and going down to the railroad bridge to watch the trains go by, Max chose the marching band. Still, it had taken him until fourth grade to decide between being a band director and a railroad engineer. The Princeton director planned to name Max an alternate for the big contest, Max's first year in the band, until several upperclassmen who'd noticed Max's persistence and his passion for bands lobbied hard to keep the little kid with the big grin in the show. Princeton placed tenth that year. They didn't place as high in subsequent years, but Max still loved coming to State Fair each August, loved seeing the other bands, felt proud of his band and its lineage.

When Max went to Ball State University in Muncie to study organ music and become a band director himself, he learned to make finer distinctions between bands and their performances, and between directors. Several of his teachers at Ball State showed him how much further he could push himself, and his students, in pursuing excellence, while one of the upperclassmen taught him what he'd never, ever do to a student when the student leader corrected Max's posture one day by kicking him. After years of teaching himself on the organs in his father's churches (and accompanying the services), Max studied the organ for the first time at Ball State. It was an unusual major instrument for a band-director-in-training, but on it, Max learned to hear the voice of every instrument. He experimented with balancing their colors and with dynamics. If he wanted more from his upper register, he pulled out the knob marked "flute." He'd later say that studying organ had developed some of his best talents.

As Max began his career, the Princeton program that had started him on his path faltered and failed. In 1972, Princeton came in 72nd in the State Fair contest. The following year, the band registered for the contest but didn't show up. Max, who was by then the band director at Winchester, wondered why some programs continued to flourish even when directors changed, while others couldn't survive such transitions. But he understood the power of bands, even mediocre ones, to transform kids' lives.

Winchester, as it turned out, was a good example of the changing

order in marching bands. Winchester Community High School opened
in 1966, consolidating six smaller rural schools. The next county over,
Jay County High School replaced seven schools, and the band director
for one of them, Dave Humbert, took charge of the new Jay County
Marching Patriot Band. The number of schools competing at Band Day
dropped to fifty-four in 1973.

Another central Indiana band, the Richmond Red Devils, won the
band contest in August that year. They became the last band for whom
a State Fair win gave them the right to call themselves the champion
high school marching band of Indiana. Later that fall, another marching contest was held at a high school north of Indianapolis. The format
was different: Instead of marching from left to right down a narrow
track, parade-style, bands entered from the sidelines of a football field
and used the entire field throughout the performance. And they
marched using the low-to-the-ground drum-corps step. Max Jones and
the Winchester band were at the forefront of both the new style and the
new contest.

Max was only twenty-four years old when Winchester hired him,
and one year older when he was tapped to join the governing body of a
regional band-director organization for southern Indiana. A few years
later, he was asked to be part of a group that combined his regional association with a competing organization from the north and formed
them into a statewide entity called the Indiana State School Music Association. The next year, Max became ISSMA's first elected president.
One of ISSMA's charters was to set up and run band contests and festi-
vals that gave directors clear feedback to improve their band programs.
Unlike the older State Fair contest, ISSMA separated schools into
classes: A for the state's biggest schools, such as Ben Davis, down to D
for its smallest. ISSMA also created a judging sheet that many directors
immediately preferred for its pedagogical usefulness.

The state's biggest schools and strongest programs gravitated to the
new format. Ben Davis retooled its State Fair show in 1973 to enter the
fall contest; in 1974, the school registered only for the field shows.
Max took Winchester to the new contests and became a dominant
force in Class B. By the end of the decade, ISSMA had assumed the
kingmaker role for marching bands. In 1988, only twenty-four bands
competed in State Fair Band Day.

Some of the communities that sent bands to the State Fair couldn't easily afford to compete in the field shows and fall contests. Central Indiana towns formed the backbone of the State Fair contest, but had been weakened economically by decades of plant closings: GM had systematically closed down its operations in Anderson; Richmond had lost its major employers and the greenhouse companies that had earned it the name "City of Roses." A summer track circuit had developed that gave those communities a cheaper and more contained marching season, with Band Day its culminating event. Some longtime Band Day supporters also saw no reason to mess with a contest and a format that had worked so well for so long. In the communities that had never stopped sending bands to State Fair, some complained that too many people in other parts of the state had forgotten that the high school marching band was part of the community. They argued that the band should march in Fourth of July and Labor Day parades, and entertain football fans with new halftime shows each week, not spend its time preparing its own show for its own competitions. Whether tradition or economy was the pull, the numbers of participants in the State Fair contest had gradually inched back up. Thirty-six bands had competed that morning for a chance at the night show.

Over the years, the other State Fair bands had learned that although Concord was a big program and a powerful competitor in the field shows, the Marching Minutemen were unlikely ever to win the championship the smaller bands cared about—not with Concord's mud-in-your-eye humor and clown-show routines. Max Jones's unorthodox shows eventually became familiar and even anticipated, and the band stopped being greeted with boos from the stands. The previous year, Concord's "fun" song had been the foot-stomper "Shout." The vocalist (Evan Jarvis, the one with whom Max had goaded the band the night before) had yelled out, "Indianaaaaapoooolis! The Concord band loves ya!" The crowd had risen to its feet to return the sentiment. Fans of other State Fair bands knew that Concord could be counted on to give them a good time and to play very, very well.

Now, the preliminary competition over, students gathered on the track to hear whether their bands had made it into the "Sweet 16" or one of the two exhibition slots, or whether they'd earned a night on the midway and an early ride home.

The announcer drew out the suspense. He told his audience it was his forty-sixth year at State Fair, which dated him back to the same year that Max Jones had barely squeaked into a spot at State Fair in the Princeton band. After asking his listeners to forgive an old man for taking his time, he read back from 25th place, the lowest ranking that earned a cash prize. The Concord students and directors listened closely. If they'd known their visual rankings, they might have been particularly anxious. One visual judge put Concord 32nd out of the 36 bands, saying over and over on his tape, "We have non-unison efforts." The other visual judge took a slightly more favorable view of the Concord approach, ranking the Marching Minutemen 20th. As usual, the quality of Max's band showed up in the music category. One music judge put Concord 6th in music; the other ranked them 3rd, which put them 5th overall in music. One of them said into his tape recorder, "Concord, always a pleasure to hear you. You can't march, but you sure play great."

When the announcer read off the alphabetical list of the bands that would return at nightfall for the final Band Day competition, he said, "And if we can, we'd looove to see Concord again." Concord's combined score put them at 15th overall. One day, Max knew, Concord wouldn't make the evening lineup, but they were in the Sweet 16 at least one more time.

Max loaded the buses and took the kids to the quiet of nearby Butler University for dinner. (If any of the Concord students had actually expected to spend some time at the fair, they were mistaken.) He gathered them around and told them what he'd noticed that afternoon. "My take on it was," he told them, "you played it safe. You played it scared. Now you're veterans. Go for it. Your job is to get smiles on people's faces."

The evening moved faster than the afternoon. Instead of marching third from the end, they were up fifth. It seemed to Adilene that as soon as the buses returned to an emptier field, they were back in line, walking to the track. The midway was lit up now, the grind of machinery drifting through the cool air. Two Ferris wheels spun slowly, their neon spokes throwing colors into the air from opposite ends of the fairgrounds. The signs on top of the Coliseum glowed red and white. The lights for the *P* and the *e* in "Pepsi" were out, so the smaller sign now read *psi Coliseum*. The sun setting behind the building was putting on quite a light show as well. Clouds piled up above the Coliseum, over a brilliant band of pink sky that went indigo at the horizon.

The stands were filling quickly. Nearly empty at 7:15, by 7:30, when the last of the daylight caught the metal seats, they were halfway to capacity, and people were still streaming in. The seats, painted in broad rows of blue, white, and red, soon held a rainbow of partisan colors.

The Coronas hadn't made it to Adilene's first public performance. Juan had been needed at the greenhouse until 3:30 that day, and Camelia had picked up a summer job decorating cakes at the Meijer grocery store. They left Concord with Adilene's brother, Esau, shortly before 5:00, not entirely sure when Concord performed but aware that the evening competition began at 8:00. Coming into the fairgrounds, they got turned around trying to find the right parking lot. It was already 8:00 when they reached the fairground gates. They heard a band playing and hoped it wasn't Concord. The Coronas couldn't know that Max would have been happy to march Concord in an exhibition slot. His students would have gotten to perform twice in one day, they wouldn't crowd a band out of the finals that had practiced all summer, and their buses would get back to the school before midnight. So the Coronas didn't understand the full extent of their luck when they slid into seats in the middle section in time to watch the last of the exhibition performances, below a crowd wearing pirate eye patches and carrying gold flags that said, "Grab the gold."

The announcer said, "Now we get underway for the big gold trophy, with Hagerstown, the first band up." Camelia, Juan, and Esau could look down the lighted track and see bands lined up under the darkening sky. The breeze, still strong, gusted cold now, as if coming off a glacier. People sipped hot chocolate and pulled on Windbreakers or tightened the hoods on their jackets.

Nearly eleven thousand people packed into the grandstand. The bright lights of the fair, that evening, narrowed to sixteen bands.

Concord appeared in the walkway to the track, stretching back and back. While the Hagerstown band played, the Concord ranks stepped quietly onto the track. There wasn't enough room for all of them. They had to wait until the band directly in front of them moved into starting position.

The gray-uniformed Noblesville Marching Millers offered a contrast with the loose-limbed Concord group, especially now that Concord had added its final State Fair accessory: red and green blinky lights. Max, always on the prowl for State Fair costumes, had found the lights at the Elkhart Jazz Festival the year before. He'd seen blue lights blinking in the back of a booth along the St. Joseph River. The guy at the booth showed him how to twist on the tiny lights and how to use their built-in magnets. Three lights for three dollars, one for each ear and one more for good measure, or three on a shirt collar or floppy hat. Max ran some rough math while he pulled money out of his wallet: three times two hundred and forty, give or take, for the band and staff. Well, really three times five hundred, because some of the band parents would want them. No, probably more like three times a couple thousand, because other kids would want them, too. But six thousand dollars was way too much for blinky lights. The next night at home, Max typed "blinky lights" into his computer and found what he wanted for sixty-seven cents each. He ordered three thousand blue lights, then thought again and added an assortment of orange, red, and green—eight thousand total. During the football and basketball season, band parents sold the green lights for $2, an easy fund-raiser for the band. The lights had gone over so well that Max had ordered several thousand more for the coming year. As night came on, the lights sparkled around the faces of the Concord students like fireflies.

Concord moved into position to the sound of Noblesville's "Let the Sunshine In." The students' white sneakers and socks, which had blended in with the dirt during the afternoon performance, now glowed against the dark brown of the track.

Max, lights blinking at his ears, talked to the official responsible for starting the clock. State Fair gave Max an excuse to indulge a taste for camp that surprised those who knew only his efficient, disciplined side. He made a big show each year of pretending to bribe the starters, men who were usually retired band directors. He handed the official a tie-dyed T-shirt and some blinky lights. Max knew nearly everyone in the Indiana band world, or knew someone they knew. And everyone, it seemed, knew Max Jones.

The green flag went down. The blinking Minutemen stepped over the line. The sequined hats were positively stunning under the lights. Who would have guessed such campy materials could be transformed at night into sparkling spectacle?

At the quiet beginning of "Gabriel's Oboe," the trumpet fanfare from Jay County's warm-up drifted in above the melody line from

Concord's bass clarinets and synthesizer. The distant horns, oddly, added a layer to the music, and to the experience. It was a classic State Fair moment, part of what people came for.

This time, Max watched from the side of the track opposite the grandstand, on the stage where the final awards would be handed to drum majors. It gave him a new perspective. People around him laughed at Concord's clowning, but Max ignored the silliness for the moment and concentrated on the music. He was often more critical of his band than judges were. Still, he was pleased with Amanda's solo. He'd bet well on her ability to hold the beginning of a show together. But when he looked at the band section by section, he was less pleased. He noticed the drumline losing the pulse during the ballad; the large band, which stretched the full length of the grandstand, almost broke into two separate bands going at competing tempos. Max had tried to work with the drum majors on how to avoid such a problem, or, barring that, how to fix it. He could see Patrick Doherty, the senior drum major, making extra-big movements for the separate beats, but what Pat really needed to do was to bark out the counts and bring the two halves of the band back into a whole. The bass and snare drums weren't in sync. Nick Stubbs would also be hearing from Max.

Now the full band joined the ballad and the sound swelled, filling the grandstand. One of the music judges allowed himself simply to enjoy the song. "Yeah," he said, sighing as the band played. "Yeah . . . yeah." A few seconds later, as the song reached its final crescendo, he said, a bit sheepishly, "I'm not saying anything critical because you're doing such a good job." The other judge, talking into his tape recorder on another platform, agreed: "Your musicianship qualities are superb. Always a pleasure to see you here, Concord. Have a great fall."

On "Lucretia MacEvil," the T-shirted musicians swayed back and forth, twisting down to the ground and jumping back up again. Cameron on saxophone reached for more melody. He and the other saxophone jumped onto the center drum major platform to play their final notes and wave to the crowd; Pat Doherty pretended to take their picture with a throwaway camera. Max was still unimpressed. He'd given the two soloists the room to make something of their moment, and they hadn't delivered. He thought their duet could have rivaled "Shout" from the year before. In his mind, the two seniors had taken the easy way out.

The short Dixieland snippet of "The Saints Go Marching In" got the crowd clapping, though. Max watched Grant perform, doing everything the Concord way. He pulled Max's eyes to him, just the way he leaned back and held his horn up a little higher than anyone else around him. He wasn't flashy the way some other fine trumpet players were, but Max saw plenty of showmanship there. Grant high-stepped into place in the N. A judge mistook him for one of the drum majors at that point and complimented him on his old-fashioned back-bending style. "Wish we saw more of that," she said on the tape.

The letters kept their shape better in the night show. Camelia Corona heard an approving murmur in the stands as people saw what they spelled and liked the nod to tradition. But the other visual judge now lost his cool: "Maintain form! If you're going to put your school name out there, maintain form!"

Camelia had watched Adilene through the entire show, as much as she could keep track of her. She recognized her daughter's slim body and her dark hair underneath that ridiculous hat. She watched Adilene dance around waving her clarinet—that new clarinet, more than a thousand dollars they'd spent on it just last year, and here she was almost poking someone in the behind with it? But then, she looked like she was having so much fun, among all those young men and women. She watched Adilene running to her letter, sliding into place, but once Adilene had marched past their seats, Camelia could no longer tell which tie-dyed T-shirt belonged to her daughter. Still watching, knowing that one of those departing backs was her daughter's, Camelia felt tears spring to her eyes. She was so proud.

Camelia noticed that Esau, who had taken beginning band the summer before, was intent not just on Concord's performance, but on every band that marched past the grandstand. Camelia had come to see her daughter; Esau, she realized, had come to see his future.

Eleven more bands performed after Concord left the track. Richmond, marching tenth, played selections from the movie *Pirates of the Caribbean*. A tractor pulled out a flatbed trailer and a fifteen-foot-tall pirate ship. At different points in the show, fog billowed from its portholes, and its deck became the stage for solos and sword fights. Before the performance, the Richmond band members had placed 1973 and 1988 pennies in the toes of their shoes, hoping for good-luck magic from Richmond's two previous State Fair wins. Befitting their Patriot name, Jay County recited the Pledge of Allegiance over a drumroll, a show of patriotism that played well to the crowd. By the time the last band, tiny Centerville, had left the track, babies had fallen asleep in strollers and on laps, and young children had curled up on the metal seats. Some in the audience wrapped themselves in blankets as if they were watching a late-season football game.

Down on the track, however, the teenagers congregated one last time. Kids in some bands had brought school banners with them and raced back and forth in front of the grandstand showing their colors. One of the Concord kids hoisted a huge overstuffed fish that he had somehow found time to win at the midway and ran around the dirt track with it over his head.

Max had told the Concord students to leave the track as soon as they heard Concord's place and not wait until all the names had been read. He wanted all eight Concord buses to be on their way back north, driving past the pretty houses and the suburbs, while the rest of the bands idled an hour or more in traffic trying to leave the fairgrounds.

The announcer recognized two band directors who had recently retired: Jay County's first band director, Dave Humbert, still there after thirty years but due to retire at the end of the coming school year; and the recently retired director from Anderson. Max, of course, knew them both. Now the retiring directors weren't old guys to him. One was even a few years younger.

As following the prelims, the announcer read the results from the bottom up. Hagerstown was 16th. The Concord kids whooped loudly—they weren't in last place! Fifteenth went to Anderson. Concord had moved up since the afternoon! Fourteenth: Noblesville, the gray-clad band that had played "Let the Sunshine In" just ahead of them. With each name, the Concord upperclassmen cheered more loudly. Later, on the way to their obligatory stop at White Castle, where Max would grin devilishly while the summer staff dutifully choked down the greasy, onion-filled gray patties, the directors would listen to judges' tapes from both performances and read the numbers on the scoring sheets over their two-way radios. Their overall rankings from the night show would follow the same general pattern as from the day show. They placed 16th in the visual category. This put them dead last among the Sweet 16, but Scott Spradling, remembering the 32nd ranking they'd received earlier, quipped, "Hey! We've come up in marching!" They were 15th in general effect. But they had actually moved up in music, coming in 4th in that category. Back on the track, the announcer called out the 13th-place band: "And from Elkhart, that great music city up north, the Concord Marching Minutemennnn."

Thirteenth place! Better than 15th! Better than last year's 16th! Concord students hugged and pumped their fists in the air. If you just registered their pleasure and excitement, you'd think they'd won, or at least made the top three or five. Adilene, along with many of the other freshmen (and some number of teenagers from the other bands), didn't get it. Why all this excitement about 13th place? She was confused. She knew Concord had won a state championship the year before, the big championship. Shouldn't they be closer to winning State Fair than 13th place? In a few minutes, she'd board bus #4 along with the other clarinets, still bewildered by the behavior of the older students. The buses would pull up to the music-department entrance after three a.m. Adilene's father would be waiting for her, asleep in his car. She'd be silent on the way home and go straight to bed, exhausted, not even wanting to think about the long practice awaiting her the next evening. Brent Lehman and a handful of trombone, tuba, and baritone players would toilet-paper low-brass director Bryan Golden's house before going home. Grant Longenbaugh and Cameron Bradley would grab a cheap breakfast at Taco Bell and try to make each other laugh with full bites of empanadas in their mouths.

But right there, on the dirt track in the cool night air, hugging kids they'd barely known a month earlier, Adilene and the other freshmen mostly felt relief. Grant and Cameron and Brent and the other upperclassmen cheered for State Fair. The older students knew that State Fair was the end of the summer, in more ways than one. After State Fair, everything would get harder.

6 ⋆ Learning the Drill

Nick Stubbs was Concord's crown prince of drumming. He was a band director's kid, a drummer's kid, part of a family in which grown-ups actually played drums for a living. His father's drumline had led the Richmond Red Devils to a state championship three decades earlier. Wayne and Jackie Stubbs had taken their firstborn to drum-corps shows before he could walk; he started playing before he could talk.

Nick's father had bought a drumset in high school, back when blue-tinted plastic drumheads were all the rage. When Nick was a toddler, Wayne reassembled it in a corner of their basement; even then, the set was so old and battered that the name of the manufacturer had completely worn off, and duct tape held the shells together where they'd split. A framed picture that Wayne kept on his desk showed Nick grinning, his blond hair still baby-fine, perched on his father's lap above the dingy drums. He was stretching forward over the blue plastic with a drumstick in each hand. He held the sticks like he'd been born to them.

In time, Wayne passed on some of the lessons that he'd learned as a young drummer to his son. When he'd wanted to take drum lessons, at age eight, his instructor had insisted that he first understand fractions. When he finally started, he discovered that much of his time went to a form of musical math called subdividing. Years later, he taught his son how many quarter, eighth, or sixteenth notes went into each beat in a measure; and how to divide beats into multiples of two, three, four, and more complex combinations.

Wayne explained to Nick that a drummer, more than any other musician in a group, has to know where he is. If you can't count it, he told Nick, you can't play it. He taught Nick the importance of hand position and schooled him in the artful balance of holding his sticks firmly and loosely at the same time. That Zenlike quality of playing drums would come to fascinate Nick and hold him.

Over the years, Nick heard plenty of dumb drummer jokes: *How can you tell there's a drummer at your front door? He rushes. How do you get a drummer out of your house? Pay him for the pizza.* Nick knew that a lot of people thought of drummers as dimwitted slackers, but his own experience didn't fit the stereotypes. He had his father, a serious musician who had become a band director, then a school administrator. And he had his father's cousin Jeff, who had been the drumline captain at Richmond a few years ahead of Wayne. Jeff Hamilton had gone on to become one of the most versatile jazz drummers of his generation. He'd long been a fixture of the L.A. jazz scene, had played behind jazz singer Rosemary Clooney, Lionel Hampton, several small ensembles that bore his name, and recently for Diana Krall. People who knew jazz said he made drums melodic as well as rhythmic. Jeff's touring schedules were often discussed around the dinner table in the Stubbs household. His most recent project wasn't a tour, however, but a cameo, playing a 1950s version of himself, in a film being put together by Rosemary Clooney's nephew. Nick didn't know much about the movie, except that Jeff didn't have to say a word, just do what he always did with the sticks.

Nick came to understand in those dinner-table conversations that for his father, Jeff's life traveled the road not taken. He knew that his dad had felt the pull of the professional musician's life. Wayne had wanted to join a drum corps out of high school but had needed to earn money for college instead. During a summer break in Michigan playing in a jazz trio, he'd been asked to go on the road with a big band, a siren song that Jeff Hamilton had heeded only two years earlier. But when the phone calls came from Indiana, urging him to finish his education first, Wayne had taken the advice.

For a number of summers, the Jeff Hamilton Trio played at the Elkhart Jazz Festival, and Jeff stayed with Wayne and his family. One year, Nick looked at Jeff as just another relative. But the next year—the summer before Nick started sixth grade—Nick suddenly saw him as a celebrity. Nick was playing in the beginning band at Concord and had started to think of the hours he spent on his father's basement drumset as something more than play. If drumming ran in the blood, he wondered then, how strongly did it beat for him? But just as the family drumming legacy was coming into focus for Nick, his accomplished uncle cut short his questions about technique, music, what it felt like to play in front of a big crowd. Later, though, after a few hours of playing pickup basketball in the driveway, Jeff turned to Nick and asked, You want a drum lesson? Down in the basement, Jeff listened to Nick play. When Nick stopped, Jeff talked to him like a fellow drummer. Some of what he said Nick couldn't absorb, even though he strained to hold on to every word. A few things he understood, and remembered. Jeff praised him for the lack of clutter in his kit, and he offered Nick corollary advice: Try to do with very little what others will try to do with too much.

Jeff told his young pupil that most people, even many drummers, assume that the drums are the key to setting rhythm in a group. But that isn't always so; in fact, it isn't always what a good drummer wants. The crucial beat can come from unexpected places. He showed Nick how to keep rhythm on the ride cymbals, using a flick of the wrist and a bounce that was like fingers snapping, just what you'd naturally want to do, listening to a jazz melody. It was subtle, even subversive, this beat that was nimble and flexible, tying everything else together while keeping so much in the background that its actual sound almost disappeared.

Jeff's influence turned Nick toward a minimalist, classic style. Each pointer he gave became another Zen koan, working in Nick's mind.

By then, Nick was already balancing seemingly opposite impulses. He saw himself as destined for greater things than the people around him. He cast himself in the role of a rebel, and pushed against the boundaries he felt growing up in a place like Concord. He spent an entire summer trying to re-create the battle scenes in *Saving Private Ryan* with his closest friend, Matt Tompkins. They pretended to be generals in wars they fought in their backyards or under the scraggly pine trees, rejects of a former Christmas tree farm, that dotted their subdivision. They kept themselves apart from other kids.

But when he got to junior high, Nick learned that he didn't need to remain completely separate. In the band, he felt part of something bigger than himself. Now, the eighty or a hundred kids who'd played together in beginning band no longer dispersed to four different elementary schools when band was over. They formed a formidable force inside the junior high. For two years, as far as Nick was concerned, they were part of the coolest thing around. The band kids ate lunch together. They traveled back to the elementary schools to give concerts, where they were looked up to as eleven- and twelve-year-old celebrities. But then half the girls who played flutes seemed to decide overnight that cool resided elsewhere, a bunch of the boys chose sports over band, and other kids who were struggling were relieved to give up the fight. Only about half the kids who had filled the ranks of band in seventh grade continued in high school.

Nick never wavered. Even before he tried one on, he loved the idea of wearing the Marching Minutemen uniform. He stood in profile before the bathroom mirror to make sure he held his chin at the proper angle.

He'd heard his father's stories about making the drumline right out of junior high, and wanted to do the same, even though it was practically unheard of at Concord for a freshman to join the part of the percussion section that marched on the field. Nick auditioned at the end of eighth grade against some twenty other kids, most of them older, most of them already experienced marchers. He made it through two preliminary rounds but not the final cut. He was still digesting his disappointment when one of the bass drums dropped out, and Nick was in.

The percussion instructor recognized Nick's talent and placed him on the second largest of the five basses. The fourth bass, as it was called, got the off-beats, the second and fourth beats in a four-beat measure. Because marching automatically emphasizes the first and third beats—in traditional marching bands, step-offs always come on the first beat—the number four was considered the hardest drum to play in the bass line. Nick understood the compliment.

At first, the upperclassmen hazed him. What did he know, even if he was a band director's kid? Nick accepted the hazing as impassively as he accepted the compliment. It was clear to him that a freshman on the drumline should be an exception; the line should remain difficult, demanding, elite. He kept his mouth shut.

After the first band practices, he took home his drum and his music. He'd never seen a bass line score before. Bass drums in a marching band are each tuned to a different note, so that together they can play melody lines. The trick is in how well the group can play the "split line"—how well different drummers can sequence those notes. Nick highlighted the fourth bass's note every time it appeared among the other notes on his score. Then he tried to hear the entire line in his head and play his note at the right time in the sequence, from memory. It was hard and discouraging work, and he couldn't keep it up for long, but the other drummers noticed and eased off.

In spite of his talent, or maybe because of it, it took until the end of Nick's first summer in the band before an upperclassman finally invited him to one of the drumline parties.

The show his freshman year contained just two pieces of music, a trumpet fanfare and the "Peterloo" Overture. The overture referred to an episode in English history in which a peaceful demonstration for parliamentary reform by farmers and laborers, many of them treating the event as a family holiday, was violently broken up by soldiers. Nick, who often read his father's history books and biographies, imagined acting out the story on the field.

"Peterloo" gave Nick his first experience with "locking." When a drumline locks, each person can hear only one drum, one rhythm. But it's not the same as if only one person is playing. In a tightly locked sequence, each note contains extra resonance. To those making it happen, time itself seems to alter, to slow down; the notes seem to vibrate at a special frequency, or become almost visible. Other groups experience something similarly transcendent. Rowers call it "swing"; dance partners can feel as if they're moving as one; hockey and basketball players sometimes feel it during the flow of a fast break. "Locking" requires absolute precision, absolute accuracy, but also lightness, confidence, a groove. There can be no stuttering or muddiness, and no holding back. Even the slightest variation in timing can end the sensation.

It happened during a rehearsal of a particularly difficult passage, a part of the show that signaled the beginning of the massacre. The sound from the percussion section grew faster and more violent, until it

completely overwhelmed the lyrical melody the woodwinds were playing. The bass players had been unsure of their parts, a split set of fast-
moving sixteenth-note triplets, and the lack of confidence showed.
Practice was nearly over. Bass drums are heavy, and Nick and the others were ready to give their backs and shoulders a break. But the college student working with them that summer had them repeat the two
worst measures again and again and again. The line couldn't stay together. After one botched try, the instructor grabbed a mallet from the
second bass and heaved it twenty feet into the parking lot. The unexpected gesture made Nick and the other bass players laugh. They tried
the tricky section again, one more time.

Nick felt it before he understood it: the feeling of one voice from
many throats. The rhythm seemed to come from inside him and outside
him simultaneously. He didn't dare to look at anyone else. He just
played to the end. Then they all whooped. The instructor immediately
made them play the measures again. Nick wished he wouldn't. He
wanted to hold on to the feeling a little longer before he lost it. But
there it was again. After that, the bass line could play that section better on some days than on others, but some magic had occurred. Soon
they were able to string other long, complicated runs together with the
same precision. Drummers from other schools came to watch their
practices. Concord won every percussion award leading up to state finals that year. And Nick discovered what to shoot for.

Over the next two years, he worked his way up the ranks, from bass
as a freshman to snare as a sophomore, and then to captain-in-training.
In jazz band, he quickly earned the seat behind the drumset in the top
ensemble, where his graceful style and subtle technique earned the
praise of judges. In all of it, Nick was practicing for the time he would
set the beat for the entire marching band.

His growing role in the band took on deeper dimensions during the
dinner-table conversations at home, where Nick was forming his sense
of the world. Growing up the son of two teachers—his mom taught
second grade in Wakarusa, twenty minutes south into farmland; his father was now studying for his superintendent's license—he'd absorbed
the pleasures of learning. The year Nick started high school, the family
moved to a new house in a newer subdivision with bigger lots. The new
house held bookcases full of his and his father's shared passions: music,
military history, biographies of presidents, biographies of generals.

Nick didn't touch his father's management books; Wayne left the classics—the *Odyssey*, the *Iliad*—to Nick.

Nick was particularly drawn to the books about the military. As a child, he'd listened to his grandfather's stories about the great-grandfather who wore a gas mask in World War I, and about relatives who fought in the Indian wars. He'd read biographies of Alexander the Great, Napoleon, Rommel (whom he admired for a doomed dignity), and MacArthur (whose two-fisted attack on life inspired him); he'd read the classics of military literature, *The Peloponnesian War, The Art of War*; he'd dipped into strategy, political maneuvering, diplomacy. A poster of George Patton glowered from his bedroom wall. No one in three generations on either side of his family had served in a war. And Nick's slight build and fine features suggested "poet" more than "fighter." But the life of a soldier seemed epic, romantic, and meaningful.

Shortly after the end of his junior year, Nick and his father watched a History Channel show about West Point. Nick knew about the military academy—it was the training ground for many of his heroes—but until that night, the school had seemed like a place for young men from another era, or at least another part of the country. After the TV program ended, Nick said, "I wish I could go to that school," with an intensity that surprised them both. He told his father, "I don't want to be just a high school teacher."

"Then you should go to West Point," his father responded, choosing not to be offended.

But Nick wasn't sure a family of teachers could afford such a dream; he knew the school was selective, so it was bound to be expensive. After his father had gone to bed, Nick looked up West Point online. He saw the uniforms, sensed the discipline, leadership, and intelligence behind the long gray lines, and felt that he belonged there. He read through lists of illustrious alumni and careers West Point graduates had gone on to: astronaut, judge, governor, CEO, president, general. He read through the admissions process, learned that he needed to be nominated for application by a congressman or senator or the vice president of the United States, and learned that if he was admitted, his tuition was paid for. He woke up his father to tell him that West Point was free to anyone who got in. There was a selection process, including a physical aptitude test. He would start it right away. He went back to the computer to fill out a request for an application. A thunderstorm rumbled through town, bringing heavy winds and rain. He took each crack of lightning as an affirmation of his resolve.

All summer Nick ran nearly every day, several miles on the curving roads of his new and old neighborhoods. Their names came straight out of the suburban name-book—Catalpa, Chestnut, Meadowlark, Flicker—the flora and fauna of an American pastoral. He followed the asphalt where it led him, circling the cul-de-sacs with their look-alike houses arranged like lawn chairs around asphalt swimming pools. He monitored the dew with a professional's eye, gauging how long it would take the sun to burn it off. Nick mowed some of the lawns in the neighborhood. He'd made a lot of money mowing during the past couple years, but he privately thought that Concord had a strange obsession with lawns. People mowed their lawns, he thought, the same way they went to church: because everyone else did it, and because not doing it meant being different, and therefore ostracized. Max Jones was one of Nick's most particular customers. He insisted that his lawn be cut to an exact two and a half inches. Whenever Nick showed up at the Joneses' immaculate ranch house, the lawn mower was already set out for him, alongside two pre-mixed gas cans. But Mr. Jones wanted his lawn mowed because he was an orderly man, Nick sensed, not because he worried about what the neighbors thought. Nick respected that.

Max's example notwithstanding, Nick bristled at the prevailing herd mentality, and ran faster as a result. He finished off his runs with wind sprints in the backyard or by going down into the basement where he'd built a pull-up bar out of two-by-fours and a length of pipe. He timed pull-ups, sit-ups, push-ups and recorded them in a small notebook he kept next to the mat.

He was heir, now, to the family tradition: drumline captain, responsible for leading the battery—six snares, three tenors, five bass drums, and five cymbals—and section leader for the entire percussion section. He was at the center of the band, the nerve center behind its pulse. But he was also looking beyond the music. He saw the band as a chance to exercise leadership. He thought of himself as in training as a leader of warriors.

Nick's community was full of patriots, judging by the magnetized flags and "Support Our Troops" ribbons on the back panels of cars, the Bush-Cheney signs already sprouting in yards all over town. But Nick's patriotism was grounded in an idealistic belief in the power of individuals to change the course of history, and he questioned many of the decisions made by his country's leaders. He wanted to understand context, background, and the wider ripples of actions in the world. Even as a high school student, he was independent, thoughtfully weighing different sides of issues. He was also quite willing to hold unpopular opinions. He'd taken on the evangelical students in Mrs. Greene's class. Among his friends, his was a lone voice questioning the Patriot Act.

Throughout the summer, his approach to leadership in the band had been romantic, as well, and individualistic: about him, Nicholas Stubbs. He started out assuming that everyone on the line would want to win as much as he did, that they'd be motivated in practices by his example, and that he merely had to model correct behavior and good musicianship in order to lead the drumline. He couldn't have been more mistaken.

ON THE FIRST morning of school, Nick drove his black Grand Am as fast as he dared on the straight roads, window down, stereo cranked up to Led Zeppelin. He'd paid half the cost of the sports car with lawn-mowing money. The car had eighty thousand miles on it when he'd bought it, and it sucked up most of his cash now, but he loved the way he felt when he drove it fast. One day the road ahead of him would lead out of town, out into the great unknown.

He pulled his car into a space close to the pine trees where the snare line had spent so much of the summer practicing, not far from the entrance to the music department. The parking lots that would fill rapidly in the next half hour sat mostly empty. He liked being ahead of the crowd.

Around a far corner of the building, at the curving middle of the official school entrance, double-glass doors opened onto the high school's main lobby. Two rows of portraits hung on the walls on either side of the entrance, valedictorians on one side, salutatorians on the other. Most seniors, Nick included, expected Grant Longenbaugh to take his place on the wall with the other valedictorians after their class graduated. But Nick and the other band students rarely saw those pictures; they started their days in the music wing, among their own trophies and awards and reminders of excellence.

As early as Nick was, Max Jones had arrived before him and was standing just inside the entrance to the music department. He greeted Nick and grinned in response to Nick's polite "Good morning." Max took paternal pride in monitoring the music wing. He spoke to some of the students and seemed to light up around Nick and the few others who dared speak to him. But mostly he observed. All year long, he noticed who walked through the door carrying an instrument, and who therefore might have practiced at home. He saw who rushed in at the last minute and who avoided looking at him. He would come to know which students regularly met a boyfriend or a girlfriend in the band room, and which were making the music department a home away from home, drifting in and out of the directors' offices and talking so much to Shirley Dyer, the music secretary, that she had to send them on errands just so she could finish her own work.

Nick and the other drummers had their own private reserve, a dark cave hidden off the short ramp into the band room where the percussion instruments were stored. Even Amy Davis, the instructor responsible for everything related to the percussion section, stopped at the doorway whenever students were inside and asked if it was OK to come in. Nick knew that at least a couple of drummers really did hide out there, taking naps or avoiding classes.

The long music hallway ended in a wide arcing turn into the hallway outside the cafeteria, where the freshmen lockers were clustered. The high school no longer symbolized Concord's suburban newness. More yellow-brick boxes—a new gym, the performing arts center, the bigger band room—had been added over the years, but the school remained essentially the same one that had removed Concord from the ranks of township schools. Concord Community High School was as dated and serviceable as the classic rock that Nick listened to, the music the same age as its central buildings.

The students had the same hard-to-place look about them. They looked mainstream, like a generalized idea of teenagers almost anywhere in the country at the turn of the twenty-first century. But in how they dressed and how they acted, they also seemed to recall an earlier, more innocent time—a role Midwestern teenagers had been playing for the rest of the country for generations. Concord students dressed in an all-American casual that seemed little affected by brand names or celebrity fashion. Boys and girls wore jeans, sweatpants, and sweat-shirts, even in the sticky August heat. Boys wore their hair shaggy over their ears and collars, just as many of their fathers had done in the seventies. Girls wore pants a little lower on their hips than their mothers had, their hair pulled into the universal American-girl ponytail. But other, edgier styles—piercings, tattoos, sexed-up clothing—seldom appeared in the yellow-brick hallways. The school had a dress code, and it was enforced. Max Jones had reminded the band students about the code during band camp: sleeveless shirts and dresses had to cover shoulders, no bellies or midriffs could show, no spaghetti straps, no underwear visible, not even the patterned boxers that boys elsewhere wore in combination with low-riding pants. Boys at Concord were expected to hold up their pants, if they were baggy enough to need it, with belts.

Only a few kids stood out as different. A handful of Goth kids dressed in black. One, who wrote ironic Op-Ed pieces for the school newspaper, strode down the hallways in an ankle-length black trench coat. Some students wore pants festooned with zippers and chains. But Nick passed no metal detectors on his way in, and no armed guards, and he didn't carry an identification card. Taken as a whole, the student body seemed filled with clean-cut, pleasant kids.

Once they'd left the music hallway, the students in the band mixed in seamlessly with the rest of the student body. The band drew broadly from the school population, from the school's best students to students in remedial and special ed classes. It included kids preparing for college, kids spending their mornings learning a trade, some athletes and popular kids (though not the most popular—even at Concord, band wasn't *that* cool), and kids who otherwise went through their days nearly invisible to other students and their teachers. For those kids especially, band gave them an identity.

On the first day of school, Adilene Corona wore the same hooded sweatshirt and jeans she'd worn nearly every day of eighth grade. For her, the start of school meant the chance to see her friends again. All summer long, she'd missed parties at friends' houses—parties, even, at her own home, where the kitchen counter overflowed with chips and guacamole and homemade chicken mole and steaming bowls of Spanish rice. Her friends and their parents, who were also her parents' friends, would ask, *¿Dónde está Adilene?* And her mother would say, At band. Afterward, Camelia would tell Adilene that so-and-so had asked after her, and Adilene would yell at her mother: Why are you telling me this, when I couldn't even be there? But she knew why her mother couldn't help telling her; it was the same reason Camelia had to tell people about Adilene being in band. She was proud of Adilene, proud of her for stepping outside their world where all their friends spoke Spanish, proud of her for sticking with something hard. And good Mexican-American Catholic girl that she was, Adilene still wanted to please her mother.

Adilene had also missed most of the practices for the folk dance group that was her favorite part of the Asociación Cultural Santa Cruz, a group that their friend Asael Mujica had started in order to teach the new generation the culture and traditions of the old country. Her mother had sewed most of the wide, ruffled skirts that they wore when they performed. They'd danced on Cinco de Mayo at the Elkhart plaza downtown, which had been empty except for their group, and in front of a few curious onlookers outside JCPenney at the Concord Mall. These performances were the only times she was allowed to wear makeup, and even then only a pale gloss on her lips, a hint of color above her eyes. She would continue to miss dance practices until marching band ended, but at least now that school had started, she had a way to see her friends. She could meet them in the language and litera-ture class taught mostly to Hispanic kids, and at her locker in the fresh-man hallway, between classes.

She didn't know it, but she had a surprise for them. As soon as she arrived that first day of school and met her friends at her locker, people started saying hello to her: white kids, other freshmen who'd never said a word to any of them in junior high, sophomores, juniors, and even—oh mother Mary!—seniors. Adilene, quiet as usual at school, merely smiled in response to her friends' raised eyebrows. She still didn't know if she liked band, but there was no mistake about it: The band kids saw her as one of them.

Nick, as a senior and leader in the band, was in a different place. He walked into his second-period English class not sure what to expect. The teacher, Chris Judson, had visited Mrs. Greene's class at the end of Nick's junior year. Though Judson had been at Concord for years, hired by the previous principal after graduating from Grace College, he had only recently started teaching AP English, and Nick had heard conflicting reports about the class. Unlike Mrs. Greene, Mr. Judson had made no effort to connect the class or the summer's assignments to the lives of the students he'd soon be teaching. He had merely told them that they would be reading *Middlemarch* and *Crime and Punishment* over the summer. Even physically, he seemed utterly different: tall and thin to the point of gauntness, with an impassive face that intrigued Nick.

Now, with little preamble, Judson handed out square Post-it notes about half the size of a postcard. He gave a short quiz that focused on their summer reading. They were to write their answers on the small squares. For the final question, he asked if they'd finished their assignments. Nick answered truthfully. Yes to *Crime and Punishment*. No to *Middlemarch*. (Grant Longenbaugh also hadn't finished *Middlemarch*, but couldn't resist having a little fun. Before the test, Judson asked if anyone wanted to talk about the book's main themes. Quoting the back cover from memory, Grant intoned, "*Middlemarch* is the quintessential Victorian novel. . . ." The other kids murmured—Grant, getting it right again—but Judson raised his eyebrows. Grant held up the back cover of his book, busted, and the discussion ended.) Nick would be surprised and angry when his sticky note came back the following day with a C marked on it, the result of forty points taken off for not finishing *Middlemarch*. He would notice As going to others he knew had not finished the reading, and immediately think it unfair, and that the first lesson from Mr. Judson's class was that honesty didn't pay. Of course, honesty had paid; it had bought him a mediocre grade.

Band ran as a fifth-hour class. As the single biggest class at the high school, it was the first each year to be scheduled. No honors or AP classes were allowed to conflict with it. Because it was the last class of the day, Max Jones could run longer band practices during marching season, and avoid holding additional afternoon practices. All during the fall, when other students were getting out of school at five minutes to three, the band would stay out on the field, practicing for another twenty-five minutes. The scheduling was part of Max's efficiency, and it put the band's work ethic on display every day.

The first day, though, was a shortened school day, giving them only thirty-seven minutes of in-school time for a band practice. Max wasn't going to waste them. The band room was too small for 244 students, the new huge number, not including staff, so he assembled the entire band by sections in the Beickman Performing Arts Center. The flutes sat in the front on one side, the clarinets behind them. Brass filed into the middle. Percussion took seats in front on the other side. Nick sat in the middle of the first row, surrounded by his battery.

Max introduced three new students. One of them, an exchange student from Germany named Christine Fischer, had arrived in Elkhart at midnight the previous Thursday, and less than twenty-four hours later had been out on the practice field. Her host family had a daughter in the color guard. They'd asked Christine if she wanted to be in the band and she'd said yes. She'd taken flute lessons and played in a youth symphony in Germany. But that first night, jet-lagged and still thinking in German, wearing a thin white cotton T-shirt with Mickey Mouse on the front that still managed to look European, she was stunned by what she saw and heard: the motion, the music, the voices of the directors all reverberating against the buildings, the bugs flying around the lights, the warm night, the strange vocabulary that she understood, but not in the context of music: *drill, chart,* fundamentals that meant marching, not scales. The few words that stood out for her—*tenuto, forte*—she knew but had trouble translating there. And so big. So many of them. She'd been told to expect new experiences, had wanted to be an exchange student for exactly that sense of vertigo. She just hadn't expected marching band to feel so foreign, so American.

Max formally introduced her now. She stood, shyly, and the students in the theater seats applauded loudly. Having an exchange student made band feel somehow cosmopolitan.

Nick, though, sitting in the front row with the other snares, was feeling a different kind of vertigo. His season as drumline captain wasn't going at all as he'd thought it would. It hadn't been romantic or heroic or inspiring in the least.

His problems were numerous and seemingly intractable. Working under Miss Davis—Amy Davis, the percussion instructor—had turned out to be surprisingly difficult. She was Nick's third percussion instructor in four years. She'd replaced someone who'd worked at Concord less than a year, who had himself been a replacement for another teacher. After so much turnover, Nick had been ready to learn under one person for his remaining years in band. Davis had performed in drum corps, a mark of distinction, and in a world-champion corps at that, the Cadets of Bergen County. She was known as a skilled cymbalist; a cymbal manufacturer sent her around the country to give workshops and clinics between the end of school and the start of band camp. All of which sounded great. But from Nick's point of view, Miss Davis had a touchy-feely approach to teaching that ran counter to his image of the drumline. Her only tool for teaching, or so it seemed to Nick, was praise, applied liberally.

It was true that she preferred to focus on the positive, and her feedback to her students lacked the same specificity of problem and solution as the other, more experienced directors. But she was also fighting an ingrained culture. Some of the students who'd started out under other teachers were vocal in their lack of respect for her. The ones who appreciated her gentleness, who had wilted under the harshness of the previous instructors, kept quiet.

Nick knew going into his final year that one of his challenges would be holding together the divided group. There was a fundamental difference between the battery and the pit—that is, between the members of the percussion section who marched on the field and those who didn't. The pit functioned like a traditional concert-band percussion section, its members moving between large stationary instruments like marimbas, xylophones, and timpani, and smaller noise-makers like triangles, wood blocks, and hand drums. Because they didn't march, and because most of them didn't play every note, the students in the pit had a tendency to slack off. A more efficient and disciplined instructor, Nick thought, could run rehearsals for both the pit and the battery, plus keep that slacker tendency in check. But in the early weeks of the season, Nick noticed how much the kids in the pit hung around chatting while the drumline and the rest of the band were working hard. He'd also noticed Max Jones watching from his tower. He could have sworn he'd seen Mr. Jones's jaw grind in disapproval.

Max had taken Nick aside at the beginning of the season and told him that "Roots of American Music" would ask more of the percussion section than any show Concord had ever performed. Every piece would feature the battery or the pit, or both, and in a different way. "Gabriel's Oboe" contained distinctive, chantlike African drumming, augmented by the pit; "Africa" was fast-paced, with a traditional drum break; "New Orleans Jazz," "Swing, Swing, Swing" . . . where wasn't the percussion section central? But Amy Davis was responsible for writing the percussion score, and already the parts seemed muddy to Nick, without a clear line to follow. It seemed to him that she was overwriting, doing too little with too much.

Even harder for Nick to accept was what his instructor had done to the drumline. The snare line now had a freshman in it. A *freshman*. Nick had felt that his making the bass line as a freshman had been extraordinary—but frankly, he'd been a special case. Nick worried that Miss Davis wanted to make the drumline no more elite than the rest of the band. And while Nick heard Max Jones's reminders that the band was a community that included everyone, he had always silently exempted the drumline. The drumline—any drumline worth the name, Nick thought—had to be a cut above everyone else.

Still, Nick's respect for authority overrode his other feelings. He yesma'amed Miss Davis and was courtly in his politeness. He'd been stunned earlier in the summer when the college student who'd worked with the drumline had been asked to leave. Nick had liked how the young man had treated the drumline as the elite corps that Nick believed it should be. But Max had caught the young staffer encouraging the drumline to mock Miss Davis. Nick, the idealist, had been willing to be a pragmatist: The young man's work with the drumline had met a high standard, even if his behavior had not. Max Jones, pragmatic in so much of what he did, had been the idealist in that situation. Max was clear about Amy Davis's strengths and weaknesses as a teacher. He supported her attempts to bring the drumline more in line with the larger democratic goals of the band. He'd found the college student's insubordination unacceptable. His drumline captain would simply have to realign his perspective.

Now, Nick sat in the front row of the performance center with the other snares. And struggled to find his place.

THE BAND PRACTICED that evening under the glare of the lights. Max reminded them that they had just ten evening practices before state finals.

He'd already handed out the first drill charts for "Africa," the show's second song, which he'd told them to memorize by the start of school. He wanted to mark those charts on the pavement that night, and then play through the entire piece. They'd get the rest of the

"Africa" charts the following week. Once those were also marked on the pavement, he told them, half their show would be on the field.

That sounded good, but Max also told them that Elkhart Central was close to having taught its entire show already. North Wood, fifteen miles away in Nappanee, had just held its field-show preview the weekend before school started. Those two schools, along with other rivals who were as far along, would now have the rest of the season to clean and polish their shows. A band director's rule of thumb allowed for one week of cleaning for each minute of a show. If Max could get "Roots of American Music" down below eight minutes—he was still fiddling with his arrangements, trying to trim and tighten—keeping to that rule meant his kids needed to have finished learning the show by the beginning of September, two weeks away. That wasn't going to happen. Max was holding to a schedule that still gave them five weeks to clean, an improvement over the previous year, when they'd had a mere—and scary—three weeks. And this show was harder. "It all depends on how you work together," Max told his students. "You will move at the pace of the slowest member of the band."

Nick and the other seniors knew what learning the drill meant. For the next month they'd live in a swirl of drill books, coordinate sheets, drill charts, and paint sticks. "Drill"—the synchronized movements of the musicians and the color guard on the field—defined modern marching bands. Once locked inside its right-face, left-face military origins, drill in most of the country's marching bands now meant complex, fluid, and non-linear choreography. In such shows, each student had to march, and memorize, a completely individual, unique path. All the students had to move, and work, together, yet in the end, each was on his or her own.

For the students, the process started with being assigned a two-part ID. Grant Longenbaugh was T1, for Trumpet 1; Adilene Corona C31, for Clarinet 31. Nick was the fifth snare drum, or SD 5, and so on.

Putting the drill on the field required two pieces of paper. The first, the drill chart, was a picture, in the exact dimensions of a football field, made up of the individual IDs. The first chart for "Africa," Chart 17, looked vaguely like a line drawing of a tractor. Nick's symbol, a picture of crossed sticks above a snare drum next to the number 5, formed part of the "tractor seat." The drill writers weren't trying to make a picture of a tractor on the field, and the form depicted in Chart 17 would hold that shape for exactly one step. Between Chart 17 and Chart 21, the "tractor" shape would gradually change, until by Chart 21, Nick would be marching the outer perimeter of a curving line.

The second piece of paper the directors were now handing out was a coordinate sheet. The sheets, individualized for each student, identified their exact placement on the field at the start of each drill chart. The language of the coordinate sheets needed decoding: "4.0 Outside N15, 6.5 Front of Front Hash"—Diana de la Reza's coordinates for Chart 17—meant that she was to stand four steps from the north fifteen-yard line, toward the ten-yard line, and six and a half steps in front of one of the two dotted lines, the hash marks, that ran lengthwise down the field.

If drill seemed confusing, it was. The charts and the coordinate sheets were complicated enough for Nick and Diana and the other seniors. (And, truth be told, for the directors as well. Bryan Golden regularly got himself turned around when he tried to decipher his students' coordinate sheets. And Max sometimes told the kids that he didn't think he could do what he was asking of them. There had been no personalized, individual drill when he marched in the Princeton band. He'd had the security of knowing that the students all around him were doing the same thing.) For freshmen like Adilene Corona, the entire process was nearly impenetrable.

Before the start of the season, Nick and a handful of other band members had repainted the practice field with guiding lines for the drill, a complete grid of white dots every two steps. They'd also painted the yard lines that mimicked the football fields where the band would perform. They'd actually painted two sets of hash marks, one in white and one in yellow. The white hash marks matched the width of the high school football fields that would be the location for all of Concord's performances—except one. The yellow dashes marked the slightly narrower width of the Indianapolis Colts' playing field at the RCA Dome. The band would guide off the yellow marks only once, but it was a matter of pride to have them painted on from the beginning.

Each student needed to transcribe the information from the two sheets of paper into personal drill books, which were stacks of spiral-bound file cards that most students looped with string and slung across their bodies. Diana helped Adilene write down her coordinates for the new drill.

Only after they'd gone through the laborious process of translation and notation were the students in the band ready to mark drill. That first evening practice of the school year, Max sent the seniors to the sidelines for paint sticks, repurposed all-weather livestock markers. "OK, we're ready to mark Chart 17." Using their drill books, the students found their places in the "tractor" picture. Diana and Adilene stood at the bottom of its back wheel. When Max gave the word from the tower, each person marked a simple dot and a small circled number designating the chart onto the pavement, then rubbed both marks into the asphalt. Grant, helping the freshmen at the hub of the front wheel, liked the rich oil smell of the sticks and how they felt like extra-big, extra-soft crayons when he marked the nubbly surface. The bright pink and orange paint stained the tips of everyone's fingers. By the end of the season, some places on the field would be covered with marks from multiple points in the drill, all within a few inches of each other, some even piled on top of others—hot zones of drill-chart placement.

The band could reasonably mark a new chart in five minutes. The schedule that night gave them ninety minutes to mark nine charts, twice that long per chart. But the forms were difficult to read, and the energy on the field, at the end of the long first day of school, was diffuse. More than once, the directors had to call the group to attention to refocus them. By the time Max had to move on to reviewing the State Fair show the band would reprise at Concord's first home football game, they were one chart shy of the mark.

They would have to wait until the following week to know how "Africa" actually felt on the field. But Nick had already seen enough to be concerned. He noticed that after Chart 21, the snare line remained behind the band, back by the forty-yard line. It would be hard to maintain the pulse of the band from there. If he could have seen the next charts, he'd have been even more anxious. The snare line kept moving away from the rest of the band, practically into band Siberia.

Friday evening, though, during the last run-through before the football game, Nick's concerns were no longer on paper. Again and again, Max lit into him in front of the entire band: Nick wasn't getting into place quickly enough after the Dixieland snippet to make the roll-off for "Anchors Aweigh." The snare line at the bottom of the second C in C-O-N-C-O-R-D was crooked. The drumline wasn't setting a clear enough beat for "Gabriel's Oboe." Kids in the pit were talking while Max was talking. All these were Nick's fault, apparently, and Max rode him hard.

Their relationship was complicated. Nick looked up to Mr. Jones, and respected his director's talent and authority. He'd been brought up to recognize good band directors, and Max Jones was one of the best. He had felt proud as the new drumline captain at the start of the summer, when Mr. Jones seemed to single him out for approval. But more and more, he felt that Mr. Jones pegged him for criticism, picking on him for the mistakes of others. Nick remained politely deferential, just as he was to Amy Davis. But privately he seethed with resentment.

For his part, Max recognized Nick's exemplary conduct and musical ability, and also that those traits alone were not enough to make the drumline captain a leader. Max could see that Nick was holding back. Max needed Nick to communicate his expectations to the rest of the drumline, and to the entire percussion section, as a peer. He knew that Nick's pushing would be more effective than his pushing. But from the tower, Max looked down and saw the drummers and the pit, and saw Nick holding himself separate, and all of them separate from the rest of the band, the mass of students disengaged, unmotivated. Max worried that Nick was afraid to step out in front of his friends, to challenge them.

But it wasn't as simple as that.

Nick had approached his role as drumline captain as a personal, intellectual exercise. He had imagined himself as one of the leaders he admired, imagined himself acting on the world stage with similar success. He had compartmentalized the role. Outside of the band, he was reluctant to talk with his friends about what was going on in the section. He liked to joke around with them, liked joining in with their teasing. He associated only with the kids he liked. Unless he was teaching, he didn't have much use for the newest kids, or the struggling kids, either. Outside the bubble of the band, as far as he was concerned, they were nothing.

He had only a slight, growing awareness of the context in which his own leadership occurred. On the small stage of the Concord marching band, the context included working with a teacher he didn't respect, a director he admired immensely, and a group of peers, some of whom were his closest friends, some of whom he actively disliked, and some of whom he thought didn't even belong there.

If he could have found words for the feeling, he might have understood that he needed to get his uniform dirty.

By the end of the final run-through of the halftime show, Nick was having a hard time maintaining his composure. Max scolded him for setting the tempo too slow for—of all songs—"Anchors Aweigh," the school song. "Nick, buddy, you got to get it together." For a brief moment, Nick lost his cool. He looked up at the tower. A snarl twisted his normally controlled face. He flicked his drumsticks up in a manner that could only be described as insolent.

He recovered quickly, finished the practice, got ready for the game, sat in the front row of the pep band section with the other snares, did the roll-offs when Bryan Golden asked him to. But inwardly, he continued to fume.

After the game, Nick gunned the Grand Am out of the parking lot. His father had waited up. Wayne saw that something was wrong. Nick didn't want to talk about it at first, but once he started, all his wounded feelings poured out. If Mr. Jones thought he was doing such a bad job, why had he put him in the position in the first place?

Wayne let Nick vent. As he listened, memories of his own frustrations as a drumline captain rose to the surface.

"Do you want to quit?" asked the father.

"No!" said the son.

7 ★ Downbeat

When Max met with his drill writers and choreographers in early June, he believed that the 2004 show would surpass any show he'd ever created.

It was his third season working with the team he called "the LC guys." The three men worked full-time for Lawrence Central, one of the large suburban high schools ringing Indianapolis. They created shows for their own program and for a handful of other schools around the country. Max drove down the Friday after Concord's graduation for the meeting that would kick off their work on the 2004 show, "Roots of American Music." The Lawrence Central band room was a bigger, shinier version of Concord's. Banners and plaques lined its walls, commemorating Class A marching-band championships, Bands of America Grand National championships, concert-band championships, and dozens of appearances at parades and lesser contests. Here was another community that gave generously to its music programs, and out of deeper pockets.

The LC guys had flown in early that morning from Los Angeles, where they'd previewed their itinerary for the 2005 Rose Bowl parade, to which Lawrence Central had been invited. They arrived a few minutes late for the meeting, puffy-eyed and sleepy. Matt James, the head of the team and its main drill writer, hadn't changed out of his freebie Disney T-shirt; Greg Hagen, the team's conceptual mastermind and choreographer, and Todd Hinton, who would create Concord's color-guard routines, both sported sunburns along with their tattoos and earrings. They looked scruffy next to Max, in his pressed T-shirt and shorts. Unlike Max, they were young enough never to have rehearsed a band on a hot summer day wearing a suit coat and tie. But Max appreciated their younger-generation understanding of trends in marching band and their facility with the tools people now used to create the shows. Although he wouldn't have allowed them to dress so casually had they been on his staff in Elkhart, he was willing to look past appearances for the edge the three men gave his program.

Thirty years earlier, when Max began his long championship run at Winchester, he'd been a one-man band director. He'd arranged each show's music and marked out marching drills by hand on graph paper. He'd been thrilled by winning, then; by the standards of that era, he'd driven himself and his students hard. But by the time Max arrived at Concord, one-man operations no longer won the championships. Computers had eased the tedium of writing and revising drills; in the paradoxical pattern of new technology, that ease made drills themselves harder, more complicated and quick-changing. Choreography in turn became more sophisticated. And Max, who by then had stretched the Winchester dynasty past a decade, had discovered the deeper rewards beyond winning, and had started to form the educational structure that he would develop more fully at Concord.

After the first hard years at Concord, Max realized that he was in danger of falling behind his competition. And even though he no longer needed to win for himself, he thought the kids in the program needed to have the opportunity to win.

Max knew his limitations better than people around Concord might have guessed. He didn't pretend to be a choreographer or even a particularly good drill writer. But from the beginning he'd been willing to try new ideas, and he had an astute eye. In addition to his extraordinary skills as a teacher of music and an organizer, he brought a magpie genius to creating marching-band shows. He excelled in collecting the shiniest new ideas and stringing them together in the most interesting and compelling patterns. Still, he knew he needed someone else to take his shiny bits and form them into the coherent whole of drill and dance.

He started looking for drill writers and choreographers to work with the Concord program. Music arranging, the part he did best, he kept for himself.

For fifteen years, he searched for the right match. The drum-corps drill writers whose work he admired on the field could charge $20,000 or more for their skills, and many schools lined up to hire them. But he couldn't justify paying such high fees. They were out of scale in a place like Concord, and as a matter of principle he disliked the advantages conferred by being able to buy the best talent. The teams that he assembled during those years often lived in different parts of the country, and communication became as big a challenge as the drill itself. Charts and choreography arrived late, incomplete, badly coordinated.

During this time, he watched the Greenwood Marching Woodsmen, from a bedroom community south of Indianapolis, replace Winchester as the Class B power, in large part because Greenwood's head director, Jon Sutton, had brought on three talented assistants—Matt James, Greg Hagen, and Todd Hinton—to design his shows. Sutton continued to use the three men even after they'd left Greenwood for Lawrence Central.

Max envied Sutton's coup—drill writers just down the road, a real team that worked together, and one that understood Indiana marching bands—but he wasn't about to poach another director's team, especially when that director was a friend and Class B colleague. The LC guys were off-limits. But the 2000 season made Max even more determined to find a team he could work with over time. Max built his field show that year around a selection the composer described as "Bambi Becoming Godzilla." The three far-flung members of Max's design team seemed, in Max's mind, to turn into Godzillas themselves as the season progressed. That season, for the first time, in spite of what Max considered a superb effort on the part of his students, a Max Jones band did not make it to state finals. Max took the students to the Dome anyway, as spectators, where they watched Greenwood win another Class B championship.

A year later, Max tracked down Jon Sutton. Every December, band directors from around the country came to a conference they called "Midwest" (officially, the Midwest Clinic for Band and Orchestra), where they mingled, listened to performances, and strolled booths. Midwest was Max's best approximation of his old drum-corps–chasing days, a crowded bazaar in which he routinely found new music and new ideas. He arranged to have breakfast with Sutton. Over eggs and a Coke, he asked if Sutton would be willing to let him work with the same drill-writing team that Greenwood used. Sutton knew about Max's troubles. Over the years, he had told the Greenwood staff, and sometimes the students, that Concord could play music, all right, but they didn't have the total package. Even though he knew that his drill-writing team would give Concord that package, he gave Max his blessing.

The next year, using the LC guys for the first time, Concord placed second, Greenwood seventh. That December, Max again ran into Jon Sutton at Midwest and asked him to breakfast. Sutton replied, "Not if you're going to ask me any more questions like last year's!"

Since then, of course, the LC guys had helped Concord to the state championship. The only competition, now, was themselves.

The first visual aid Max brought out was a slide show put together by Jim Faigh, the Concord super–band dad who had been the creative force behind the colorful tarps and guitar platform in the 2003 show. Faigh, a freelance marketer who counted Elkhart's music-instrument companies among his clients, had matched each segment of the show to a historical moment. He'd already worked out the props and the costumes for the color guard—and had the music in mind, as well, had Max asked him for it. One image showed a spreading African acacia tree rising from the back sideline of a football field. Its roots flowed onto the field over a massive tarp. The roots left the tree as earthy tan and brown. But as they moved away from the tree, the colors flowed darker, into deep blues and purple. The still photographs and graphics that followed showed the roots, so to speak, of Faigh's thinking: He picked up the earth tones of the roots closest to the tree for dashiki tunics in the pit; he'd found grainy photos of a New Orleans brass band leading mourners down a city street and images of African-American women dressed for church in big hats for Dixieland's jambalaya of funeral and parade, black and sequins. The tarp's roots flowed into arcs of brilliant cerulean and royal blue, suggesting water, not earth, and signifying the end of the show's journey through American music: the cool blue of jazz.

One of the LC guys—who knew Jim Faigh from the year before, and understood the management challenge an energetic parent like Faigh could present—commented on the thoroughness of Faigh's design ideas.

The tree and the roots represented the African roots of American popular music, and gave physical form to Max's idea. The show was practically a history of American music and dance up through the 1940s. But it was a very particular history. No nod to Sousa or Copland or Charles Ives, here: this was the America of Ken Burns and Wynton Marsalis, who saw jazz as the nation's great art form, founded at the intersection of race and opportunity, freedom and constraint. That the history would be conveyed by a nearly all-white marching band from Indiana was a strangeness unremarked by the drill team, or by Max.

Max's American music was the Methodist hymnal, was Sousa, early rock and roll. He had catholic tastes. He enjoyed many varieties of music, including the more melodic and danceable forms of jazz, like swing. But he'd never been to New Orleans, never heard a real New Orleans jazz band. As did many band directors, he took most of his musical culture through the bowdlerized, watered-down versions of original compositions that comprised the bulk of the school-music diet. He hadn't watched the Ken Burns jazz documentary; race was not his filter, history not his interest. But like all talented arrangers, he knew a great piece of music—and knew a great combination of music, a great show—when he heard it in his head.

Before he showed the other clips, Max recounted his frustrating search for the pieces that would anchor his theme. His original opener had been a wordless chant over African drumming that was both authentic and a beautiful piece of music. But when he couldn't secure the performance rights to that piece and another from the same CD, he settled on a Robert W. Smith piece to which the band already had rights. Max thought "Africa" was an example of "serious" music so common in the public school music-industrial complex, obvious in its musical concepts and lacking forward movement and depth. But he could work with it. He was still searching for an opener when someone suggested "Dry Your Tears, Africa" from John Williams's *Amistad* soundtrack.

That recommendation moved Max from pieces that kept their historical antecedents close to the surface, to "African" rhythms heavily spiced by Hollywood schmaltz. But judges might recognize the film score and make the African connection, and it did have the melodic and percussive elements Max was looking for.

He sent away for permission. He didn't have to wait long for a reply. John Williams, the copyright company informed Max, did not want his music played by marching bands. Guessing that the composer might believe a marching band was incapable of handling the nuances of his score, and would therefore dumb it down, Max sent another letter explaining that he was willing to play the arrangement exactly as Williams had written it. Concord would play it as a concert band on the move. The response was, again, swift and clear: Concord could receive permission to play the song only by agreeing to play it sitting down, in chairs. That exchange had occurred not quite two weeks earlier. Max said to the LC guys, playing the track for them anyway, "This was going to be our music until John Williams hurt our feelings."

"Here's where we are now," Max told them, introducing "Gabriel's Oboe." He showed the same video he would play for the Concord students during band camp, played several selections from the soundtrack of *The Mission*, and explained how the percussive overlay in one of the versions of the main theme could work as the African opener.

Still, as they listened to the long phrases of the ballad, he couldn't keep from expressing some anxiety: "I'm not actually sure you can march to this. We *are* going to have to march at some point, against my better judgment." The LC guys laughed. They knew, as Max did, that even though it was hard to march fast, it was even harder to march slow, because it allowed judges to pick out mistakes as easily as owls spotting slow-moving mice. And they all knew that Concord was not going to win any championships based on its marching.

Even without the vocals, the extended solo in "Gabriel's Oboe" was risky, but Max felt like taking some risks with the show. And it truly was beautiful, hauntingly so. He was less happy about recycling "Africa," but he would play its musically more developed concert-band version, and keep it a transitional piece to the true middle of the show, the Dixieland medley. He'd known from the beginning that he wanted "Swing, Swing, Swing" as his finale. Ironically, it, too, was a John Williams piece, a pared-down version of "Sing, Sing, Sing," the "hot jazz" song that had made drummer Gene Krupa famous. But for some reason, possibly because it was based on another piece, or because it was from a rare Steven Spielberg flop, the movie *1941*, Williams allowed marching bands to play it. Max's toes started tapping as soon as the Dixieland music started. He grinned like a boy, toes going crazy, all the way through the end.

After the viewing, Max, Matt James, and Greg Hagen moved into James's cramped office. The band directors' offices at Lawrence Central were small dark cells off the rehearsal rooms. (Indiana's capital city had yet to build one of its band directors a better office than the one Max occupied at Concord.) Max listened as the drill writer and the choreographer turned the concept, the music, and Jim Faigh's visuals around in their minds, beginning the process of translating Max's vision into movement and forms. The issues they brought up, now, gave voice to concerns that Max had been grappling with, more or less alone, back at Concord. Max felt that his own staff was too junior, too torn by family commitments, and, he suspected, not interested enough to truly share the details and the painstaking process—the obsession—of putting together a show. The more Hagen and James talked through the challenges and possibilities they saw, the more Max relaxed. The more he relaxed, the more excited he became. His grin grew wider. He started to bounce on the balls of his feet. He cracked jokes.

The first and most obvious challenge the LC guys faced was the size of the Concord band. Concord's numbers tested the designers' abilities on several fronts. On the purely operational level, they'd have to manipulate almost twice as many spots on the field as in the Lawrence Central band, their own band. And needing to work with so many marchers would limit the forms they could use. Most important, knowing Concord's historical weakness in marching, they'd have to find even more ways to disguise "dirty feet"—out-of-step marching, missed stops and starts, delayed turns.

The LC guys were all over it. Ideas came rapid-fire. Greg Hagen said, "Whenever we have a high-velocity moment, we need to have them stacked up tight, so all you're seeing is the form." He reassured Max that he understood the issues, and that he had solutions: "We'll want to use the mass of people as a way to communicate."

After the previous championship, it had gotten back to Max that a student from another school, waiting to compete after Concord, had complained, "How can we compete with a rock concert?" Now Max felt the same pressure to entertain, but also recognized it as an opportunity. He told his collaborators, "We want to be blatant and have a good time doing it." As an educator, he wanted to expand the musical and cultural horizons of his students. But personally, he was impatient with scores—with anything—that appealed strictly to the mind. He wanted to bring the joy of music to his students, wanted them to feel the pleasure of making music. In the meeting, he called it "wanting more of the State Fair circus." But, he told the LC guys, "We want to be sophisticated enough to get credit."

Greg Hagen got it. "I think the band last year set itself apart," he told Max. "I think statewide, Midwest-wide, it was understood as a presentation that didn't look like marching band as everyone knows it to be." That was especially so, he said, among the bands of Class B, a group that traditionally focused on cleanliness and straight lines. "But that sense of pageantry . . . ," he said, then paused and seemed to roll this description of the 2003 show around inside his mind. Liking it, he repeated it. "The pageantry in that show took the idea of a marching-band show to a new level."

Mulling the new concept out loud, Hagen told Max, "You need theatrical ways to create energy, gridded ways to create energy. I hesitate even to say this, but your beginning is very *Lion King*–ish." He meant the roots, the tree, Africa as a symbol for humankind's first home. He compared the new Concord show to a performance he'd seen earlier that year at Disney World. "What we're saying with this show is that it's a theatrical event. If you look at this set, you've got the African bush back there and this modernistic dance hall down here. Even if the show hasn't been announced yet, you're going, 'It's a transition from this idea to this idea.' It becomes a stage."

He'd hit on an important insight into the new show, and their route to the next level. Now the model they were emulating was Disney, Broadway—a show. He developed the idea with enthusiasm: "This is a timeline moving from here to now." The timeline would advance down the tarp, until the show ended at the front sideline. One more step, and they'd be into soul, R & B, rock and roll, fusion, the splendor and confusion of the modern world.

The talk was of transcending marching band. But, Hagen warned Max, "That's what the music is saying to me. Then when you start rehearsing it and we're looking at the computer and we start mathematizing everything, it becomes more structured and leaves the creative realm and it starts to become more what it can really do."

Max still owed them final numbers and the final arrangements, but he would start seeing drill in mid-August, right after State Fair. He felt buoyed as he left the meeting. He'd hoped for a confirmation of his high hopes for the show, and he'd gotten it. He liked everything he heard, liked how he and this team seemed to push each other, to inspire each other. There was pleasure in the process. Even though the "Roots of American Music" show would be the grand summary gesture of his career, there was no need, yet, to tell James, Hagen, and Hinton that it was the last show the four of them would ever create together.

AUGUST ENDED AND September ticked past the Labor Day parade, toward the start of the field-show season. Max started seeing a different reality than the one he'd hoped for back in June.

The drill dribbled in from the start. The charts for "Africa" came in from the LC guys a week later than Max had expected. Greg Hagen had promised he'd come up and teach the entire band the choreography for "Gabriel's Oboe" on a Wednesday so he could take advantage of both the afternoon and the evening rehearsals. But he called and canceled, and canceled again. Max understood the pressures on the LC team. He knew they had to juggle the needs of several clients in addition to their own show for Lawrence Central; he knew the Concord show was complicated and ambitious. He wasn't surprised when Matt James told him that they'd rewritten the end of the "Africa" drill three times before they were satisfied with it. But he couldn't be patient indefinitely.

At any rate, he and the rest of the Concord staff had their hands full with "Africa." The band was moving through its charts much more slowly than Max had hoped. "Mixing bowl" pinwheels stymied the younger marchers, then rotating blocks. Two days in a row, they worked through only one chart, several other days only two. At that pace, he snapped at them, they'd finish mapping out the show by November—long after the season had ended.

Even more discouraging, Max had learned in the past two weeks that many students, and not just freshmen, could not play the music they'd worked on all summer—not while also marching to it. They'd started testing on "Gabriel's Oboe." The band had started working on the field-show opener during freshman band camp and had performed it at State Fair. But when the students played the music in small groups in front of the directors and added in step-offs, halts, and marching single-time or double-time, it quickly became apparent that they didn't know the music or the marching as well as they, or their directors, had thought.

Adilene Corona failed her first test, as did nearly every freshman clarinet. She'd scored 15 out of a possible 100. "If I fail," she asked Steve Peterson, "do I march?"

"Nope, you're out," he said.

"Can I still go to California?"

"Nope. You're out. If you bake me cookies, you can go to California."

The band trip that year was to California. The stated purpose of the trip was to march in the Hollywood Holiday parade the day after Thanksgiving, but Max, as always, had wrapped sightseeing and side trips around the main event. Adilene wasn't particularly interested in the Getty Art Museum or the Crystal Cathedral, or in Thanksgiving dinner aboard the *Queen Mary*, but she very much wanted to go to Disneyland and to the beach. Her parents still hadn't decided whether she could go. The trip cost twelve hundred dollars.

She walked away from her test, not sure if Mr. Peterson had been joking, or how much he'd been joking, which was his intent. Peterson didn't want to give her the lowest bar she could get over. He didn't want her to give up, and he didn't want her to do less than she was capable of. He wanted her to get it, period.

Handing back drill books at the beginning of yet another afternoon trying to untangle the intricacies of "Africa," Steve Peterson told the woodwinds they had to put more effort into practicing the parts of the show they'd already learned. "It's how you play by yourself that tells you how well you know your music. Whatever your system of practicing is, it's not working. Not enough minutes, not enough intensity. It's your section. I'm on the same team you are, but I can't play your instruments for you."

He took Diana de la Reza aside after practice and told her just how badly Adilene and some of the other freshmen had played. They'd managed to play at most ten measures of the entire composition.

Diana defended the freshmen. "I know they're better than that."

Her director gently disagreed. "When they go home and practice, they're not going to go after it," he told her. "That was a good example of their performance. You've been working with them, right? Have you been getting them to play for *you*?"

He'd already set up "pods"—small groups of upperclassmen and freshmen—to foster the extra teaching and learning that clearly needed to happen. He knew that Diana de la Reza was taking her role seriously, but he saw much less effort from other seniors. Later that night, at home, Peterson asked his wife, "Why do we need to push them every year? Is it me?"

After the first round of testing, Max told the band, "We're having good rehearsals, so we think. But when you get right down to it, individual for individual, we may not be as solid as we need to be." He gave them a chance to redo their "Gabriel's Oboe" tests and pushed out the testing on "Africa" by a week. Everything now was slipping.

Some of the kids were failing to meet Max's basic requirement for marching band: giving their best effort. A week into the new school year, he started bringing the biggest problems, one by one, into his office. Directors and students, alike, referred to such meetings as "The Talk." Often, simply being face-to-face with Mr. Jones, having to meet his eyes and his direct questions, was enough to bring straying sheep back into the fold.

Jon Faloon, the only senior in the pit, was near the top of Max's "Talk" list. Jon still nursed a grudge over not making it onto the drumline for his final year in band and had become a bad influence in a group primed to go that direction. He was the kind of kid who seemed to flirt with trouble even when he didn't mean to, the kind of kid who stuck blinky lights on either side of his nose, and then had to be taken to the ER to get the magnets extracted. Max also knew that he was a naturally talented, if undisciplined, musician. Max didn't yell at him in their meeting, or tick off the many rules he'd broken, the work he'd left undone, a list Jon himself could have given. Instead, Max told Jon that he saw the younger students emulating him. He knew they valued what Jon knew about music, knowledge he could pass on to them. Max told him, "You can make a difference in their lives."

Max didn't get the charts for "New Orleans Jazz Portrait," the Dixieland segment, until the Wednesday following Labor Day, two weeks behind schedule. He expected Greg Hagen to come that night to teach the choreography for the first part of the show, but Hagen called before fifth hour to cancel for the third time in as many weeks. Already, the delays on choreography meant that they were about to compete in their first invitational, at nearby Goshen, with an incomplete first section. They would have to stand and play the Dixieland music without marching, and they'd have to keep using "Anchors Aweigh" to end the show.

Max pleaded that week, "Please mount a challenge." This was the moment in every season when it became clear how committed the students were, or were not. Three weeks into the school year, course-work and other activities were beginning to pile up for some kids as boredom set in for others. But the show wouldn't come together unless the students started putting in extra hours on their own.

That extra work had a name: sectionals. By tradition, the leaders of each instrumental section determined when the extra practices were nec-essary, and how the work got done depended partly on the personality of the section. The flutes and high brass were the Type As who knew they played the most difficult instruments in the band, and thought that meant they were better than everyone else. It was a truth grudgingly rec-ognized by the other students that those instrumental groups frequently produced the band's best musicians and leaders. The students who played low brass—trombones, baritones, tubas—prided themselves on their collective ability to get the work done and then relax, something they suspected the more tightly wound high brass were incapable of do-ing. The clarinets played a similar role relative to the flutes, although they sometimes wondered if they truly were second-class citizens. The students on the drumline *knew* they were better than all the others, and the kids in the pit were just happy when practice was over.

So it wasn't surprising that Grant Longenbaugh and Amanda Bech-tel, the high-brass and flute section leaders, had already started holding sectionals. Grant had asked the seniors to hold mini-sectionals with one or two younger students. He'd worked with individual students, with small groups of students, and with every freshman in the high-brass section at one time or another. He and the other two amigos were bringing along the sophomores and juniors who were trying to learn to lead. At home, after homework, he found most of his section online, and others in the band as well, jostling with each other for the chance to talk to him, and he played Concord's Dear Abby into the night. At the beginning of the season, with so many distractions swirling through his mind, he hadn't felt sure he could muster the energy to care for and nourish so many people, or even that he wanted to. But halfway into the season, he was finding great solace in his role in the band. At least here he knew what he needed to do, and he liked the clarity.

Brent Lehman, aware that some of his low-brass peers suspected he was a high-brass wannabe, had also started holding extra sectionals. He had managed to get most of the freshmen to attend, but not nearly as many of the sophomores and juniors as he would have liked. So he

worked hard, often driving kids home after rehearsals. Two years earlier, when his brother was a senior and the one with the car keys, they'd
clashed over how far their commitment to the band should extend, and
Brent had lost the argument. Now he had the keys. Sometimes he
paused for a moment in front of the house or trailer or apartment into
which a bandmate had just disappeared and tried to imagine the world
through that person's eyes. He often came up blank. But once or twice
he'd had a flash of insight—a sophomore's struggle to make better
choices, the way a messy divorce was messing with another kid's
head—and it kept him trying.

He'd hoped for more help from Brandon Schenk, the gregarious junior who had such an easy touch with people, but Brandon seemed to
have quit putting in time as a leader. Brent knew that the trombone
player didn't need the extra repetitions, but he thought the junior
should understand how his negative attitude affected the other students. If Brandon didn't run back to his spot, neither would the freshmen. That was just how it worked. But Brandon, who had just been
given the male lead in Concord's fall play, saw it differently. Theater,
not band, was part of the future he'd mapped out for himself, and he
was frustrated by the lack of room in Max Jones's system for kids like
him, kids who might enjoy marching band and even be able to contribute, but didn't see it as their main identity.

Brandon saw Brent trying to do the right thing, but he wasn't crazy
about the obviousness of Brent's effort. And Brandon couldn't rid his
mind of a scene from the year before, when Brent had lost his temper
and slammed his trombone onto the ground. And why? Because he'd
wanted to practice *now,* and everyone else had wanted to play soccer
first. Brandon couldn't forget the outburst, or see that Brent had truly
changed.

After practice, Scott Spradling talked to the upperclassmen in the
high-brass section. Eight freshmen trumpets had failed their "Gabriel's
Oboe" tests. "We lose freshmen now because they think they can't do
it," he warned them. After Spradling left, Grant held back the seniors.
One by one, he asked them how their mini-sectionals were working.
Some, like Keith McCrorey, had worked almost daily with their students. Others hadn't met once with their small groups.

Grant thought, but didn't say, *Maybe you should start cranking.* Instead, he said, "Maybe it's time to add full sectionals."

AT LAST, SEVERAL weeks later than Max had planned, and only a few days before the fall season's first competition, the band started work on the Dixieland segment of the show. Max had hoped to have marked all the drills for the important middle portion of the show by then, and be deep into rehearsing the drill and the choreography. He knew that the Goshen Invitational was drawing only four bands in Class B, and only eight bands overall, and he didn't expect tough competition. He was more focused on Concord's own invitational, coming up a week after Goshen. They had to get the heart of the show on the field.

With the two Dixieland tunes, the band left the African continent and moved into the American Deep South. Both pieces in the medley pulsed with a syncopated "swing" rhythm, meaning that the accents driving the melodies fell on the second and fourth counts of a four-beat measure. Around Concord, the white-bread kids, particularly the kids from East Side, were said to "swing" on one and three—that is, they couldn't emphasize the offbeats, and were thus hopelessly square. The staff joked that Max, who lived in the East Side elementary district, was a true East Sider, too.

The joke pointed up the difficulty of teaching jazz. Steve Peterson sometimes worked with his jazz students over an entire season before he saw them begin to internalize the rhythm. And these were students in the *jazz* band, the *top* jazz band. A swing beat underlay blues, ragtime, New Orleans parade bands. In all those forms, the 2-4 beat often "swung" a bit to one side or another, seeming to speed past the exact second or fourth count or lollygag behind it. Played correctly, the beat constantly surprised expectations. Even Peterson's most dedicated jazz-band students—Grant, for example—didn't always grasp the more advanced lesson of how to drive a rhythm forward or, alternately, to slow it down, using those offbeats. And only the rarest of students could make the rhythm feel natural, as if they always knew where they were in relation to it. So to try to teach every kid in the marching band how to swing, even the kids who struggled to find a straight-ahead 1-3 pulse, could seem a doomed effort. Noble, perhaps, but crazy. If the directors were lucky, after the fact, the effort would look inspired.

Anybody listening to the New Orleans anthem, "When the Saints Go Marching In," would recognize the swing rhythm in a heartbeat, but even hymns such as the medley's opening, "A Closer Walk with Thee," had it. The trumpet and the trombone came from the dance hall; they were secular instruments. At some point in African-American music history, they'd married into the spiritual family. Now "A Closer Walk with Thee" was played with one foot tapping earth, one eye to the sky, the ragtime instruments carrying the conversation between people and God.

Later, working with his woodwinds on the Dixieland style, Peterson stopped and said, "Now you guys are jammin'! Hallelujah! Call it heat, salsa, skank, whatever you want. But people should be testifying in the stands when they hear you. That would have been within the city limits of New Orleans—now let's get to Bourbon Street!"

Matt Tompkins, who had played the wailing guitar solo in the championship show the year before, debuted on the banjo, the newest experiment in the Dixieland ensemble. "I like the banjo," Max said from the center tower.

"It could be the first marching banjo in history," Scott Spradling said from another tower. "Now I can die in peace."

CONCORD EASILY WON the Goshen Invitational, taking first place in every caption: music, marching, percussion, color guard, drum majors, and general effect. One judge, aware of how Concord worked, went so far as to predict a repeat championship for the still half-baked show. Afterward, Grant held his first party of the season. Leandra was there. Snacks filled the kitchen counter and the dining room table. In the renovated basement, where the new sofas had taken their places only days before, the teenagers watched a video that Grant's father had taken of their performance, getting a preview of what they'd see at school the following Monday. Several boys played Texas Hold 'Em at a card table. When Chris Longenbaugh came downstairs with a tray of her homemade Blizzards—Oreo cookie ice cream and Cool Whip mixed together in a creamy, sweet parfait—it seemed like old times.

Greg Hagen finally showed up to teach the Dixieland choreography just three days before Concord's own invitational. His arrival was so far behind schedule that he had to cover not only the two Dixieland pieces, but "Gabriel's Oboe" and all of "Africa," as well.

In a black T-shirt, black socks, black shorts, and black jazz shoes (doing the artist thing in the band vernacular), Hagen showed them how they could take the jazz history behind the medley and illustrate it on the field. He explained that a classic New Orleans funeral always included a slow march of musicians and mourners to the cemetery, but that high-spirited music, party music, accompanied the return from the graveyard. Their show would follow the same progression from mourning to celebration, starting with the soulful, bluesy rendition of "A Closer Walk with Thee," and ending with "When the Saints Go Marching In." The kids had marked the drill on the pavement the week before, but now Hagen made sense of it for them.

He stopped them at Chart 39 and pointed out that now they were separated into two smaller bands. He asked them to imagine themselves in New Orleans, at the passing of one of the funerals. While the Dixieland ensemble played in front, the color guard would dance down the "street." The rest of them—the crowd—would act like extras in a movie, miming their reaction to the parade for the audience. Hagen said, "I need people who are theatrical, who can tell a story." Many students turned to look at Brandon Schenk in the trombone line, who shrugged, gave them a sheepish smile, and raised his hand. Hagen used Brandon to demonstrate the slow-motion gestures he wanted. While Brandon gave an exaggerated, quarter-speed wave, Hagen did the voice-over: "Weee'rrre claaaappppinngggg for the paaaarrrraaade. Looooook, it's my uunnnnnnncle iiiiinnn the paaaaaaraaaaade." In his normal voice, he continued, "The movie will run in slow time while the parade's running in real time. Then the parade will expand to include everyone, and from then on it's real."

On the field, though, Hagen's explanation and Brandon's demonstration didn't translate. Few kids seemed to get it. The noise on the field grew with their frustration. The Dixieland ensemble moved back to help teach, but Grant, Brent, and the others were ignored. The merging of the crowd into the parade was muddy, and the sense of the now-whole band stepping out in syncopated celebration was lost altogether. The band's concentration broke down with their marching. From the tower, Max heard laughter and more chitchat. Max had always been proud of the way his bands responded to Greg Hagen's teaching. He knew that Hagen had been impressed by the efficiency of Concord's operation and by how the older students treated the younger ones and got them to perform. He had urged Lawrence Central's head director to come with him and watch

Concord rehearse. Lawrence Central was a national champion band, but they had changed their whole rehearsal structure because of what Greg Hagen saw at Concord. Now, standing alongside Hagen on the tower, Max felt ashamed.

The next day, before practice, he waited outside the music department doors for students to arrive for a hastily called seniors-only meeting. While he waited for all the seniors to show up, he stood with a hand on one hip, the green bag he always brought to rehearsals slung over a shoulder. One of his legs bounced, stopped, then started up again while he jingled the coins in his pocket. He didn't say a word to the students who had already gathered there, just let the bouncing leg and his silence convey his mood.

When everyone had gathered around him, he began. "Bottom line, I'm extremely disappointed in how you're doing." His voice was quiet, but he seemed to bite off each word.

"We've talked about what an incredible group of kids you are. And you are. But as far as what you're doing about leading this band, it's extremely disappointing. As a class, you are not effective. The class ahead of you and you, combined, did a better job of being in service to this band.

"So I created this."

He held up a piece of paper divided into seven days and three categories. "This is a diary or a log. I expect you to turn it in every Monday. If you don't, then I will cut your grade, bigtime. You can say on the day—for example, today, Thursday, September 16—what did you do personally to improve yourself? Say if you practiced for five minutes, or three minutes, or one minute, or I didn't do diddly. And then the second one, what did you do to help somebody else?" The final column gave them a chance to grade their efforts. "Because we've talked about this since we were in Michigan City sitting on the beach. And what's more, you've been doing it as you've grown up in the program. Some of you. Some of you have yet to lift a finger to help anybody. And that's where it is, folks. When you become the leaders, that's what your job is. It's not how good am I, how cool. It's what I do to help others be good."

He told them he'd hand back the forms at the end of the season, once they knew how it had ended. "Six more Wednesday nights, folks."

Frustrations that he'd silenced all season burst out. One irritation bled into another.

"You're all talking about state championships. I know it. 'We're number one!' Baloney! We march lousy. We play lousy. And we don't try. As a band.

"I thought you were the class of classes, maybe the all-time greatest. In my whole career—I've been teaching thirty-seven years, you aren't even close to that old, you aren't even half that old, probably—I can only name about five great classes. And I truly believed that you might be the best one ever. But right now, it ain't happening."

Max faced versions of these problems with every band. But two things made this group different: This was a defending champion band that seemed to be coasting—seemed, as a group, to think it no longer needed to work hard. And Max had extraordinarily high expectations for them.

"Anyone else has a band like this," he reminded them, "they will have fifteen, twenty, thirty adults working with them all the time. They can hardly call it their own. We are family, and it's time to do something besides for yourselves.

"Here's your log. I hope you're the people I think you are. I know who you could be. I'm not going to let you off the hook. I expect you to be great."

The talk rambled on, eventually filling fifteen minutes, an extravagance of time. Max had used the well-timed harangue to great effect over the years; it was one of his sharpest tools. But this talk edged into more personal territory. It was a barometer of Max's frustration, and a sign, perhaps, of the growing disconnect he felt with this generation of students. His irritable aside that their life experience didn't add up to even half the number of years he'd been teaching was telling. Like a parent who resorts, finally, to yelling, his speech hinted at a sense of fatigue, a sense of personal injury—*How can you do this to me?*—and, as damning for teachers as for parents, a lack of creativity. Like perfectionists everywhere, Max saw what wasn't working and wanted it fixed. His one-sided quarrel gave them no room to respond, no way to enlist, and no reason to get fired up. His appeal would reach those in the group—Grant, Amanda—who were also perfectionists and the idealists like Brent Lehman who wanted to do the right thing. But not the kids who didn't know if they could give, or were afraid to find out how little they might contribute, or who simply didn't want to work that hard. A few of the kids already believed that Max would never be satisfied, and were quietly waging personal rebellions against him and his whole program. For them, there was no solution. By the end of the talk, a number of seniors had tuned Max out.

MAX'S SABBATICAL PLANS weren't working out the way he'd hoped, either.

He had talked to his assistants as a group during the senior trip to Chicago. He presented the Purdue opportunity as the culmination of a career in music, a rare chance to help lead a top college band. In recent weeks, he'd talked to each of his assistants privately, laying out his plan in more detail. His idea was to take off three consecutive fall trimesters, which meant missing three marching seasons. He told them how he thought it could work: The remaining staff would divvy up the work that Max had handled, and they'd hire a junior staff member, maybe some-one right out of college, to offload some of their other work. Max would return for concert season; he'd still run the department and, during the rest of the year, handle the budget and all the time-consuming interfaces between the music department and the school administration, parents, and boosters. To Max, the plan was a chance for his senior directors to rehearse the role of band director for a limited run, without having to go through an audition. He wasn't going to be at Concord forever. If they ever wanted to run the full show, here was their own golden opportunity.

But the other directors saw the situation differently.

Scott Spradling, the senior member of Max's staff, had been at Con-cord for seventeen years, nearly as long as the director himself. He had hoped that Max would offer the job of directing to him alone. Max—who'd been a father figure for Spradling since seventh grade—hadn't done that. Spradling had never led a program, and worried that he was some-how deficient because he hadn't already left to be in charge somewhere else. Instead of the hoped-for affirmation of his abilities and his dedica-tion, however, he felt that he'd received a judgment, maybe a confirma-tion. But Spradling felt, too, that Max's strict control over the program and his ingrained habit of withholding information from the rest of them made it almost impossible to hand off as he'd proposed. To Spradling, the arrangement seemed unworkable, but he found it hard to say so to Max.

Steve Peterson told Max he didn't want the responsibility of being the music director, even for one trimester. It seemed obvious to him that Max's plan didn't build in nearly enough support. The hours he worked during the summer and fall, and again in the spring directing the jazz program, already stressed his family and kept him from spending enough time with his son. Adam had been born three years earlier on the day before the music department's biggest spring happening, Jazz Café. Peterson ran the popular event, which one night every year transformed the high school gymnasium into a crowded, smoky jazz club (the smoke coming not from cigarettes but from a fog machine). After Adam's arrival, Peterson left a message for Max saying that he'd be taking off the first days of the following week, missing the jazz band tour of the elementary schools. Max called Peterson at home and told him he was being selfish, thinking just of himself. He told Peterson that the kids in the jazz band needed him as much as his wife and newborn son did. The two men traded barbs. Steve said to Max, "It's just the elementary school!" Max replied, "It's just a baby." When Peterson got off the phone, he stormed into his basement. He nearly punched a hole in the wall, and the bones in his hand felt tender for a long time afterward.

Peterson now had a second child due in December. He knew not to mention family pressures to Max. He wanted to say, "Max, *you're* just being selfish, thinking only of yourself and your opportunity. What about the kids? What about the rest of us?" But he kept his mouth shut.

Steve and Kathy Peterson weren't the only ones with a baby on the way. Scott Spradling and his wife Mary had a two-year-old son and a baby due the day before the Concord Invitational. Spradling had been the announcer for the invitational every year they'd hosted it. He had training in broadcasting, a smooth baritone voice, and a sense of humor. He'd reassured everyone that he planned to be at the invitational—he and Mary had an induction scheduled for the following Monday—and that he had trained a replacement, just in case. Max was from a generation that didn't understand why family concerns should get in the way of work that needed to be done. His own marriage, an unusually collaborative partnership, had kept his career at the center. During the days leading up to the weekend, Max prepared for the invitational as if it were the only big event in any of their lives.

Max was nonplused that none of his senior directors wanted to take on the challenge, that none wanted to help him. His vision for what came next, for him and for the band, had become much more murky. Two days until their own invitational. Lord knows there was enough work to do.

8 ★ "We the People"

The morning of the Concord Invitational dawned damp and chilly. Thick, low clouds squatted on top of the buildings and the press box at the top of the football field, giving the day a somber cast. At first light, Concord superintendent George Dyer was already driving a cart around with the school's maintenance crew looking for flat, grassy areas on which to paint lines, even though the heavy ground fog obscured their search. They'd need every possible parking spot they could fit onto school property before the day was over. The institutional kitchen at the high school was already warm, crowded, and full of conversation as band moms chopped and diced, mixed and stirred, and worked through lists taped along the stainless steel shelves. Other women moved around the big table in the music office, tallying advance ticket sales and bagging and pricing blinky lights that had arrived late the day before and needed to go on sale in the concession stand at noon. The one-day Concord Invitational was the Concord Music Association's biggest fund-raiser every year. Any band director worth his baton within one hundred miles of Max's kingdom wanted to be in Concord on the third Saturday of September. The best programs from northern Indiana would be there, along with bands from Michigan and even a few from near Indianapolis. The quality of the judging, the efficiency of the operation, the level of competition—even the food—set Concord's invitational apart. The parents knew that the contest trained a bright light on the program, and all of Concord, in front of some of the most important eyes in the Indiana marching-band world. Behind the scenes, a small community worked to pull it off. It would be an exaggeration to say that the work went on 24/7. But not by much.

Numbers told part of the story: Beginning at noon and ending nearly 12 hours later, 40 bands—as many as would compete in the season's finale at the RCA Dome—would march onto Concord's football field and perform in front of an ever-changing but always packed and enthusiastic audience. The band parents planned for 10,000 spectators and more than 4,500 competitors. Already, band parents had fanned out to airports in South Bend, Indianapolis, and Chicago to pick up the 10 judges and chauffeur them to their hotels. Subcommittees had divvied up to-do lists and logistics, including how they'd shoehorn 69 semitrailers, 79 vans, and 130 school buses onto the grounds surrounding the football field, not to mention all those cars. (Jim Faigh used computer graphics to break down the parking layout and coverage; Jeff Longenbaugh, for instance, was assigned position B-1 in the last of three time slots.) The massive undertaking seemed to energize the parents.

The band dads were an in-house service department. Each season, their most visible contributions were the props, like the ramps and tarps that had linked to form the guitar in the previous year's show. But they were also the group that the directors came to when they needed a problem fixed: how to carry mutes on the field, how to transport several dozen instruments quickly. The answers—cowboy-style mute holders, rolling carts—were always designed by committee and executed using whatever materials came to hand. The band dads prided themselves on their ability to engineer solutions, usually on a low budget.

Great as the previous season had been, Jim Faigh couldn't forget how close they'd come to not pulling everything together in time. He had decided to get a jump on the 2004 season. Before band camp had even started, he'd already purchased 250 square yards of heavy-duty tarpaulin and set a crew to painting it. They'd roll out the finished tarp for the first time at the invitational that night. So far, the band dads were ahead of schedule, and Jim Faigh wanted to keep it that way.

Ten of them met at their usual booth-plus-a-table in a corner of Gramma's Restaurant, "where two eggs is always four," for their Saturday morning breakfast-and-banter session. It had been an inventive week: They'd fashioned four-inch-to-two-inch PVC reducers from a plumbing supply store into the holsters for the high-brass mutes. They'd put an Elkhart Fire Department snorkel truck to use as a makeshift photographer's platform. The annual marching-band portrait had been shot the previous Saturday, set among the rusting old steam engines and boxcars of the New York Central Railroad train museum in downtown Elkhart. The location and the band's size had created a problem for the photographers, but the band dads had solved it. It helped that the fire chief was one of them.

There'd been a certain amount of rework: There was bound to be, in the Max Jones system, even in a good year. Earlier that week, Max had determined that the large painted surface of the tarp glared too harshly under the lights. The band dads had hastily repainted the tarp and sprinkled fifty pounds of kitty litter onto it to soak up the tackiness. They wouldn't know whether the new paint job had done the trick until the band's 10:30 performance at the invitational, the event's finale.

That morning around the table, Mark Tack steered the conversation to the day's task list. "Listen up! I'm only going to say this six times!" Pushing aside empty plates and cups of coffee and using napkins as stand-ins, the dads debated whether the two sections of the tarp should be fan-folded or rolled up starting from one sideline. This wasn't make-work: Half a football-field's worth of canvas was both heavy and unwieldy, and at the first ISSMA contest in two weeks, the tarp would become part of the band's time allotment. The dads would be under serious pressure to move it on and off the field quickly. At three o'clock that morning, Darrel Yoder had sent around a lengthy e-mail in support of one folding method that made no sense to him when he got up two and a half hours later.

Earlier that week, Max had mentioned to Teri Schenk, Brandon's mother and the president of the Concord Music Association, that he wished they had someplace for the judges to rest during their twelve-hour workdays at the invitational. Two days later, Schenk called back to say she'd found him a judges' lounge: Monaco Coach, one of Elkhart's big RV manufacturers, had agreed to loan one of its midline vehicles, sticker price around $300,000. By Friday, a Holiday Rambler, its four slide-outs at full extension and its three flat-screen TVs all in working order, was parked near the concession stand just outside the gates to the field. The judges would need to walk only a short distance for a nap or a break from the bands and their directors. By the morning of the invitational, "Judge Lounge/RV" appeared on the hospitality committee's master list for food-tray delivery, as if it had always been there.

ON A DAY that put Max's high-level organizational skills so much on display, a small part stood out in relief. Scott Spradling's baby—a girl—had arrived, right on her due date, as if keeping to a Max Jones schedule. Max, already worried about so many things he felt responsible for but couldn't control, now was down a director and his emcee for the invitational. The new worry crowded out whatever other feelings he might have had about the news.

Nevertheless, the other director's absence created an unexpected opportunity for Max. Spradling had taken pains to train a replacement to take his place in the press box as announcer and had prepared Grant Longenbaugh and Craig Searer to run warm-ups for the high brass. But Max still had a directing void in the high-brass section. He decided to fill it himself.

Max had made it clear to his students that the three-and-a-half-hour rehearsal beginning at 7:30 on Saturday morning was a life raft thrown out by the band gods on the troubled seas of their past week. If they grabbed hold of it, they could rescue their good standing with him, save that evening's show, and maybe even change the course of the season. But they had to work hard, and on the right things.

Max knew that a show could leap forward with focused, methodical detail work. His method involved slowing down a trouble spot until he identified the one or two steps that needed to be cleaner, the one or two kids who needed another round of explanation. The approach only worked, though, if everyone stayed with it. If those one or two kids refused to work, or gave up, the entire effort was wasted.

He turned his attention to a difficult section of "Africa," a block of trumpets that slid across the fifty-yard line first in one direction and then in the other, rotating every sixteen counts. Max had his eye on one student in particular, a lanky sophomore named Jim Schoeffler, who missed nearly every turn and many of his step-offs. The year before, Jim had argued with his instructors, skipped sectionals, complained constantly, and told everyone that he was done with marching band as soon as the season was over. Still, he had come back. (Laurie Schalliol sniffed, "All last year he said, 'I'm quitting.' We were all, like, yay. But darn if once he got that championship ring, he decided not to.") But he hadn't changed his tune.

For Scott Spradling, Jim Schoeffler was a particularly hard case, the kind of student who highlights a teacher's weak spots. During marching band the year before, Jim's parents made it clear to Spradling that they thought he didn't like their son and was treating him unfairly, in public, in front of his peers. Spradling *was* hard on Jim; he was hard on all his students. He accepted being hated if a student also thought, *I'll show you!* and then did the hard work. Jim Schoeffler frustrated his director. But Scott Spradling didn't dislike the student; he just thought the teenager had become used to getting too much for doing too little. The week before, Jim Schoeffler's father had called a meeting with the high-brass director to ask why Jim hadn't been given one of the better trumpet parts, instead of being kept with the thirds. Spradling asked if he'd heard Jim practice at home very often. "No . . . ," the senior Schoeffler had replied.

Jim's father, president of a company that supplied add-ons for RV and car manufacturers, and reportedly one of the county's wealthiest men, traveled frequently for his work. His schedule, along with Jim's experience in the band, hadn't inclined the Schoefflers to volunteer as band parents. If they had, however, they might have seen for themselves how the directors worked with their son, observed Jim among his peers, and perhaps found common ground.

But the Schoefflers didn't want to spend even more time around the music department. Band was just one of five classes that Jim took every day, but it didn't function at all like the others. To Jim's parents, band's multiple non-academic requirements and a seemingly endless series of "voluntary" practices made it feel suspiciously like an extracurricular activity, not a class. Band's time commitment regularly conflicted with an extracurricular activity that Jim did enjoy—playing on the school tennis team. His parents thought Jim should have the right to organize his time outside of regular school hours, and that marching band should be called what it really was.

Even some of the band's best leaders shared some of the Schoefflers' frustration with the commitment it required. Keith Yoder waggishly revised the band's 2003 tagline to reflect the tension felt by many, saying, "Thank you, Mr. Jones, for changing my life. Now may I have my soul back?"

The Schoefflers would continue to meet with Spradling over his handling of their son's absences and tardiness, most of them tennis-related. And the discussions would continue to end in impasse.

Now Max possibly had an opening to resolve a long-standing conflict, and at the same time to make a difference in how the show would be judged that night. As he worked with the trumpet block along the fifty-yard line, trying to sharpen its lines and its movements, he singled out the skinny sophomore with the frown and the slumping shoulders. "Jim, you've shortened your steps because of the mute. Take bigger steps."

"Jim, on that eight where you have to cover ten, take bigger steps."

"You've got to cover ten, Jim."

"Jim, bigger steps. You're taking bigger steps toward the end."

When they still had trouble with the sequence after a few run-throughs, Max broke down the drill into smaller units. He counted out to Jim and the others when they'd reach certain markers, and where they were in relation to one another. "Jim, you're right on the forty-five-yard line on count two; Laurie, you're right behind him." He was trying to help them create an image of the form in their minds, and then to associate certain counts in the drill with particular locations and particular people.

Every student in the Concord band marched a unique drill. For parts of it, students had to pay attention only to what they, alone, were doing. But forms like the trumpet block required a deeper awareness of the group. Max kept calling the trumpet players by name and orienting them in the block by the locations of their classmates. Jim, but also others, looked up at Max and then around, as if noticing each other, and their connectedness, for the first time.

"Jim, you always stay two steps to the left of Jared."

"You hit a straight line every six counts, guys."

"You see who you're going to be behind at halfway. Jim, halfway you're behind Ellen. By the end you're behind Tyler."

"Rayna, now you're behind Jim. See that?"

Jim seemed to brighten under the steady and increasingly specific feedback from the music director. Normally, Max ratcheted up his irritation if someone didn't execute one of his commands after a couple of tries. But he didn't that morning. He stayed on his tower throughout the practice, but during the hour that he worked with the trumpet block, he seemed to be down on the ground right next to Jim.

"The work is going really well, folks. We're taking care of the small details."

"Jim, that was really good."

"Hey, trumpets, the entire block was readable. There are still some of you who are confused. But every block was readable that time."

When they heard that praise, the entire block cheered, including Jim. He had made enormous visible, measurable improvement. It was hard to conceive how much he would have missed if he hadn't come that morning. And how much he might have missed if Scott Spradling had.

Just before ten o'clock, Max took off his fleece Windbreaker and stuffed it into his green shoulder bag. The breeze felt cool, but the fog had burned off and the sky was clearing into a brilliant fall blue. A great day for marching bands.

THE FIRST BUSES arrived: DeKalb County, Garrett-Keyser-Butler Community School Corporation. The parking lot dads waved them into the best spots, in the shade of the grandstand. The Pride of Woodlan semi-trailer, a big treble clef painted on the side, swung into the lot. Woodlan's own band dads got out and started unloading the trailer. It wasn't just Concord's dedication on display that autumn weekend. All around the state, parents were driving buses and semis, feeding kids, helping them into uniforms, cheering them on.

The big metal blinds of the concession stand rumbled open. In the back of a nearby equipment trailer, an industrial popcorn popper fired up. Two hundred and fifty pounds of popcorn kernels sat inside the trailer, along with cases and cases of bottled water. The smell of popcorn and artificial butter flavoring drifted on the breeze, soon mixing with grease and charcoal as Wayne Stubbs and several other fathers got the hamburgers cooking on the grill.

As a former band director in the Elkhart schools and the current music supervisor there, Stubbs felt the need to keep a low profile around the Concord band. Unlike most of the other band parents, he avoided wearing Kelly green. Still, he wanted to support Nick, and he respected what Max did with the program as a whole, and with Nick in particular. Even if, as a father, it was sometimes hard to hear what Max had to say to his son.

Superintendent George Dyer had lent the concessions crew an old fiberglass canoe to use as a cooler. It was filled, now, with blocks of ice and bottles of water. Dyer and principal Dan Cunningham stopped by the RV and poked their heads in. Not every school would allow such a vehicle to be parked on school grounds on a day's notice. But both men believed in Max Jones and the Concord music program.

At the beginning of the school year, Dyer had held an assembly for every employee of the school corporation. He welcomed new teachers, new custodians, new cafeteria workers, and, that year, the new high school principal. He spoke a few words about the goals of their joint endeavors—not about financial goals or test goals, but about forming the minds and characters of young men and women. He'd hired a motivational speaker, a former teacher who made his audience laugh even as he described "a world out of whack," in which "we the people" allow the federal government to cut school lunch programs for kids who are hungry, but buy diet food for our pets.

"What we're talking about here, ladies and gentlemen," the speaker said, "is a matter of values. We got dough for anything in this country we want dough for, and we go around cutting school budgets." Values, that is, and hard work. He described for them a new teacher who struggled to navigate the multiple demands placed on her—Increase test scores! Establish discipline! Encourage creativity! Build self-esteem!—all these things, he told them to sniggers of recognition, when she couldn't even get markers for the board in her classroom. "And you wonder why the music department gets everything it wants." The laughter stopped abruptly. If the other teachers were tired of hearing how great the Concord music program was, or resented that Max Jones was the highest-paid teacher in the district, the speaker didn't care. He'd done his research, knew about the state championship, the seven directors, the music wing; he reminded them of the hours worked by the band directors, asked his audience to consider how much of that time was spent inside a classroom. "I don't see you taking your kids to the Macy's parade," he told them. "Once you do stuff like that, you'll get markers, too."

In the month since school had started, the music department had seen more of the new principal, at practices and in their offices, than they'd seen of his predecessor in ten years. Dan Cunningham had been a coach, an athletic director, and a principal in southern Indiana, not far from where Max had learned to march. Cunningham's two daughters had been in marching band, and he'd driven equipment tractors as a volunteer. In the music hallway, it was considered a good omen that the new principal was a band dad. The school year was barely a month old, but Cunningham had already made his support clear. Among other things, he'd rejiggered the early-release schedule for the coming week to give the band its normal full practice time. He was showing the marching band the kind of administrative flexibility that most schools reserved for the football team.

Earlier that week, Cunningham had requested a meeting with the music staff. He wanted to brainstorm how to make the rest of the school more like the marching band. He saw marching band as a model that, if followed across other departments, could return Concord to the higher level in Indiana's academic ranks from which the school had slipped over the past decade.

"You guys," Cunningham said, "with your instrumental program, you've got students teaching students, a variety of instructional strategies, kinesthetic learning. Band is like a magnet school inside the larger school."

He ticked off on his fingers the elements of the band program that he wanted every Concord student to have:

1. "Band is a small learning community—except yours isn't small."
2. "Everyone works toward common goals."
3. "The results are publicly adjudicated—and are published in the newspaper." The directors laughed at this. Cunningham brightened at their response and continued. "And read by your peers, and the parents of your peers."

4. "It's an experience that is both stable and replicable. One group goes out, a new group comes in and has the same experience."
5. "The teachers know students over time, and spend a significant amount of time with them—before the school day begins, during the school day, after the school day is over, on evenings and weekends . . ."

Cunningham let them know that he understood the difference between music and sports, and why sports teams were not the model for Concord. "The freshman basketball team is just freshmen, not seniors," he reminded them, his voice rising. "Sophomore year, half of them may get cut. By senior year, there may be only five kids left. It's all about winning!"

At that, Max's fingers had drummed, twice on the table. Although his music program was not about winning, it was also not about *not* winning.

In other circumstances, Cunningham's impassioned speech might have been the beginning of a powerful partnership. But he'd approached the band staff just as the most stressful part of their year was ramping up. Max was already putting in long days; the others already didn't have enough time for their families. No one around the conference table tried to match the principal's enthusiasm. None of the staff offered to show other teachers how to become more like band directors. If Cunningham was offended, the feeling hadn't lingered. He finished his tour of the RV and milled around the concession stand, proud of what he was a part of.

WHILE THE ORGANIZATIONAL machinery cranked up with the arrival of the first buses, the first order of business for the high-brass section after the practice was to celebrate the arrival of Mr. Spradling's baby. They quickly hatched a plan to squeeze as many kids as could fit into Jim Schoeffler's new car, buy some presents for the Spradlings and the new baby at the Dollar Store, and drop them off at the Spradlings' home. "Car" was possibly not the right word to describe a banana-yellow, four-ton makeover of a military vehicle. Jim asked Grant to drive the Hummer while he sat shotgun, and ten other members of the best section in the Concord band piled into the two sets of seats behind them. Even a Hummer wasn't quite big enough to hold them all without some squeezing, so a few sat on laps. Laurie Schalliol lingered on the sidewalk, wishing she hadn't signed up to host a visiting band. Three of the freshmen girls wanted to go, but watching the others crowding in, they held back, remembering that their parents didn't allow them to be in cars driven by teenage boys. And whatever else Grant Longenbaugh might be, he was still a teenage boy. The grin on his face said as much as he turned the wheel of the Hummer this way and that.

The boys got off-task immediately in the Dollar Store, buying soft drinks, plastic camouflage vests, swords, a bunny mask. The girls found a bib with "Baby" written across it in pink script and a card they thought was perfect: "It smells funny, makes a lot of noise, and depends on you for everything. But enough about your husband. Congratulations on your new baby." A quiet boy, one of the few freshmen who'd been put on the first trumpet part, found a card with a Bible verse, "The blessing of the Lord be upon you," and brought it to Grant for his OK. Two of the boys staged a sword fight outside the store, one of them wearing a plastic camo vest and the bunny mask. Eventually, Grant steered them all back to the yellow Hummer. "Who pays the gas on this thing?" one of the guys called up from the back. Jim admitted that his parents did, to ribbing from the back seat, and smiled sheepishly. Between Max Jones and the Hummer, Jim Schoeffler was getting more positive attention in the high-brass section than he ever had.

Grant pulled out onto Highway 33, away from the Dollar Store, past OfficeMax, Bed Bath & Beyond, and other middling rungs of brand-name America. He drove south down County Road 19, past new houses, construction equipment, lots for sale. The boys with the swords held them out the open windows, slicing the air. Scott Spradling and Mary Amador had recently moved to a nineteenth-century brick farmhouse in a stretch of country that had yet to lose its fields. It sat at the end of a narrow driveway next to an old barn and a ruined silo, the silo's rounded cone lopped off. But its isolation didn't keep Spradling's students from finding him. The kids piled out of the Hummer and got down to the business of decorating the house for the baby's arrival.

"Barbie heads, that's all we talked about in beginning band," said one of the girls as she pulled the head off a Winter Collection Barbie and impaled it on a wrought-iron fence outside the house. Spradling was famous at the junior high for his collection of Barbies, many of them headless, all of them given to him by students. He'd never pulled the head off a doll in his life, and he no longer remembered how the collection got started. But he went along with it. Like Steve Peterson's crinkled smile and his own tough-guy persona, the "headless Barbie" weirdness was partly a mask he wore to reach his students. The Barbies "lived" in an old dollhouse in a corner of the junior high band room, and he turned the arrival of each new one into an occasion.

The kids tied pink balloons to the fence railing and set up ninja dolls next to them, then balanced a Barbie head on the door handle. It was a strange celebration of a daughter's birth, and one that Scott Spradling, upon his family's return from the hospital, found oddly touching.

Grant shook his head at the tableau and said, "OK, let's go, guys."

He drove the Hummer back through half a dozen neighborhoods, dropping kids off at their homes, *The Incredible Hulk* playing on the TV screen above the front seats. He was the only senior in the group. Sometimes, leadership could look a lot like hanging out.

BACK AT THE high school, the crowd swelled. Long lines formed in front of the concession stand. The afternoon turned hot and stretched on. Wayne Stubbs and the grill dads stayed busy flipping burgers; a crew kept emptying cases of bottled water into the canoe of ice. Music filled the warm air, carried out over the cornfields and the Green Valley subdivision, echoed off the brick of the gym and performance center. Kids in band uniforms wandered in packs through the crowd. Now and then one of them carrying an instrument with a cracked reed or missing key pad made his or her way over to a booth beneath an awning where Blessings Music, an Elkhart instrument supply and re-pair store, had set up shop. Hundreds of adults and teenagers milled around in T-shirts and shorts. People seemed hungry, thirsty, and happy, as if basking in the last blast of summer.

The Class C and D bands finished up and the larger bands arrived, bringing more buses, more trailers, more spectators. Warsaw's trailer backed into its space, sporting a faded tiger and a list of community sponsors: Sprint, Ramada Plaza Hotel, Wal-Mart, Warsaw Farm Center, Metzger Trucking, Swihart Trucking, Everly Trucking, Explorer

In the twilight of a long career, music director Max Jones looks over the paved practice field at Concord Community High School from his customary perch: atop a rickety, twenty-four-foot-tall observation tower.

Banners hang overhead in the school's band room, constant reminders of past glory and present dreams. The Marching Minutemen entered the 2004 season with a veteran class of seniors and notions of creating a dynasty.

Freshman clarinet player Adilene Corona, new to the band and the community, "marks a chart" on the pavement. The paint smudge, one of thousands, will help her find where she belongs in the band.

Grant Longenbaugh, the band's acknowledged leader, hoped to leave a legacy of faith in action and a "servant" model of leadership when he graduated.

The Concord horns lay into the Blood, Sweat & Tears classic "Lucretia MacEvil" at the Indiana State Fair. The crazy costumes and irreverent shows were part of Max Jones's strategy to teach his students to perform.

Before competing, the low-brass section joins hands in a prayer huddle. Evangelical Christianity increasingly influenced life at Concord, both inside and outside the band.

Max Jones hoped that saxophone player Cameron Bradley, one of the most gifted musicians in the band, would also become one of its strongest leaders.

The Minutemen put on their "Roots of American Music" show at the Homestead Invitational. Their complex, fast-moving formations are closer to drum corps and Broadway than traditional "half-time" marching-band shows.

Grant Longenbaugh reaches for some soul with his solo of "Closer Walk with Thee." Playing as part of a New Orleans–style quartet, Concord's would-be valedictorian worked all season to think less and feel more.

Max Jones savors the view from the floor of the Indianapolis RCA Dome just before his final performance. Behind him: the elaborate fabric backdrop to the show; senior flute soloist Amanda Bechtel, already in position.

The bassline cranks up the tempo for the "killer-diller" beat of the show's finale. The piece demanded unusual precision from a drum section hoping to achieve the nearly mystical unified state known as "locking."

Drumline captain Nick Stubbs (center) displays the signature high
Concord chin as he awaits the judges' word in the 2004 state finals.

Her final marching season drawing to a close, clarinet player
Diana de la Reza reacts to the results of the championship.

In a somber rain, members of the 2004 Concord Marching Minutemen gather for their traditional post-finals celebration outside the RCA Dome.

Van, Reinholt's Furniture, Lewis Salvage, Owen's Supermarket, and two Optimist Clubs. The Marching Saints of Bishop Dwenger, a Catholic school in Class B, pulled in alongside. Painted on the side of their trailer was a little angel with a black eye and a crooked halo.

Out on the football field, fans saw the latest trends in marching band. Pirate-themed shows were big: The Richmond performance at State Fair had been merely the first of a spate of shows that flashed bandannas, spangles, and eye patches. Color-guard costumes ran to form-fitting velour that often left one shoulder bare. Over the years, band uniforms had gone mostly to black, the look seeming to reach for something out of *Star Trek*. A lot of drum majors were dressed in formal wear, the girls conducting in long black dresses. A surprising number of those dresses were sleeveless, even strapless. It was easy to see how the trend had started and caught on. These bands were attempting to play music at the level of a concert band, and concert bands wore formal attire. The fashion on display at the Concord Invitational, though, suggested prom more than symphony. After watching one young woman struggle to keep the bodice of her strapless dress from sliding down, one judge recommended, choosing his words carefully, that the drum majors in that band reconsider their choice of dress. By the time the Class B competition started, at eight p.m., lengthening shadows brought a noticeable chill to the air, and it was hard to watch some of the young women and not shiver.

Chris Longenbaugh was among the moms who served a prime-rib dinner to the directors and judges in the atrium of the auditorium. Dressed in white tops and black pants, they hovered over the diners, restocked empty trays, filled water glasses, and cleared plates. Chris knew that Max wanted to maintain Concord's reputation for serving great food, homemade food, the best food on the marching-band circuit. Two appetizers had become, in fact, somewhat famous: a bacon roll-up and meatballs in a special tomato sauce. They'd been made every year that Chris could remember, in increasing quantities, and every year both were polished off early. This year was no exception: they'd cooked ten pounds of bacon, forty pounds of meatballs, and still, by 7:45, when Chris was waiting on tables for the third dinner seating, all of it was gone.

The parents on the hospitality committee understood that, like the band itself, they labored under the weight of heavy expectations. It hadn't always been that way. Several years earlier, a mom had introduced fancier dishes into the mix. The food thing escalated after that, and seemed, now, to have taken on a life of its own. The food crew bought local Amish cheeses and hearty German bread, which they sliced alongside the cheeses. Salads, if heavy on starches and light on greens, were homemade: pasta salad, taco salad, macaroni salad, chicken salad, several varieties of potato salad.

Dick and Jolene Lehman usually cooked in the kitchen, Dick the only man present. They'd been partly responsible for the escalation: They were both creative, skilled cooks at home, and they brought sophisticated taste into the committee. The cooking had given them an opening in the band. Dick, in particular, hadn't been especially eager to make that part of their sons' life a big part of his own. There was his consuming pottery work, which involved not only running a business but tending to a reputation that was growing internationally. And then there was his complicated relationship with music. After high school, Dick had toured with a band, playing trombone for Thurlow Spurr and the Spurrlows. The band, out of Detroit, was sponsored for a time by one of the car manufacturers to perform driver-safety programs in high schools, but also played a "sacred" program in churches. Dick thought he had joined a forward-thinking Christian band that included brass instruments, electric guitars, and drums along with banjos and voices. Over eleven months, he played more than five hundred concerts. The novelty and the fun wore off quickly, though, and Dick became disillusioned by the way they always seemed to be grubbing for their money. After the tour ended, Dick put away his trombone. The experience would taint his feelings about music for a long time.

Dick and Jolene weren't in the kitchen, though. Dick was going through what they hoped would be his last round of chemotherapy, and Jolene was staying with him.

That year was Chris's eighth as a parent volunteer: four with Anne, a year off, and then another four with Grant. When Anne had first signed up for band, at the end of her eighth-grade year, Chris had been alarmed. She'd returned to work only one year earlier, and she'd heard about the long days and the seriousness of the commitment for parents and children alike. It had seemed too much like a cult. She hadn't protested, though, and halfway into the first season, she and Jeff were hooked. She'd learned that first season how Max built the show in

layers, and sat in the stands with the other band parents at the previews and the contests, marking the show's progress from week to
week. She remembered her reaction to the first shows she saw—*That's
it?*—and now made a point of explaining Max's iterative process to
new band parents.

She'd handed out water to the kids during band camp, fitted uniforms, baked brownies, and worked in the concession stand, rolling
thousands of hot dogs off the heated bars and onto buns. When she
was diagnosed with breast cancer during Anne's first year in marching
band, Chris was touched by the support she received from other band
parents. Max lectured the kids about taking care of each other, but his
words affected everyone, adults included.

Anne had been a close friend of Max Jones's son, Gavin, all through
school. Chris had seen Max Jones loosen up because of Gavin, and cut
kids just a little more slack. He showed more understanding of the pull
of sports on students in the band, when Gavin wanted to keep playing
soccer in high school. Anne and Gavin had been part of a gang of fun-
loving band kids. They'd gotten into their share of trouble. One night
they climbed onto the school roof to hang a banner wishing the band
luck at state. Max had been furious. But Chris had appreciated their
high spirits, and had even been glad that teenagers could still get into
such old-fashioned trouble. A lot of people around Concord thought
Max would retire after Gavin graduated. But Gavin and Anne had both
gone off to Purdue and marched together in Purdue's All-American
Band. They were getting ready to graduate from college now, and Max
was still at Concord—though Chris thought he had lost a point of connection with the kids.

In the band, Chris and Jeff Longenbaugh had seen Anne become a
beautiful, poised young woman, and Grant grow from a quiet, pudgy
freshman into a cowboy-hat–wearing leading man. Now Chris and Jeff
were both tasting the bittersweet pleasure of everything being the last
time. The last State Fair. The last invitational. The last band parties at
the house. Soon, the last state finals. Anne finishing her student teaching. Then Grant off to college. A new world opening up, for all of
them.

Chris, though, couldn't fully enjoy the moments. Her back still hurt.
West Side Elementary School, where she worked, tested children at the
beginning of the school year to determine which needed the remedial

literacy program that she'd put into place. She was curious about the children, and recognized in them the changing face of her community. She loved holding them on her lap, easing their anxieties about taking tests, and helping them unlock the secrets of language. But she had a growing anxiety about the pain she was feeling, which lingered long after she'd risen from the small desks and bothered her even now, waiting on tables.

George Dyer strolled into the lobby, his face sunburned, and asked if the food crew needed anything. He'd emptied ice out of all six Concord schools, and was heading out with one of the band dads to buy more ice and more cases of bottled water. The concession stand had nearly sold out its hundred cases from the ice-cooler canoe, a quantity that was supposed to cover the upcoming district competition as well. The food trays had run low, too: out of the meatballs, out of snacks, only one fruit tray with marshmallow-creme dip left. Someone else was already making a run for more cheese.

On the field, under the lights, the Class B bands marched through their programs: Northridge, Wawasee, Bishop Dwenger. Max had encouraged his students to watch all the bands and learn from them, but he saw no rivals among his peers at the invitational, and in fact few in the entire state. He wanted his kids to aim higher.

After the early Class A bands had completed their shows, the Concord kids left the stands and gathered inside the music wing to get to dressed. Moms tucked up stray bits of hair and shaved stubble that was growing toward midnight shadows. Adilene's uniform, far too big on her, drooped against her shoes and hung loosely off her narrow shoulders. As always, Grant's shako helmet sat high on top of his head, which was so big that none of the helmets fit him properly. In their hats and uniforms, though, it was hard to tell most of the kids apart. The moms ushered them out, and the directors took them to a warm-up area far on the other side of the school from their normal practice field—now completely filled with other bands' trailers—to get into position for their own show. They weren't able to see the long braided gold lines of Homestead, or watch Penn's Marching Kingsmen, in sleek black costumes, put on a tightly choreographed, clean performance filled with difficult, subtle music. Perhaps it was just as well.

In their white pants and shoes and their dark green jackets, Concord appeared so out of fashion following the *Star Trek* bands that they looked retro, almost cool, ahead of the curve. Their drum majors were dressed not in prom wear but in the old-style uniform of the band. But if the crowd and judges were expecting an old-style show, Amanda Bechtel's plaintive opening flute on "Gabriel's Oboe" set a decidedly unexpected tone. The African drummers took over, spread across the field; the trumpet block rotated, spinning off mellophones and picking up flugels as it turned; mourners pointed and clapped in slow motion as the parade sauntered by; "Anchors Aweigh"—being used the last time, they hoped, as a filler—finished it off. At the high level of modern competitive marching bands, and the high level of Max's expectations, the marching was ragged, the forms muddy, and the music uneven. But the energy pulsed. The dads took nearly four and a half minutes to roll and unroll the tarp—an unacceptable time, a fatal time, if you were at an ISSMA contest—but in the end the crowd was clapping and the kids were smiling. It was nearly eleven o'clock and it felt like a great party was just ending.

AFTER THE SHOW, the Concord staff walked over to the Holiday Rambler to hear the judges' critique. The audience was leaving, buses pulling out into the darkness—a traffic jam at midnight. People who had stripped down to T-shirts in the middle of the afternoon now clutched coats around their bodies and hurried to their cars.

The judges Max brought in that year had adjudicated drum-corps performances in a dozen states. Some had been critiquing marching bands nearly as long as Max had been directing them. Most still taught music themselves, in middle schools, high schools, universities, even a conservatory. The combination gave the judges a rare national perspective on music education, broad in scope but grounded in day-to-day experience. At no other time in the year would Max hear such knowledgeable feedback.

In a few weeks, the contests run by the Indiana State School Music Association would start. These were the contests that winnowed down nearly three hundred high school marching bands to four class champions. Starting with the district competition, a decreasing number of bands would advance to the next levels. With such high stakes, directors needed to get their shows in shape and fix problems before the sifting began.

ISSMA rules prohibited contact between band directors and judges. Directors could listen to the judging tapes from those contests, read comments on scoring sheets, and read between the lines of their scores. But no conversations were allowed, no chance to hear judges' advice about how to address specific issues.

Invitationals, on the other hand, encouraged exactly such conversations. The judges waiting in the RV had the room to elaborate on important comments, and directors could ask for clarification or more detail. Max knew well that the point was not to argue with someone's scoring or comments, but to learn enough to sway a judge at a later contest. When it went well, a critique session at an invitational could make a huge difference to a new director starting out, to a director trying to salvage a troubled show, or to a director shooting the moon.

The judges brought individual perspectives. Eric Sabach, a judge from Indianapolis, considered marching bands an American populist art form. Elite art, in his definition, pitched itself only to people who were prepared or trained to appreciate it. Populist art was obvious, clear, and accessible, even when it was high quality. He had some strong opinions about what he'd seen in Concord that night. He smiled when he saw Max step into the RV.

The Concord directors squeezed onto the love seat and in next to the five judges on that first panel. A cozy living room chat, someone joked. Out of nervousness or impatience or just his sense of time kicking in, Max dispensed with small talk. "What do you think?" he asked.

Judge Beth Fabrizio responded using nearly the same words: "I want to know what you guys were thinking." This was not what Max had expected to hear, and for a moment he seemed stunned.

Max had gone through a key session with Fabrizio at an invitational three years earlier. "Can I say something out of caption?" she'd asked him. (She'd been one of the judges in the music caption, as she was again at Concord.) She'd then told Max that his drill was awful, and that he wouldn't make it out of the ISSMA regional competition unless he did something drastic. Her advice came at a crucial moment in the season. Max worked every night, right up to regionals, rewriting the drill, collaborating with a student music teacher he'd put up in his basement. Concord pulled off a fourth-place finish in the state finals at the end of that crazy season, the first season this year's seniors had been in the band. Beth Fabrizio's advice had likely nudged Max toward his breakfast with Jon Sutton. She had subsequently become a regular guest at the Concord Invitational. Fabrizio was exactly the kind of judge Max wanted at his contest. She was knowledgeable, forthright, clear, and helpful. She was willing to say, This won't do. You have to change it or your season is over.

Such was not the case in 2004—Max was sure he had a winning show. What he needed was an honest assessment of how close his band came to executing his vision.

In the pause, Fabrizio rephrased and softened her question.

It quickly became apparent that while all of the judges were familiar with the theme music from *The Mission*, their familiarity extended only to the ballad version that was a staple of the concert-band repertoire. The piece made no sense to them as the starting point for an exploration of the African roots of American music. As far as the judges in the RV were concerned, "Gabriel's Oboe" didn't come with hand drums. It was supposed to be all hymn, no thunder.

A quiet and somber group of Concord directors walked over to the auditorium lobby to talk with the second panel of judges. Max didn't start with the same open-ended question. Instead, he launched into his explanation of the show's genesis, including his problems finding the right opener. He went through the entire timeline, including his plans for "Swing, Swing, Swing." "We'll pull out four drumsets," he told them, "and they're all blue, and they're on these circular pedestals."

Tom Roe, a judge from Henderson, Nevada, was particularly interested in Max's description of the rest of the show, particularly the drumsets in "Swing, Swing, Swing." As a percussion teacher, he saw that Concord would enact onstage the classic evolution in drumming from antiphonal drumming to a mono sound, that is, from many drummers, each drumming singly, to one drummer playing many drums.

Roe had a long perspective from which to judge marching bands. He'd started judging in the early 1970s for what became Drum Corps International, or DCI. Being a DCI judge then had been like being the sheriff in a Wild West town. Hitting judges after the contest was common enough that DCI had set a standard fine for such behavior. In those early years, directors for the drum corps took the judging so personally that some collected money ahead of critique sessions so a designated staff member could punch a judge after they heard his criticism, then hand cash to an official for the $500 fine on their way out the door. Roe had also judged in Texas, where high school marching bands fell under the umbrella of athletic departments, adjuncts to their football teams; and in the affluent Northeast, where both the quality of marching bands and the level of support they received was often quite poor.

So when he gave Concord the highest "general effect" scores of any band he saw, including the Class A bands, and praised their sophisticated awareness of their show as a "show," as something that they wanted the people watching to respond to, not just sit and listen to, he knew what he was talking about.

But the other judges weren't concerned about "Gabriel's Oboe" or the timeline, "Swing, Swing, Swing," or the ability of the Concord students to fire up an audience. They were concerned about how much work Max and his staff and students had in front of them.

"It's a clever idea," one judge said. "But . . . are you able to get the ideas on the field and teach children to march and make this happen? I find it hard to believe you're going to do it."

This quickly became the central question that the panel considered. Talking as much to one another as to Max and the other Concord directors, they dissected the difficulties in front of the band: adding another number ("another production," a second judge corrected the first, to emphasize everything beyond music the kids had to learn), teaching drill and music, and preparing the show for district competition, on top of the additional work that needed to go into the three sections the band had just performed. Max interjected, "I'll just tell you, it's typical of us."

"Really?" the disbelieving judge asked. He hadn't judged in Indiana in recent years, didn't know the Concord way or the Max Jones system. But others did, and chimed in to support Max when he said, simply, "Last year's show that won the state. . . . This is us."

"I couldn't take the stress," the judge said. Max's staff laughed at this, exchanging looks. That judge had no idea. . . .

Max didn't notice their glances or the levity. He was taking the opportunity to educate another judge. "Every minute we have is very valuable. We don't waste time. It takes major organization. The RV was an idea that happened Tuesday of this week because we were worried about Lee"—one of the judges on the other panel—"getting in at eleven o'clock and having to fly back at eight o'clock this morning. We thought, he needs to rest and these chairs aren't comfortable. So the parents got an RV."

He boasted again about the work the band dads had put into the drumset carts and covers, and couldn't resist letting the judges know that Conn-Selmer had loaned them the four matching blue drumsets.

The disbelieving judge said, "That's sort of like in my school district. I say I need another band director, and they say, 'OK, we'll take one away and the whole period out of the school day. How's that?'" Another judge added, "And you gotta teach everybody on your own now." A third said, "And now you also gotta monitor study hall."

They were describing the reality of music in most schools. But that was not Max's problem at the moment. They complimented him on the band's musicality, the students' ability to play in different idioms. The conversation wound down. Everyone looked tired, even Max. It was after midnight.

As a fund-raiser and a display of Concord's commitment to marching bands, the invitational had been a huge success. When the gate and concession receipts were tallied, the numbers would dovetail with everyone's sense that the stadium had been a crush of people, the lines for food extra long: almost 13,000 people had paid admission, 700 pounds of hamburger had been grilled, 104 cases of bottled water sold, every hot dog and all the popcorn that the music association had expected would last through both the invitational and the district. The invitational would set a new record for the music association: more than $75,000.

Their performance numbers looked good, too—the scores the judges had given the Concord band placed them far above the other Class B bands, better than all but the top two Class A bands. Max knew that some of his students would take that to mean they were back on track and that all was well, and he'd try to deflate their overconfidence on Monday by paraphrasing the judges' parting words: "We wish you well. But you're too ambitious."

The conversations with the judges had given Max reason to be even more concerned about the show. Numbers told part of the story, but only part, and Max was worried about the part they didn't tell.

At ten to one on what was now Sunday morning, he stood on a chair and turned off the last TV still on in the lobby, a college football game running late. The other Concord directors had trickled away without much conversation after the last critique session. The last of the band moms had packed away leftovers and taken stacks of containers up to the music-department kitchen. Band dads had swept through on security and cleanup. The two-way radios were all accounted for.

Max had had a lot of help. He wasn't the only person who'd worked a twenty-hour day, and some of those other long days had been true labors of love, their only payment the pleasure of seeing the invitational go well. But in the dark of a new day, Max now worked alone. He picked up one more stray piece of paper and turned out the lights.

9 ★ On Earth As It Is in Heaven

On Sunday, Grant took the back way to Nappanee. He drove across the double railroad tracks that separated Concord's east and west sides, past the subdivisions, the fast-food restaurants and the strip malls, and out onto the grid of county roads. Turning south toward Goshen, he traced the peaks and valleys of a line of squat, wooded hills. He picked a place to cut west and followed a gradual incline toward higher ground. The land opened up. Crops waited in the fields for the last of the harvest. His artist's eye registered the cleaner line of the Amish houses and barns without electrical wires strung between them. The view expanded. He crested the final rise and jogged south one more time, until Nappanee Missionary Church rose in front of him out of soybeans and corn.

He was always taken aback by its immensity. The new main building, where worshipers entered through sets of glass doors, was massive and broad-roofed. Several wings, a visual history of the church's growth, jutted out from it amid a jumble of rooflines. The complex echoed the shape and faded color of the barns Grant had passed coming in, but in its scale and stripped-down style, it sat on the land more like the supersize RV warehouses nearby. No steeple marked it as a place of worship on that side, not even a cross high on its facade. Some at Nappanee referred to their spiritual home as "the mother ship." Nappanee's pastor called his church "a miracle in a cornfield." Whatever else a passerby might mistake the church for, the shopping-mall–sized parking lot was nearly full when Grant pulled in.

Grant had heard Pastor Dave Engbrecht tell the story of taking the job twenty-six years earlier, believing he was destined for a bigger place than a four-corners-and-a-feedstore community, but unable to convince God to send him elsewhere. Nappanee Missionary Church had been a strictly local church then, located on Main Street, its pews not quite filled with farm families who had branched out from Mennonite roots.

Schisms and divisions had long been a fact of Christian life for the Mennonite and Amish believers who had settled around Goshen and the town of Nappanee. Groups split over issues that outsiders would find trivial: the teaching of Sunday school, whether members could attend or hold revival meetings, whether services could include four-part singing. Not long after Engbrecht moved to Nappanee, one of the local Amish congregations split when some of its members insisted on being allowed to drive rubber-tired tractors.

The division that created Nappanee Missionary Church had occurred in the latter part of the nineteenth century. A Mennonite minister named Daniel Brenneman had attended several "camp meetings" and felt that his church needed more of the Holy Spirit. Furthermore, he believed that the tradition he'd grown up in had erred in its almost-exclusive emphasis on the adult practice of Christian faith. In the Mennonite tradition, children were not considered capable of making deep spiritual decisions; adult baptism was a foundation of the faith, which was why the group had been nicknamed Anabaptists, or "rebaptizers." But Brenneman believed that Mennonites were losing the chance to convert the next generation; he understood, ahead of his time, perhaps, that churches could grow dramatically if they appealed to youth. Brenneman joined the movement to educate young people in the practice of their faith, separate from their parents, and brought his church with him.

A century later, Dave Engbrecht worked the same rich vein as his church's founder. Engbrecht was a natural promoter, gregarious, affable, sincere. He'd immediately moved the church to the site outside the town, which had given it ample room to grow, and grow, and grow again—twenty-six years in a row of expanding membership, and counting. Pastor Dave liked to share the good news with his congregation, often updating the church's numbers in his welcoming remarks on Sunday mornings, which was how Grant knew that membership had passed two thousand at the beginning of that year and grown by another three hundred or so since. Being involved with something so dynamic and vital was part of what excited Grant about the church.

Like Brenneman, Engbrecht felt called to youth ministry. He focused especially on teens and young adults. He had a longer reach than Brenneman because he could draw on the tools of modern corporate America. He knew that consumers formed lifelong brand attachments at that young age; churches were no different. Through his marketing and the efforts of his team of youth pastors, Nappanee Missionary Church had overtaken Beulah, its sister church where Grant's sister had gone to youth group, as the place the region's teens flocked to worship.

Grant walked through the glass entrance, past café tables once again laden with boxes of Krispy Kreme doughnuts, then passed by the open doors of the main sanctuary. His destination that morning was the new fieldhouse, part of a $7 million upgrade that included the bigger new sanctuary, children's and youth worship centers, and a grand atrium. Inside the windowless gymnasium, basketball hoops were retracted against the wall, and rows of folding chairs stretched back to a coffee bar doing a brisk business in bagels and lattes. Dave Engbrecht's newest campaign for reaching the next generation was in full swing.

"The Connection," a worship service targeted exclusively to teens and young adults, had been rolled out in midsummer. It had quickly absorbed the youth of Nappanee from the church's three other Sunday morning services. And as Engbrecht and the youth pastors had hoped, the new service had attracted new worshipers.

Hundreds of teenagers filled the gym that morning. They had come from Concord subdivisions and from rougher districts in Elkhart. They'd come from Goshen, with its strange stew of Amish farmers, Mennonite college students, and the fastest-growing Hispanic population in the state. They'd come from decaying factory towns along the St. Joseph River and from small farming communities like Nappanee and Wakarusa growing up in exurbs. Some came with their families, but more came with friends, or, as Grant had, alone. They came for the same tribal reason they drove to the big new mall in Mishawaka: because it was the place to go.

Grant, his eyes adjusting to the dark, found his seat between Cameron and Leandra in their new regular place up front. Spotlights shone on electric guitars and a bass on a raised platform in front of them. The musicians hopped onto the stage and looped microphones over their ears with a studied ease, then launched into a cover of a Christian rock song. Amplified guitar riffs filled the room. The music was no more tuneful or sophisticated than in Nappanee's other services, but it was louder—much louder. A technician worked a console near the back of the gym, changing the colors onstage and synchronizing images on a big screen behind the band. Except for the lyrics displayed on the screen, everything on the stage screamed rock concert. The audience, left to synthesize the musical experience with the spiritual, seemed oddly subdued by comparison. Except for the rows closest to the front, where Grant and his friends stood, few of the listeners sang along with the words, as they would have done in the main sanctuary. No one danced in the aisles, either, or crowded the stage up front. Many of the young adults in the dark room simply stood and watched the show without expression. None of them wore the "Sunday best" of an earlier era, although most seemed to have spent more care on their clothing than they did for school, and that added to the scene's polite feel. Gradually, though it was still far from a sing-along, a few kids started moving to the music. The lead guitarist slid into the first chords of a new song, and the words to "Undignified" by the David Crowder Band came up on the screen.

> And I'll become
> Even more undignified than this
> Some may say it's foolishness
> But I'll become
> Even more undignified than this.
> Leave by my pride
> By my side
> And I'll become
> Even more undignified than this.

Grant let the music work on him. He still craved the release from his constant thinking. Over the past weeks, the voice in his head had not gone away. It continued to rebuke him; it still told him he had to choose between Leandra and God. But he was fighting the voice less these days. He was letting himself live with the conflict, at least for the time being, however undignified that might be.

The music streamed into him. That week, working on his essay for a National Merit Scholarship, he'd written about his friendship with Cameron Bradley and a bluegrass festival they'd gone to. He wrote, "I often envy Cameron's exceptional musical ear." But not at the festival. "The Creole scared him, and the music rubbed him wrong. I couldn't hear that it was out of tune or 'twangy'—I only heard the truth, I heard life, I heard music straight from the earth and heart." He was drawn, he wrote, to bluegrass's honest imperfection.

With the screaming guitars and the feedback for cover, Grant sang loudly and off-key. He knew his singing voice grated on his friend, and ever so slightly pointed it in Cameron's direction. Leandra looked over and smiled. The first present he'd given her, back in the spring, had been a David Crowder CD, with "Undignified" on it. The band wailed into the song's final refrain, over Grant's voice. By now, bunches of teenagers were swaying in unison, their hands raised above their heads. On the screen, the lyrics changed, the song ended.

I will dance, I will sing
To be mad for my King.

The band pounded out more covers: a song by Switchfoot, an older number by U2. And then it was time to pass the red bucket—no plush-lined collection plate here. As with the lattes and the music, Dave Eng-brecht catered to the shifting tastes of his young congregants. He'd embraced new media during an era when "new" meant mailing out sermons on tapes. Now his sermons were also burned onto CDs, linked in digital audio to the church's website, and aired on radio stations that Nappanee owned and ran. Pastor Dave's message reached people all over the world.

The Connection ran concurrently with the last service of the morning in the main sanctuary, where Pastor Dave was giving the day's sermon for the third time. Rather than try to hook up the gym for a real-time broadcast of the service, Engbrecht had taped his sermon during the second service for rebroadcasting. Senior youth pastor Terry Bley vaulted onto the stage with a microphone. Pastor Terry, tall and broad-shouldered, carried himself like the football player he'd been in Nebraska, and he wore his dark polo shirt and creased slacks like a travel uniform. Bley had read the popular historians who defined periods in American history by their "generations"; he believed that what they called the Millennial Generation was standing in front of him. Looking out over the crowd, he could pick out the varsity athletes, musicians, top students—so many good kids. The current seniors, a core group of about fifty, had faithfully attended church and youth groups and had impressed him with their seriousness. He believed the Bible's predictions that God had greatness in store for them. He hoped the young men and women were ready, because what he saw of the generation coming up behind them frightened him. He'd marked the group that included Grant and Cameron as the last before the turn.

Bley introduced Pastor Dave, or rather, introduced the video of Pastor Dave. The Nappanee pastor appeared on the screen perched at the edge of a tall stool, a gold-edged Bible resting on one knee, even larger than in real life.

Grant winced at the image of his pastor leaning toward him. Sitting through Pastor Dave's sermons had been an uncomfortable experience lately. He hadn't been able to articulate the source of his discomfort. He still responded to Engbrecht's directness and down-home manner, but something didn't feel right. Grant just knew, increasingly, that the sermons made him feel bad.

On the screen, Pastor Dave introduced them to a new series called "Next Level: Living with Impact." The sermon that day was their fly-over. "My prayer that burns in my heart," Engbrecht said, "is that over the next ten weeks the Holy Spirit's gonna show you where you are below the bar, strategies to get over the bar, and to become the person that God has called you to be."

Engbrecht dipped into the Bible to illustrate his points. He read from Deuteronomy: "You have stayed at this mountain long enough. It is time to break camp and move on." In John, he found Jesus' command to his disciples to bear much fruit. He framed the verse as the problem of "being a spiritual underachiever." He found a motivating restlessness in Nehemiah; from Revelation, a sense of urgency.

The camera moved in for a close-up, but Grant only felt the distance of the screen. The video lacked the emotional impact of Pastor Dave's live sermons. Maybe for Grant, that was just as well. Once again, he was hearing that he was "below the bar," "a spiritual underachiever." More and more, the image he had of God when he was at Nappanee was of a huge mountain soaring up through clouds off in the distance. He, on the other hand, was mired in dense jungle. All week, using Pastor Dave's sermons as his checklist and his guide, he tried to hack through the underbrush toward the mountain. But every Sunday he returned to Nappanee and felt as though he'd made no progress. He felt that he was wandering in the jungle again, alone, even though he knew that people around him were trying to reach God, too. Grant had begun to wonder: Why was God always up there, far away, and not inside him or next to him, leading him? Did he have to go through the journey alone?

Pastor Dave listed three steps on a white board. The study guide inside Grant's bulletin provided three lines to write them.

1. Know where God wants you to be.
2. Discover where I'm at.
3. Identify the barriers.

The pastor ticked off obstacles they might confront during the series: a lack of personal discipline, lack of endurance, rebellion, fear, and a list of what he called "hidden issues." In that secondary list, he mentioned spiritual warfare. He told them, "The power of God will help you untangle those issues."

He didn't urge them to search their conscience or feelings for guidance. A key part of Dave Engbrecht's message involved not trusting one's feelings. Each week, he found ways to demonstrate that feelings were sinful and selfish and led people astray. Sometimes his examples were down-to-earth and humorous. Earlier in the sermon, he'd described "lack of endurance" as "usually a feelings deal—as in, 'I don't feel like changing. I feel that it's my God-given right to plant myself on this couch and watch TV.'" Sometimes he was more forceful, as he had been in July: *You gotta go against your feelings.* Each week, nonetheless, Grant accepted as a basic statement of Christian belief that his nature was flawed, his understanding nothing, his desires sinful. He was being taught not to question the Bible, not to challenge what he heard or read, not to trust his feelings. Grant didn't know where God wanted him to be, or even, any more, where he was at. Were his feelings for Leandra a barrier to his relationship with God? It was his most pressing, consuming question. Pastor Dave, finishing his sermon on the screen, seemed to offer action but no answer.

In their relentless focus on self-improvement, Engbrecht's sermons shared a resemblance with Dr. Tim's workshops. They shared with Max's senior logs an impulse to organize and categorize human behavior: Identify the problem; tell me what you're doing about it. But unlike Max's reports and Dr. Tim's workshops, Engbrecht's steps stopped at the individual.

Engbrecht made it clear that he was talking about "the normative Christian life." To be a Christian was to be asked, continually, to break camp and move on. At times, it seemed that he was picturing an audience of adults set in their ways, resistant to change—people, possibly, like himself (a man who said he'd just as soon eat the same dinner every night, who thought one of the cool things about the forty years the Israelites spent wandering about the desert was that their clothes never wore out, so they never had to change them). He addressed the teenagers as if they needed to be prodded out of comfort zones, were incurious, and were unwilling to change or be challenged.

But the assumption got some important things wrong about the kids from Concord. Amanda Bechtel, who played her flute in at least one of Nappanee's regular services most Sundays, had a skeptical relationship with the church. She attended because her parents had chosen it, and she obeyed their authority. Before her family had moved to Elkhart, as she was starting fifth grade, she'd attended a private Christian school in Ohio. The experience had given her partial immunity to what she called "happy-face" hypocrisy. The sermons at Nappanee did little for her; what she wanted was to be heard and taken seriously.

She commonly conducted regular and animated conversations with God. Sometimes she swore during them—"Holy crap! Why do you want me to do that? No way!"—and He swore right back. Her current ease, however, had been hard-won. A period of self-doubt earlier in high school had started during such daily banter. Her parents had just bought her a new flute. *Would you be willing to sell the flute?* Amanda immediately thought of the verse in her Bible that said, "If you want to be perfect, go sell everything you own! Give the money to the poor, and you will have treasure in heaven. Then you can follow me." It was common at youth group to pose the "Would you?" questions: What would you give up, what would you do, for God? In those sessions, Amanda always hoped that she lived in a world where God was the most important thing in her life. But she found herself begging, *Please, don't make me do that.* Her parents would be so mad if she sold the flute after they'd spent so much money on it; and in the world where she actually did live, playing the flute was the one thing she had to her name. Her resistance had led to further questions and doubt, and the struggle had lasted several years.

When Amanda didn't feel compelled to practice her flute on the trip to Israel, she felt that something in the Holy Land had given her the strength to give up her music if God asked her again. After the trip, she'd wanted to talk to people at Nappanee about her new geo-religious understanding of God's covenant with Israel, and her new sense of mission. But she'd felt brushed off by the pastors—only a teenager, only a girl—and disheartened by the indifference of her peers at youth group. She'd returned to playing the flute, however, with renewed energy and joy. Now it wasn't her identity, but a gift from God that she could give others.

Grant's friend Keith Yoder, also not the teenager Pastor Dave had in mind, was not at Nappanee that Sunday. He was back at Ball State, in his senior year at the academy for gifted students. Throughout the late-night conversations the summer before his first year there, Keith had couched his faith in the language of evangelical fundamentalism. The Bible was the inerrant word of God; the practice of faith a process of adhering to absolutes. He took his authority from what he heard at Nappanee, from Pastor Dave, the youth ministers, and the college interns who rotated through the church. An intern from Bethel College told Keith that the leading biologists didn't believe in evolution anymore, and that the true agenda of the radicals pushing evolution was to disprove the existence of God. Keith had believed him. It had offended him that the Concord school library catalogued books on evolution as nonfiction. He'd left for the academy girded for spiritual battle, determined to fight Satan, rescue homosexuals and other sinners, and maintain the purity of his faith.

Right away, he found his views challenged with an intellectual rigor he hadn't confronted before. Classmates who said they were gay or exploring their sexuality (an unfamiliar concept for Keith) rebuffed his rescue efforts. His teachers heard his argument against evolution and responded with questions of their own. He relished the challenges, even as he felt the bottom of his world giving way.

His free fall did not end as he'd feared, nor did it land him back where he'd started. It was, he wrote in the shared journal, as if he'd fallen through air and landed in water, and then discovered that he could swim. Now, in the fall of his senior year, he was enrolled in AP biology. He'd come to believe that evolution was not a plot but a science—good science, widely accepted science—and he no longer worried that accepting it contradicted his faith. Although his fundamentalism had been shattered, his sense of wonder at Jesus' "good news" and his desire to spread that news—his evangelism—remained intact. He was starting to read books that described a Christianity strong enough to welcome inquiry into areas that threatened most believers he knew, such as scholarly research into the Bible, evolution and scientific inquiry in general, the role of women, whether homosexuality could be morally acceptable, and perhaps even fluid enough to tolerate ambiguity and uncertainty in its answers. As usual, he wanted to discuss and argue his way to understanding the new ideas. At a bonfire in Grant's backyard earlier in the summer, he held forth on his exploratory certainties regarding the Bible. His talk of mythology and historical context offended Leandra and Cameron, but it made a certain intuitive sense to Grant.

Soon, Grant found himself talking to Keith about things he'd never dared consider. They talked about God, but also about taking a year off before college. Maybe go west again, take an outdoor course, go back to the Boundary Waters. Maybe Leandra would come, too. He felt Keith pushing at him, the way a brother does. He felt himself moving, but he wasn't sure where he was going, yet. The voice in his head still pushed him, but he was pushing back.

At The Connection, the service winding down, Pastor Dave called them to join him on the bus, bent his head for a final prayer. Grant sat on his metal chair, Leandra on one side of him, Cameron the other. He felt Keith there, too, in spirit, in some new place. Grant knew Keith was a true person of faith, but wasn't sure what he thought of the turn Keith had taken. Keith was now making a point of saying to Grant,

"Take it easy." He'd recently joked that if his freshman self and his current, senior, self were to meet somehow, neither one would like the other. He had changed that much. Either way, Grant missed his friend.

If any other friend turned Grant's ear when it came to faith, it was Cameron Bradley, whose ideas differed markedly from Keith's. Unlike Keith, Cameron wasn't driven to make sense of his religious beliefs. He simply liked Nappanee, without second thoughts. He'd been coming to Nappanee with his family since second grade; it was home to him, and it appealed to him. He liked that the church had a sheen on it, and that its pastors gave off an aura of well-tended success. Pastor Terry lived in a nice house, with a pretty wife and kids who were good at sports. Cameron believed that God had rewarded Nappanee's pastors. He hoped for the same life and same rewards for himself someday.

Cameron reserved his criticism for the praise music, with its endless chords in G, C, and D. He'd wondered, "Are these the chords that God's most likely to listen to?" But he appreciated the devotion behind music that offended his ear. In youth group, he didn't mind how the other kids phrased their prayers. He said, "Prayer doesn't have to have perfect pitch."

Cameron had felt the presence of Satan on a mission trip to Peru the year before. The Peru trip was well known at Nappanee for its intensity, notably for its encounters with the demonic. Cameron and his Nappanee friends spent hours during that trip riding on a cramped bus that shuttled them to different mountain villages and to Lima to teach in summer Bible schools for local children and to pass out Bibles and witness in village plazas. During one of those long drives, talk turned to movie scenes depicting Satan and demonic possession. The students on the bus retold stories passed down from kids who'd been on previous trips of feeling the power of Satan descend and prayer breaking the spell. Later that evening, the feeling overtook them. One kid, and then another, called out against Satan. Some of the teenagers prayed fervently. Others started to cry. Three or four threw up. "It was like on TV, but people I knew," Cameron would say later. Cameron felt the heaviness fall over him. He couldn't breathe. The crying and the screaming reverberated inside the bus. He sensed that he was witnessing spiritual warfare firsthand. Later, he would talk about Satan having been there on the bus; about Satan's dark power searching him, seeking a way in; and how the group's ardent prayers had passed the same test as the groups who had come before, using the same weapon: prayer and belief. His most powerful experience as a missionary had occurred not in interaction with natives of the country but inside that bus, within the hermetic atmosphere of shared belief and shared fear. On his return, Cameron described his experience in detail to Grant. Even though Grant hadn't been on the bus that day, and had never gone to Peru or on a mission trip, Cameron's encounter with the devil remained vivid to him.

Pastor Dave invoked his faith's Trinity dozens of times in that day's sermon, but mentioned Satan only obliquely, in passing. He rarely uttered that name for the being his faith placed in opposition to God, or any other: the Devil, archangel, demon, Beelzebub. The programs laid out by Nappanee's youth pastors focused more on developing strong Christians than on developing a clear cosmology of heaven and hell. But a belief in Satan was central to their theology. The existence of a counterforce to God, whatever you wanted to call it, was why everyone had to work so hard, and what made the endless ten-week series more than self-help.

The feeling among the kids from Concord was that Satan was everywhere. You could hear it when they talked to one another, and it came out in the youth groups. If God was the hard taskmaster who assigned you a lifelong research project and expected you to finish it, Satan was the tempter who never stopped looking for ways to pull you from your task. Of the two forces, Satan could seem much more present than God. Every day was a battle for your soul. Mix the incendiary elements of a belief in Satan's omnipresence, the heroics of the battle, and the easy examples of modern American culture, and you didn't need fire and brimstone from the pulpit. All you needed was a small spark and a mass of teenagers to fan the flames.

The pastors took an encouraging view of the vomiting and chaos on the buses in Peru. In part, they'd set the kids up for it. (Cameron and the others had been told that Peru's "less sophisticated, more emotional" culture would expose them to more direct battle with Satan than they had experienced at home.) One of the biggest benefits of the mission trips, from the pastors' point of view, was the bonding that resulted. What happened on the bus formed extra-strong mortar.

If Nappanee's pastors made use of smoke and mirrors—the sulfur of the Devil, the mirrors of a rock concert—to keep the church's young people safe, the question arose, was this a problem? If you accepted, as Dave Engbrecht did, that youth culture was separate; and if you accepted, as the Missionary Church had since its founding, that converting the next generation of Christians meant teaching them separately from adults; then maybe you needed to accept some earsplitting music, some mass hysteria, some youthful obsession about sin and salvation, if what emerged at the end of the process were Christians for life, and possibly lifetime Nappanee members as well.

Some of the parents of the teenagers who attended Nappanee possibly weighed their own fears about their children's safe passage into adulthood against whatever concerns they might harbor about the new service or the tales their teenagers told them (or didn't) about being pursued by the Devil. Even if the parents knew what their children were hearing and saying about Satan; even if they knew that their children were quite frightened, in fact, about taking a wrong step that would cost them their immortal souls; even if they knew their children mistook normal adolescent urges or failings as those wrong steps— might the parents not still say, Better to be afraid than be in trouble. Better a fear of Satan than getting pregnant or getting someone pregnant, or taking drugs or drinking or getting into the wrong crowd or simply messing up. Jeff and Chris Longenbaugh, who saw what the fear was doing to their son, felt themselves in the minority.

At The Connection, the service ended with a prayer. The teenagers stood, and the energy level in the room jumped. Someone who saw the crowd and didn't know a church service had just ended could have been forgiven for mistaking the gathering for the beginning of a high school dance. Friends found friends and milled about, talking excitedly and checking each other out, checking out the scene. Chatter spilled out of the gym and spread into the foyer, where the youth of Nappanee crowded around the Krispy Kreme doughnuts.

Grant, standing with Leandra and Cameron, missing Keith, was trying to understand what he thought and how he felt. The video-recorded sermon, which hadn't provided the deep, fundamental guidance he sought, had left him feeling bad again. The mortar was softening between the bricks of his belief. Child of Nappanee, son of Concord, Grant was starting to try to figure it out for himself.

———

UNTIL NOW, MAX JONES had focused his students' attention tightly on the work in front of them. Learn fundamentals. Entertain at State Fair. Memorize each piece of music. Mark drill. The Monday after the invitational, he jammed everyone into Room 406, and asked them for the first time to look all the way down the road. They had thirty more days of practice before state finals. "Only four Wednesday evenings left," he warned.

They'd travel next to Mishawaka for the Penn Invitational. A week later, they'd need to pass their first ISSMA test, districts, hosted that year at Concord; the following Saturday, they'd travel to Homestead for the season's final invitational and the directors' last chance to hear directly from judges, a last chance to correct course. Max wanted his students to look ahead to Homestead. For the first time that season, he turned their eyes to their competitors and asked them to linger on the view.

He knew word had gotten out about Concord's high score at its own invitational. He wanted to give them some perspective. "Please, don't put this on the Internet," he pleaded. "We *killed* Class B." He paused a beat. "In the north." He paused again. Waited. "If you went south, it wouldn't be the case. We'd be in a fight for our little lives."

"Greenwood," he said, bringing up their perennial rival from downstate, "practices from two to five every day, and one night to nine, or eight, maybe two nights."

"Northview"—a central Indiana band and another rival—"thought they'd win state last year." There had been talk, down that way, of having been robbed when they placed only fourth in 2003.

He mentioned an opponent closer to home. Northridge had a small band, about a hundred kids, and had yet to make the state finals. But they had an aggressive young director and high-caliber students. The people who would have moved to Concord a couple of decades earlier had instead been buying bigger homes fifteen miles east, in fancier new subdivisions built out of the Amish farmland around Northridge. Max thought it only a matter of time before its band rode that wave and surpassed Concord. "Northridge has a good show," he said. "They're up and coming. They think this is their chance to beat us."

If some of the students had trouble keeping the names of all the schools straight, they weren't alone. Amy Davis had a hard time remembering whether Northridge was from Nappanee and North Wood from Middlebury, or the other way around. She knew Lawrence North was in Indianapolis, but was North Central as well? During Davis's first year at Concord, natives Scott Spradling and Steve Peterson made her a visual aid, which they called the "Boom Boom Davis Band Map." The names of several dozen schools, all with "north" in them, ran down the side of a line drawing of Indiana, connected by lines to their locations. It included the "norths" of Fort Wayne—North Side, which was on the north side of the city, but still south of Northrop. The list included the strange and wonderful "norths" from the southern part of the state: Bloomington North, Columbus North, North Decatur, North Daviess, Northeast Dubois (the home of the "Marching Jeeps," and in spite of its name located in the state's southwest corner), and especially Evansville North, North Harrison, and North Posey, none of them more than fifteen miles from the Kentucky border. Davis kept the map taped to her wall.

In any event, still referring to Northridge, Max reminded his students that judges rated performances in two broad areas: ambition and execution. Both were necessary. But a band that perfectly executed a less ambitious show nearly always beat a more ambitious but flawed show. He drew out the point for them. "All they have to do is be better at doing their show than we are at doing ours."

He told them that they'd remain at the Homestead Invitational after their performance, to watch the excellent Class A bands—Avon, Homestead, Penn. He wanted the Marching Minutemen to measure themselves against that competition, not the bands they'd beaten so easily on Saturday. At Homestead they'd all get a sense of where their band truly stood.

The LC guys still owed Max a few last charts. But five more pages of drill had come in, and Max wanted to push the band to get "Swing, Swing, Swing" on the field that week. After so much pushing already, it was an optimistic goal.

"You have to be aggressive," he said before releasing them to get paint sticks. "And you have to help each other. If you're first chair and can play your part pretty well, that's not good enough."

He had just collected the senior logs he'd handed out the previous week, and he knew where to aim his comments. Amanda Bechtel's report was detailed and to the point: She'd stayed late to work with these students and gone over choreography with those; she'd practiced her solo and listened, again, to *The Mission* CD. Diana de la Reza had stayed after to work with Adilene Corona, and had given up some of her own practice time to work again with Adilene and other freshmen clarinets between the rehearsal and the invitational performance. But Cameron Bradley, in the "service to others" category, had written "fixed 406 stands, chairs." He'd straightened the arcs of chairs and music stands in the main band room and picked up trash on the floor. It was precisely the type of labor memorialized in Dr. Tim's "toilet flushing" speech and in one of Max Jones's maxims: "Leaders straighten the chairs and pick up the trash." But Cameron's leadership, beginning and ending with tidying up, was a conscious act of rebellion.

Max had hoped—had expected—that Cameron would lead the saxophone section the way Grant led the high brass. He knew the two were friends; had assumed, perhaps, that Grant's dedication would rub off on Cameron. Cameron had an opportunity, Max thought, to make a difference in the saxophone section. Max had written demanding parts for the saxophones in the field show. The section was young and inexperienced, and Max knew he needed its seniors to step up. But Max had been irritated by Cameron's care-not approach to his State Fair solo. And, even more, he'd been disappointed by how little Cameron had invested in the section, which remained one of the weakest in the band.

Cameron's issue with Max Jones had developed during his junior year, after winning the state championship. He'd been thrilled to win. He believed that the marching band had won precisely because the students in the band had been given the latitude to decide how much they wanted to win. But then Cameron thought his director became greedy. It seemed to him that during the concert-band season that followed, Mr. Jones decided his top concert band should also go after a championship. Cameron, along with some others, felt they were given no choice in the matter. Their practices became contests of wills. Cameron resented being singled out for not working hard enough.

He had been unusually direct when he completed his sign-up form for his final year in the Concord band program. "This is the most apprehensive band commitment I've made," he'd written. That had caught Max's attention, but the next sentence lost it: "I simply am not enjoying any of the program at the moment, simply because there was no fun." *No fun.* Max had dismissed the comment as naive. At the end of Cameron's form was a statement, though, that he might have taken to heart: "It seemed the focus was no longer on the love of music but on the accomplishment of music."

Cameron took "love of music" as seriously as anyone in the band. He felt music keenly and heard it clearly. He had what those around him called perfect pitch. He—perhaps alone in the band—knew that his ability to pinpoint sounds on a scale didn't quite reach "perfect." It came close enough, however, that wrong or out-of-tune notes physically pained him. He could tell that most kids with poor intonation had no idea that their playing was off, but to him it was obvious what a C should sound like and how the half-tone step to C-sharp or the whole-tone jump to D should follow. Sometimes friends asked him to demonstrate his pitch, as if it were a parlor game. But pitch was only the smallest of building blocks for what Cameron really cared about, which was how music moved him.

His ear demanded a certain perfectionism. But it wasn't the disciplined, sweaty perfectionism of Amanda Bechtel or Grant Longenbaugh. Cameron's notion of "perfect" centered on a link between music and emotion. If playing a composition, or phrase, or even a note didn't trigger a corresponding emotion in him, it was nothing but an empty shell. Music deserved his full respect, which he believed meant playing it, not breaking it into rote exercises. And playing to win was particularly disrespectful.

Early that week, as the band continued polishing "Gabriel's Oboe," Cameron effortlessly made the right entrances, hit the right tempos with perfect intonation, moved seamlessly from *piano* to *fortissimo*, and had breath left over at the end of the long crescendo. He was by far the best saxophone player in the band. He marched with impeccable style, even the backward marching that was so deceptively difficult that other seniors still faltered trying to get it right. Without trying, he seemed to carry himself so that people's eyes were drawn to him on the field. He loved to perform, and the fun he had during the show was obvious. On the field, he could seem to do no wrong.

But he resisted practicing and had refused to lead in the manner that the Max Jones system required of seniors. Two months into the season, he'd set up no regular outside practices, not with individuals and not with the group. He'd called no section meetings as Brent Lehman had done with the trombones, no meetings with the senior saxophones as

Grant had with the high brass or Amanda Bechtel had with the flutes. And he made it clear to the other saxophone players that he would not push them to practice. He said, "If your heart's in it, you're probably going to play it right. If you practice but your heart's not in it, you'll never get it right in a thousand years."

Which was great, and probably true—if you could play the saxophone like Cameron Bradley. But the advice ignored the needs of a take-all-comers band. During the practices heading into the competition at Penn, Cameron played beautifully while the section around him sounded hesitant and unsure, still laboring to get the notes right and the timing down.

Cameron compared his experience in band unfavorably to his experience in the Nappanee youth groups. He believed that Max Jones's approach to band was "too worldly," which meant too wrapped up in the world, full of sinful pride, open to Satan's influence. Cameron believed wholeheartedly in the goals of the youth groups. He appreciated that whether he was a freshman or a senior didn't matter there, that nobody came with expectations about who would lead whom. What mattered was their devotion to God and to following Jesus.

In private, Cameron wished that his relationship with God came as naturally to him as did his music. His prayers, in fact, often included music, music he made on an instrument few people even knew he played. Two years earlier, he'd bought a guitar and taught himself the chords. He found that prayer sometimes went more easily, or went deeper, if he let his fingers work it out on the strings. The music he played on his guitar was between him and God. It had become his best instrument, even better than the saxophone. He kept a prayer journal in which he jotted words and chord changes. The Bible became a source of new inspiration, especially the Psalms. He felt he understood the Psalmist when he read in Psalm 104, "I will sing to the Lord as long as I live."

Max only saw Cameron's behavior in the band and thought of him as selfish. Max had gone out of his way a couple of times, just as he had with Nick, to give Cameron pointed advice on how to lead his section. When Cameron didn't respond, he let that be Cameron's choice and Cameron's lesson.

In spite of what Max thought, Cameron believed that he was taking good care of the students around him. When kids needed rides, he took them home, and if the right moment presented itself, he asked his passengers if they wanted to join him in prayer. As he had done with Grant in seventh grade, he extended invitations to Nappanee's youth group. One of the younger saxophone players had recently accepted Jesus as his personal savior. "And all because I marched next to him in drill," Cameron marveled.

He would honor his commitment to the band and finish out his final year, but he would stand on principle against playing to win. Cameron never mentioned the comments on his commitment form again to his director, and Max never responded directly to them. But invisible among the many other challenges the band faced as it pushed the field show forward, the document stood between one of its best musicians and the head director, like a wall.

IT WAS A stressful week. On Wednesday night Greg Hagen finally came up from Lawrence Central to teach the choreography for "Swing, Swing, Swing." Over the next two practices Max spent very little time on any other part of the show. On Friday, he still hadn't decided if they would perform the show's final segment the next day at Penn. "Some of you are probably thinking," he told them at the beginning of practice, "'He's making us take this out and we're gonna look like fools in front of a thousand, two thousand, ten thousand, a million people. And we're supposed to be Concord.' I will not put you out that way, but I am pressing you hard. We are going to try to get this on. If we fail this afternoon, we will take it out. But it will not be in our best interest."

The consuming work on "Swing, Swing, Swing" forced Max to pick precious few other spots in the show to work on. Early in the week, he'd found a recording he wished he'd heard back in the spring. In it, a flute solo soared over African rhythms. It had everything they would have needed to start their show, and because it didn't have the complex layering of rhythms of Morricone's "Gabriel's Oboe," the beat would have laid down better. It was far too late to switch the opening music, but he shared the recording with Amanda and asked her to play around with the feel of it in her solos. "It should be like a bird singing," he told her. He might also have been describing the sound of a true musician. He continued, "If you add on that freedom. . . ."

He scheduled some of the precious time for the Dixieland ensemble. On Friday afternoon, he brought the group together under his tower, while the rest of the band continued to work on "Swing, Swing, Swing." The ensemble had started as a group of four: a clarinet, a tuba, Brent Lehman on trombone, and Grant soloing on trumpet. Max had already added Matt Tompkins on banjo. Now, continuing to fiddle, he added Nick Stubbs. He was trying to solve the problem of how to get Nick from his spot in the drumline to his drumset for "Swing, Swing, Swing," and was thinking of adding some sparkle to the Dixieland group along the way. "I want you to dance your way down, Nick," he said. Nick dropped his head to his chest: the drumline captain, jangling a tambourine, dancing.

Grant's solo was to carry the melody—"The tune everyone's gonna whistle," Steve Peterson had told them during a session focused on style—starting with the drawn-out bluesy plea at the center of "A Closer Walk with Thee":

> Just a closer walk with Thee,
> Grant it, Jesus, is my plea,
> Daily walking close to Thee,
> Let it be, dear Lord, let it be.
>
> I am weak, but Thou art strong;
> Jesus, keep me from all wrong;
> I'll be satisfied as long
> As I walk, let me walk close to Thee.

The others in the ensemble did more than add ornamentation. They formed a conversation, a community, around Grant and the melody. Brent sounded a response in a lower register to the call of Grant's horn; the clarinet player skated across the top of the melody; the tuba pushed the song along. Peterson told them to weight their notes, to feel the pull and grit of life in each one as they played it.

"Saints," by contrast, was lightness, crisp and quick articulation. "Dance right over the notes," Peterson told them. All of them, in both songs, were being backed by a 240-piece band. Everyone had to play the same style, but the ensemble needed to carry it.

Peterson had been working closely with Grant on his solos. The director had explained the importance of the "scoop" notes in "A Closer Walk," how Grant could manipulate pitch to start flat on a note and then slide or squeeze into it. There was pleasure in delaying the gratification of hitting the correct pitch until the last moment. He'd talked to Grant about adding heat, passion, to his playing, about what he called "stank." He'd taught Grant in jazz band for three years. He knew Grant was an intelligent musician who understood theory and technique. There were all sorts of technical ways to play soulfully. Grant could use accents, play with his breathing, vary his tone, experiment with valves and fingering. But Peterson knew that more was required to play well in any jazz idiom. "You're preaching out there," he told Grant. "Think of the soul behind the music." He listened to Grant play, and sensed that the trumpet player was thinking too hard.

Peterson had a sympathetic ear, perhaps more than Grant even knew. He was struggling to live his faith in the world, too, just as Grant and some of his other students were trying to do now. Peterson had grown up Catholic, had started going to St. Vincent's in high school a few years before Chris and Jeff Longenbaugh joined as a new family. His faith had been activated at DePaul, a Catholic university in Chicago, where he'd gone to study music after graduating from Concord. He discovered that he preferred talking about the meaning of life to partying, and became involved in campus ministry.

During spring break of his junior year, he went on a university-sponsored mission to Harlan County, Kentucky, in the heart of Appalachian hill country. He and several of the others on that trip vowed to return after they graduated, but he was the only one who kept the vow. For three years, he lived in a small town in the center of the state, working for the Christian Appalachian Project and living in a volunteer house with six other twenty-somethings. They gardened, recycled, prayed daily, and performed community service in addition to their volunteer jobs. Peterson was assigned to emergency assistance with a local woman. The skinny white boy and the big black woman bonded immediately. They worked in the field as social workers, befriending the poor and witnessing to them. The work gave him his first contact with poverty. He saw rats scurrying around one trailer. It scared him, but later he'd remember that the woman who lived there always greeted him kindly—"you da purdy boy"—and that the trailer was surrounded by flowers of surpassing beauty. For his labors, he received fifty dollars a month, health insurance, housing, and food. He met Kathy, another volunteer who worked in a schools-on-wheels program. It was an exhilarating time, going against the status quo, being part of an active group of believers who were helping others, living a "full-contact life."

He returned to Harlan County as a newlywed to become the band director for the Evarts schools. To move to Evarts, he and Kathy drove south down Interstate 75 and took a two-lane highway to Kingdom Come Parkway, built to haul coal out of the hills. One of the last exits off Kingdom Come dumped them onto a narrow road that seemed to take them directly into the bowels of the earth, but actually deposited them in the town of Evarts. Over four years, Peterson built the band program there from twenty kids across five grades to more than a hundred, but his lonely labor in the poor school district wore him down. He returned home to work with Max Jones, happy to be part of a team. His first Concord flute class, alone, contained fifteen kids, Amanda Bechtel among them. The students all had their own instruments, they brought their music every day, they had parents who drove them to school for summer practices and picked them up again, on time. Who needed him there?

Seven years after leaving Kentucky, he still thought about Evarts. He sometimes asked himself who would be more at a loss, Evarts kids in Concord, or Concord kids in Evarts? And he wondered if he'd given up too easily. Personal salvation was "fire insurance," he'd sometimes say, thinking of the hereafter. "But how do you live your life?"

Each year, he told the beginning band a story from his time in Kentucky to introduce a piece called "Possum Holler." He told the sixth graders that he and his wife noticed a rancid smell wafting up through the floor of their trailer. To investigate, he pulled on a baseball cap, tied a perfume-soaked bandanna around his face, and wrapped trash bags over his hands. He crawled under the trailer and stuck a hand right through a dead possum. In a touch worthy of Scott Spradling, he lingered on his description of the maggots that swarmed over his arm. Needless to say, students who came up through the Concord music program remembered "Possum Holler." But otherwise, he talked very little with Grant or the other students about his life in Kentucky, or what had motivated it.

Peterson understood jazz at a deeper level than Max Jones did. He knew what Grant needed to do—to bring the opposing poles of his nature, the bluegrass side and the analytical, into his playing—and how hard that would be. Max, already taking Grant's playing as a given, focused on more pressing matters.

At the end of Friday's practice, Max stood on the tower and announced that they could finally drop "Anchors Aweigh" from the ending. "Swing, Swing, Swing" was in. Down on the field, the students cheered.

THE BAND PERFORMED its uneven show at Penn, against other bands that were also still working out the details of their own shows. Again, they won; again, they cleaned up the awards, including the "people's choice" award as the most entertaining band.

In the postmortem huddle with the band the following Monday, Max told his students, "Obviously, we pressed really, really hard. You had to have been unclear how it was going to turn out." He was happy they'd pulled it off, but concerned about the feedback he'd received from the judges. Once again, the music judges had been confused by the rhythm in "Gabriel's Oboe"; once again, they'd questioned the percussion score. Once again, Max was holding his band to a higher standard than merely winning competitions.

He asked Amy Davis to rewrite the percussion part, again. She'd first written the "Gabriel's Oboe" percussion score in June. Since then, she'd gone back to it more times than she could remember. She stayed up the rest of Saturday night after Penn, trying to get it right.

Homestead was less than two weeks away. Max told his students they'd be playing on AstroTurf, that the press box was high, almost high enough to see all of Concord's show. The year before, the week heading into Homestead had been their breakout week. He hoped it would be again.

Amanda's changes to her solo became even more important. After addressing the band, Max took her aside again. "Right now the judges are telling us it's not Africa," he told her. "They've heard too many people play it without the African stuff."

"The drums . . . ?" Amanda asked.

"They think it's wrong. 'Why are you taking this gorgeous piece and putting drums behind it?'" Max had listened to the soundtrack from *The Mission* again, thinking that possibly he'd been wrong about the original composition. "But they are wrong," he told Amanda, speaking of the judges. "Their horizons need to be expanded."

On Monday, after the postmortem, they had one hour and ten minutes left in the day's practice. It was all the time they'd have that week to start putting a shine on "Gabriel's Oboe."

Grant was working with third trumpets, the dos amigos with the rest of the section. It was the second time in two weeks that Grant had taken attendance, conducted warm-ups, organized the section into working groups, and basically served as a staff person. Scott Spradling had been out part of the previous week following his daughter's birth. Over the weekend, she'd had to return to the hospital. Spradling would be out again for a few more days. Max had asked Gerry Knipfel, the former band director at Elkhart High School, to cover for Spradling until the high-brass director could return to work. Knipfel had been Dick Lehman's band director in the 1970s and was now a private instructor for Grant and a handful of other trumpet players in the Concord band, another reason the high-brass section stood out. But Knipfel hadn't stood in front of a class in more than twenty years, and Max knew he didn't care for marching bands. Max was counting on Grant to help the substitute and keep the high-brass section from faltering.

Grant had responded. He still wanted another championship. He still wanted to institutionalize a new leadership system within the band. He still wanted to live his faith on the field. He liked the stress, was energized by it. This was what it had been like junior year. You need us to work this hard? *Yeah! Give us more!*

He stayed after every practice now, working with the kids who were struggling. He had started wearing the brim of his cowboy hat flipped up, and the face underneath it was lighter. His energy was out ahead of the others, and he needed to get them to rise to it. You wouldn't know to look at him that he was the best person for the job. It was still hard to catch his gaze straight on, and rarer to catch the brilliance behind it. It wasn't obvious how someone so quiet was the band's best leader. But after a while you might notice the extra measure of respect that he was given, the focused attention when he did speak, and how, even when he tried to blend in, people's eyes followed him. All of it made him seem like royalty there.

Outside of band he was changing. In the last few weeks, he'd skipped some classes. He was becoming less patient with the make-work he'd always diligently completed to keep his string of As, and had started blowing off some of it. He still wanted to be valedictorian, but he was taking more risks.

During that practice, Jim Schoeffler, who had been trying harder in Scott Spradling's absence, cracked a note during one of the long crescendos in "Gabriel's Oboe." He slammed his horn against his leg and turned away as if leaving. Grant said to everyone, to Jim, "Stick with me on the hard stuff, OK? It's going to be hard the next few days, but we're gonna get this."

One of the small freshman boys said to Jim, "Just do what Grant wants." Jim started to sputter, "I can't do what Grant—" The ninth grader interrupted. "Yes, you can."

On the practice field, Grant kneeled down on the pavement, along with the rest of his section. Greg Hagen had explained to them that they were the trees, putting down roots, and that they had to convey to the audience the "roots" of their show. The tarp would do some of the work for them, but they needed to bring the image alive. Grant sat up onto his knees and thrust one hand out, then the other, and tensed them into claws. He clawed against the pavement, putting down roots. Slowly he moved onto his feet until he was standing upright. This was where the roots came out of the ground and became limbs. Grant threw his arms up into the sky, up to the heavens.

He was almost ready to start moving. He clawed again, but through air this time, as if cutting his way through a jungle.

Finally, he joined his hands above his head, swaying them side to side as if in a breeze. Then he reached down by his side and picked up his horn, and was marching with it.

They had less than thirty minutes left that week to polish the opening number. Amanda Bechtel, improvising, played higher, tried sweeter, kept pushing. Nick Stubbs, facing a new percussion score, led the section through triplet eighth notes during the same time that the woodwinds played a quarter-note. The drums arrived at the same destination, the same beat, as the woodwinds, but by a different path.

The piece was starting to swing. Cameron Bradley blew his saxophone beautifully. Steve Peterson watched his woodwinds, looking for passion. Grant lifted his trumpet, feeling for soul.

All of them referred to the piece as "Gabriel's Oboe," but Morricone had actually named the version "On Earth As It Is in Heaven."

10 ★ Bonfire

At Districts, the Marching Minutemen lost a music caption for the first time during Max's reign at Concord. The band won every other Class B category, still came in first overall, and cleared the low hurdle of advancing to regionals. But music, what Concord had always been known for: That award went to Northridge.

The judges appreciated the ambition of Concord's show. They singled out the abilities of the band's best performers—Amanda, Grant and the Dixieland ensemble, Nick and the set drummers. From a band of Concord's size, however, they expected more volume to reach the judges' box. More important, their comments suggested that the show's unusually high demands in drill, choreography, and performance siphoned too much of the students' attention away from the music. The comments included harsh recommendations to "reduce the exposure from" or "rewrite the drill around" the students who were struggling—in other words, cut them from the show. In some elite bands, Adilene Corona and a handful of clarinets; Amanda Himes, Jim Schoeffler, and other young high-brass players; and possibly half the saxophone section would have lost their places. Eric Sabach, who had last seen the show in the warm sun of Concord's invitational, didn't bother making such a suggestion. He understood Max and his program. Nonetheless, he minced no words: "You guys are on a different level. You've set the bar high for yourselves. Now it's a matter of the performers understanding that. It's a little out of their reach."

Losing in the music category was a huge deal. Rumors spread among the students over the weekend, fueled by the Internet, that penalties had cost Concord the award. On Monday, the music hallway buzzed with freshly minted facts: Amanda Himes had practiced her trumpet after the ISSMA quiet period had started; a sophomore had been caught letting his girlfriend fool around on his bass clarinet. Max asked the band before practice, "What do you think of the penalties we got?" Murmuring started instantly: *So it was true!* He held up a hand to quiet the talk. "The penalty we got in music was: We can't play the show. We can't play the music together." Max didn't address the specific slanders, none of which were true. He just said, "We got the penalty together."

He handed out sheets of paper similar to the reports he'd asked seniors to fill out for the past two weeks. If the band wanted to win—and he reminded the students that Concord had yet to manage back-to-back championships, even though the '93 band had come within a fraction of a point of pulling off the feat—they had to understand the effort it would take. Before he played the judges' tape for them, he told the students to list its relevant criticisms in one column; in the next, to write their "personal plan to improve" each area of weakness; and in the final column, to explain how they were helping others or who was helping them.

Kids laughed when they heard one judge call out, "More banjo!" But otherwise, the mood in the band room was somber.

"I don't care about the caption," Max told them after they'd handed in the forms. "Our goal shouldn't be to do better than some other band." He grimaced at the thought. "Our goal is to be the best— the best *we* can be. These goals carry over, you understand? I hope you have the best marriage, the best job, the best grades. But you have to learn how to give 150 percent effort. I don't care if we don't make finals, as long as you give it your best effort, as long as you take care of business, as long as you care about and help each other."

His admirable goals seemed to sour, though, as he talked. He sharpened his comments: "So you care the day before state finals. It's too late. You should have cared in August." He'd created a perfect show on paper and now had to watch his students waste their opportunity. But what he talked about was losing the chance to win.

The teenagers could be forgiven if they heard mixed messages. As always, Max told his students that winning was not the goal. He wanted them to reach higher than they thought possible, and only he—because he alone could hear and see the perfect show in his mind—could set the goal high enough. At the beginning of the season, he had told the seniors that the freshmen couldn't know until October what was being asked of them. In fact, all of them were learning lessons they might not understand until years later. He wanted them to know the difference between where they were and where they wanted to be, even if that knowledge pained them. He wanted them to strive for perfection, even knowing they'd always fall short.

But that's not what they heard. Instead, many of the band students—maybe all of them, at some point—felt they'd never be good enough for Mr. Jones. Parents routinely needed to talk their children out of quitting, or into believing they could do what their director asked of them. Excellence, Max Jones–style, required the faith of many.

Max repeated a litany of mistakes and corrections for the students in the band every Monday once competitions began. He was measuring the gap for them between performance and perfection, but it was hard to remember at such times that Concord had actually won the Penn Invitational, the Goshen Invitational—in fact, usually all the contests on the way to state finals.

Almost like Pastor Dave at Nappanee, Max was trying to point toward a kind of perfection, and trying to give the young people in his charge the tools to achieve it. Both men accepted that in the course of their lessons kids were likely to feel bad about themselves. Both thought the higher goal was worth it.

But while Pastor Dave prepared his followers for the ultimate victory, where they either earned salvation or they didn't (the final judgment didn't work on a point system), Max Jones truly believed the results were in the process. If he spoke a lot about winning, it was because to Max a perfect show and a winning show were synonymous. His challenge involved not only the inherent imperfection of humanity, and the usual imperfection of communication, but the widely varying needs and psyches and personalities in a group of some two hundred teenagers.

On that Monday morning, he seemed to be searching for a way to motivate the students in front of him, or to motivate more of them than he had to date. He gave the sense of someone who was no longer sure of his tools. An undercurrent of uncertainty ran through his talk that anyone who knew him well would recognize as new.

Once again, he talked much longer than he'd planned to. His final words before he released them to a shortened practice expressed his two emotional poles. "If I have made a dent, this time will be worth it." he said. "If I didn't, the time doesn't matter anyway."

In a staff meeting later, Max told the other directors that Concord hadn't been nailed that thoroughly by judges in a very long time. "We got walloped," he said. But he accepted the harsh criticism as a gift from the judges. Eric Sabach and several of the others had stepped "out of caption" to comment broadly and frankly on Concord's show, as Beth Fabrizio had four years earlier. Max said, "They want us to win."

He was on more solid ground with his staff. His confidence seemed to grow back as he outlined a lengthy list of specifics that needed more work. Although some items on his list included minutiae and others fell into the category of field logistics and transitions, the list as a whole came down to fixing timing, timing, timing, and loosening the parts of the music-plus-everything-else tangle. And—even though none of the judges had mentioned any problem with the ending, and even though just two weeks remained until state finals—Max told his staff he thought he might tinker with the finale, maybe even add a new one altogether.

The judges' comments confirmed for him that he had the show. But he no longer knew if he had the students. Or maybe he had the students but had lost the ability to reach them.

AT THE END of the shortened practice, Nick Stubbs asked the rest of the drumline, "Is there anyone who absolutely has to leave?" A sophomore who played the tenor drums said he didn't want to miss his ride. Someone else offered to take him home. Everyone stayed, even Amy Davis, who had to keep an eye on the clock for the staff meeting. They played through the umpteenth version of "Gabriel's Oboe," the version that was less than a week old and about to change again. Davis listened and gave them feedback. "It's better," she said after the fourth run-through. That was enough for several of the kids to put their drumsticks away and start undoing their carriers. Davis quickly packed her things and left for her meeting. Before the others could leave, though, Nick called out, "Wait!"

For the past month, ever since his father had asked him if he was going to quit, Nick had been trying to turn things around in the percussion section. He'd started right away by asking his father for advice. He'd sought the counsel of the two drummers he trusted most, senior Lisa Bennett and junior Jen Bollero. He'd known Lisa since sixth grade, when she'd moved to Concord from California and immediately become a Goth princess. Through junior high, she'd clomped around in army boots, wrapped chains around her wrists, and occasionally carried a mouse in the hood of her sweatshirt. The only time she even acknowledged Nick's existence, back then, was to talk about drums. By the middle of freshman band camp, however, she'd switched to shorts and T-shirts, and hadn't gone back. Now, kids at the high school said that Lisa Bennett looked like Paris Hilton, only prettier. But she still stared down boys who expected her to act like a babe just because she resembled one. Nick had learned to think of her as one of the guys, and that seemed to get it mostly right. He regarded Lisa as his drill sergeant. She was a stickler for detail and process, the person who urged him to come down harder on the others when they were late or when they goofed off.

Jen Bollero, the daughter of a percussion instructor, was the drumline captain-in-training. She was smart, too, but quiet. She asked Nick questions more than she gave him advice, but her questions worked as insistently in Nick's mind as any command. She'd asked him, for example, how he planned to simultaneously run both the drumline and the pit. That had prompted Nick to ask Jon Faloon, the pit's resident senior, to take charge of the section. Jon didn't always remember that he was the leader, or what it meant to lead, but the honor had energized him. Nick could see that he was trying.

Nick had also realized, on his own, that he needed not only to work with Amy Davis but to support her. Two weeks earlier, he'd asked her to hold percussion sectionals for everyone on Tuesday evenings, plus one more night a week in smaller groups, all of it mandatory. Then he'd tried to keep everyone focused while they were there, even when Miss Davis couldn't. He thought it was helping.

The push to get "Swing, Swing, Swing" on the field had pressed the percussion section tremendously. The show's final piece was a drumline feature. It started with the drumsets and opened up for two drum solos. "Nobody gets to do this," Max told them, referring to other bands around the state. He was stretching the truth slightly: A few other programs at the highest level might take on a drum-corps showpiece like "Swing, Swing, Swing," but only a very select few. "By the time we get to this part of the show," Max said, "everybody should be wishing they could be in the drumline at Concord." He was riding Nick and the other drummers hard. Being featured meant they were even more under the critical gaze of a director who, for all they could tell, thought they were doing a terrible job.

Max's criticism of the percussion section had, indeed, seemed to intensify. He yelled at the bass line for sloppy feet and missed drill changes, the tenor drums for spacing problems and incorrect timing, the cymbals for missing entrances—the snares, too. During one practice of "Swing, Swing, Swing," he told them, "I hear the drumline falling apart every time, front to back." As the drumline captain, Nick had the responsibility to fix it. Max told him, "Nick, you better have some marching rehearsals, because this is hideous. The heartbeat of the band can't even march."

As if he'd needed it, the harshness of the judges' critique reminded Nick how far the section still needed to go. "We still can't play this musically," Nick said to the others now. "That's why we lost the caption."

He'd tried several times already to set up extra practices. He'd put the suggestion out there. The others had seemed to sign on, and had talked about schedules, jobs, Not that time, Let's do it this time, No, that doesn't work for me. And then a few kids needed to go to class or someone had to go home and nothing happened.

So when he now said, "Wait!" it wasn't with a suggestion. He told them he'd be at the school every morning at seven-ten, ready to practice half an hour on whatever needed work. If they kept that schedule every day, they could practice more than seven additional hours before finals. It could make the difference. "I don't know if you want to sleep in or not. I kind of want to stop sucking before it's too late."

Everyone agreed. Plans were rejiggered, rides arranged.

"Want to play it again?" one of the others asked. They reattached drums to carriers, all but Brandon Dascoli, the only senior on tenor drums and one of the section's weakest drummers. He started to leave. One of the other tenors called after him. "Brandon, you have a car. Why are you leaving?" Others joined in trying to call him back, but he didn't turn around. His departure deflated the others. They played through "Gabriel's Oboe" again, but with less care than they had while Amy Davis was there, and then quickly dispersed.

In the dawning gray light the next morning, Nick had the pick of the parking spots closest to the performing arts center. By quarter after seven, only a few of the drummers had shown up. Not even Nick's advisers, Jen and Lisa, made it in. The enthusiasm of the previous afternoon hadn't carried. Eventually, Nick and five others strapped on their drums and went outside for a fifteen-minute practice.

Nick had made his choice. He was not giving up. But he could see that having made the choice only got him part of the way. Now he had to figure out how to get the rest of his section to go with him.

THE COLD WATER of Districts and Max's continuing countdown energized others besides Nick.

After practice on Tuesday (fourteen practice days to state finals), Diana de la Reza asked Steve Peterson for advice on her group of underclassmen. She'd been holding extra practices with them ever since the woodwind director had set up the pods. "Is it OK if I tell them they have to show up every morning at, like, 7:15?"

"Sure, it's OK."

"I know they're not practicing," Diana said. "They say they are. But I can tell they aren't."

Only a few minutes before, Peterson had pulled Adilene aside, along with four other clarinets, and told them that they had to pass the "Gabriel's Oboe" tests they'd failed a month earlier. Adilene had retaken her test and improved her score, but she still hadn't achieved a passing grade. "If you don't retest and pass, I will take you out of the show." Adilene's eyes had flicked up to Peterson's face, startled and wide. She looked for a moment as if she might cry. "You guys aren't the failing type," Peterson told them. "So take care of it." But he knew they needed help.

Diana had started the season thinking she'd work hard for the clarinet section leader, who was also a friend outside of band. Diana hadn't thought of herself as a leader then, and she didn't think of herself as one now. She felt dumb standing next to Grant, who she knew was a real leader. But at freshman camp, she'd been surprised that the section leader had picked students to work with who were already strong players. Diana had been given the biggest challenges. Or maybe she'd been drawn to them. She'd picked out Adilene from the start. Although Diana didn't like to draw attention to her background—she and her twin sister, Daniela, had been raised mostly in America but had been born in Bolivia—she felt a connection with the Hispanic girl. Adilene reminded Diana of Daniela at a younger age: the long hair, the pretty face, the shyness, even the necklaces and earrings she wore. During band camp, Diana enjoyed marching next to Adilene during fundamentals and had liked finding ways to make the younger girl smile. When Mr. Peterson had created the practice groups of upperclassmen and underclassmen, Diana had been glad that he put Adilene in her group. Another quiet, unconfident girl who had become a friend of Adilene's was in the same pod, along with a space-cadet freshman and one of the better sophomores.

All season long, Diana had heard Mr. Jones call out the clarinets for being out of step, for not rolling their feet and for not turning their shoulders to the front, for not playing to the box, for not playing loud enough, for not entering on time and not stopping on time. Sometimes it seemed that the clarinets were the worst section in the entire band. Diana felt responsible. And though she didn't think of what she was doing as leadership, she felt she had to do what needed to be done.

But the first morning of Diana's special session went badly. She got lost trying to find one of the girls' houses and then was held up further by two trains. At seven-fifteen, Adilene waited in the music hallway, her clarinet ready. She waited five minutes, debated whether to put her instrument away, debated again at ten minutes, and had just pulled her case out of her instrument locker when Diana and the others rushed in. By then it was too late to get any real work done.

In Nick's sectional, three members of the drumline didn't show up: a bass drummer, snare drummer Derek Richard, and Brandon Dascoli. The ones who showed up spent part of the morning talking about Brandon. He had marched bass the previous two years. The consensus in the drummers' cave was that he'd marched horribly and played not much better. But Miss Davis had moved him to up tenor quad anyway, the drumline equivalent of passing a student in spite of failing grades. Good intentions, maybe, but they all felt the move had backfired: Brandon wasn't meeting drumline standards, and he didn't seem to care enough to try. Lisa and Jen had both tried recently to work with him, an hour one day, an hour and a half another day, each time on one chart. The next day, he'd marched and played as if the extra drilling had never occurred.

Better to cut him and march a hole, Lisa Bennett said, than to have him mess everything up. No one spoke up for the missing tenor. In the meritocracy of the drumline, effort was the minimum for acceptance.

Despite the bumps, by midweek something in the band seemed to be changing. On Wednesday five trumpet players came down during resource period to work with Scott Spradling. Some of the saxophone players who had less clout and ability than Cameron Bradley started to step in and fill the teaching gap he'd left. They understood that their section would be only as good as its most struggling member. Students from almost every part of the band, alone and in groups, ran out early to the practice field to grab a few extra minutes before the afternoon rehearsal. After they'd finished on the varsity football field, more students stayed to practice on the grass turf. Even in late afternoon, the air held its warmth, adding a buoyancy to the work. Between the sun and the smell of warm earth, it could still have been summer. The run of sun and clear skies was a gift. Only the yellow and orange on the trees along Minuteman Way gave away the lateness of the season.

The sweet smell of paint mixed in with the warmth. Over on the practice pavement, band dads were again painting a tarp. In spite of Jim Faigh's early start, in spite of the band dads' efforts to respond to concerns about glare and grip, Max had given Faigh bad news on Monday. The Concord show would still be called "Roots of American Music," but the roots themselves had been excised. He was pulling the "roots" tarp from the show. What Max wanted now was a large arc, like a dance floor at a jazz club, that would spread beneath the pit on the fifty-yard line at the front of the field. It would still be blue, of course, but it would be edged by outer rings in the original tan and orange earth tones. Faigh took all of it in stride. As he told the rest of his group, the kids had needed to relearn new music and drills as well. At least the dads had good drying weather, for now. They'd entered a time in the season when the weather often changed abruptly.

Faigh had also needed to redesign the first attempt at the African tree. Its faint, sheer fabric had unintentionally silhouetted the Concord color guard during their costume change. "We don't want people to think the highlight of the Dixieland segment is the girls changing clothes," Max had told the band dads. Jim Faigh had tracked down a billboard company in Michigan that could screen the tree onto heavier fabric under a tight deadline (for $1,500) and was personally driving up there later in the week to pick it up. In addition, the band dads had been working like crazy to figure out how to camouflage the drumsets until the proper moment during the show's finale, at which point a curtain or cover of some kind would drop to dramatically reveal shiny blue sets. The first contraptions had been too sloppy, or the curtain fabric too stiff, but they'd finally engineered a system with an aluminum hoop and PVC posts and pipe clamps and rubber bands and a releasing gate-latch mechanism that seemed to do the trick. They'd unveil the system for the first time at Homestead later that week.

With one of her podmates, Adilene played her part for "Gabriel's Oboe" and marched the step-offs for Steve Peterson—her retest. She still hesitated at most transitions and almost missed one halt, but her tone had improved. On her first test, back in July, she'd stopped playing for long stretches, and had gotten through the marching only by imitating the other test-takers. On this test, if anything, she was the stronger marcher, the other clarinet player following her lead. Both girls passed. Peterson gave Adilene's shoulder a squeeze before he let her go.

Grant had made up a schedule of high-brass sectionals through the following week and handed it out that afternoon after a rowdier-than-usual group huddle. He'd asked the other seniors to try to make every sectional, but also to give even more to anyone they saw who was struggling. The first extra practice was right then, between the afternoon and evening practices; the next at seven the following morning. And on Friday, a day off from school, a two-hour sectional would lead into lunch, or even a high-brass picnic if the weather held. His energy was ramping up.

Max had spent the first part of the week painstakingly working through "Gabriel's Oboe" with the band, adjusting the size and extent of the dynamics, the layering of sound. At times, he worked note by note, balancing not only high voices and low voices, but the various parts of the middle range as well. "I need you, flugels," he said on Wednesday afternoon. "You're missing in this chord." The piece needed every voice, and all the parts, to work. "I need you in here, seconds and thirds."

He was as exacting as if he stood behind a concert podium. But then he'd say, "Now let's play that way on the move," or tell the trumpets he could hear their feet in their sound, or caution the clarinets not to bounce. In addition to the phrasing and breathing and tonal qualities he was lavishing attention on, he was also asking them to march across the length of a football field at twice the speed of their music. His tone was softer than it had been a couple of days earlier. The band was starting to respond.

That night, the energy spiked higher. Max put them into sections for a quick brush-up on marching fundamentals and a last round of work on the show's opener. Students ran to their groups and stayed quiet once there, without a director having to remind them. Diana de la Reza and the other first clarinets stood in a circle, playing the ballad's long phrases and practicing their step-offs. Each time they started again, they widened the circle, making it harder to hear each other, making it more realistic. It had been a while since Diana had practiced with other first clarinets, and she rarely marched near them in the show. She felt a comfort, for the moment, in being inside that charmed circle.

When the band came together to work on "Africa," the energy that had been building up inside the separate sections combined into something bigger. Max and the other directors looked out over the field and saw many kids running back to their spots after a chart, not just Grant and his high brass, not just a few section leaders or the snare line. They heard people counting for each other, and upperclassmen telling the less experienced or more timid when to come in, when to halt. Down on the field, the students buzzed. Every champion band Max had directed had reached a point where his endless insistence on perfection shifted from being a burden to a challenge. Some of the upperclassmen felt it now. They called it the "magic." It was what Grant had referred to during the first senior meeting on the dunes. It started with the crazy energy of caring, and not minding that others could see how hard you were trying. And when enough people felt that way, and worked that way, the feeling electrified the group, raced through it like a fire catching and spreading.

You could almost see it reach Grant. He'd lost weight in recent weeks. (It happened every year to many of them, thanks to the extra exercise and a schedule that left little time for teenage snacking.) His jeans hung loosely on his frame. His cheekbones and jawline had sharpened. An intensity had come into his eyes. For the first time all season, anyone could see how badly he wanted to win. On Wednesday night, when Max sent them to their spots for a complete run-through, Grant didn't just run, he bounded, he charged into position. He counted for people around him with gusto, and his encouragement carried up to the towers. His exuberance was infectious. Before long, others around the field were counting and encouraging loudly as well. As the evening wore on and the air lost its warmth, the band's energy and focus grew stronger. They seemed to get what Max was telling them more quickly. Their footwork started to snap.

From their respective towers Max and the other directors exchanged glances. This was what they'd been waiting for.

THE BONFIRE AT Craig Searer's house had become the band's one purely social event of the season. Craig was one of the few kids in the band from a rich family, and the long driveway, massive house, and sweeping, manicured lawn gave the setting a feeling of elegance. Each year that Craig had marched, his parents had hosted the entire band, including the staff and band parents. They erected a party tent at the edge of their property, between the family's pedal-car museum and a cornfield. By the time kids started arriving after Thursday's rehearsal, soft drinks filled rows of coolers. Band dads had thrown hamburgers and hot dogs on the grill, and band moms had laid out bowls of chips and plates of cookies on tables beneath the big tent.

Nearly everyone in the band turned out for the party—maybe because everyone knew it was Craig's last year in the band, or maybe because word had gotten out that this was an event not to miss, or because nearly 250 kids were starting to gel into something even bigger. The food disappeared almost as quickly as it appeared. Then the tent emptied, and the party moved outside into the dark night, to the bonfire and the big lawn. Groups that had arrived together reformed and blended into new groups. Shy Amanda Himes talked to a freshman boy who played tuba. Girls from the color guard, the most isolated group in the band, dancing to music being spun by a band-dad DJ, were quickly joined by girls from the flutes and clarinets. Smiling faces glowed in the orange light of the fire. Laughter rose into the night sky along with the sparks and flying embers.

Some of the kids who had the hardest time during practices seemed to relax. Brandon Dascoli and other boys from the brass and percussion sections played tag football in the dark at the edges of the party, where the cornfields came up to the mowed grass. One of the band dads nudged another and pointed out a freshman from the pit among the group of football players. The men watched without speaking, arms folded, side by side. They'd noticed how the kid held himself apart from the other students and from the band, and they had, until now, worried about him. One broke the companionable silence, saying, "Looks like a field of dreams out there, doesn't it?" Another said he half-expected to see John Philip Sousa walk out of the corn rows.

The word "Spradling . . ." drifted out from a ring of high-brass players off to one side of the fire. The boys, comparing notes on the many ways in which their director had pushed them over the years, sounded as if they were complaining. But there they were, at a party, with the chance to talk about anything, and all they could do was talk about Scott Spradling. The band dads could see Jim Schoeffler among them. Jim was the kind of kid who pulled his shoulders in and frowned around adults. To the dads, he seemed to float at the periphery of the band. Now the dads saw him in another light, alone with his classmates, laughing and joking and looking for all the world like one of the guys.

Jared Nymeyer and Craig Searer found Steve Peterson and started talking about the upcoming jazz season. They were eager to try to make it into the finals of the Essentially Ellington jazz band competition, held by Wynton Marsalis and the Lincoln Center Jazz Orchestra in New York City. The previous spring, Peterson had entered Concord's top jazz band in the contest for the first time. They hadn't made it to the fifteen-band finals, but all of them, Steve Peterson included, had been thrilled by the positive feedback they'd received. None of them had ever studied Duke Ellington beforehand, not even Peterson. Now they all knew his music, played it, listened to it, liked it. Jared and Craig wanted to know what Ellington songs they'd be playing next. "Happy-Go-Lucky Local," Peterson told them. "Isfahan."

"Let's have Grant play it!" Craig said, and the two of them fell into their routine.

"Grant can do it," Jared replied.

"Grant'll show you how!" said Craig.

Almost in unison, they said, "Grant's perfect."

The edge to their voices had been unmistakable. Peterson shook his head and gave a faint smile.

Near the end of the evening, Jared's dad put on the CD from the 2003 show, and almost everyone got up to dance. The color guard girls reprised their routines. Brandon Schenk joined them. The upperclassmen remembered their choreography, mimed playing their instruments and step-offs, or simply danced. The whole scene—the happy faces in the firelight, the throng of energy, the tight packs of teenagers—evoked a timeless, feel-good sense of high school everywhere. Here, though, the kids were dancing to music they'd made themselves; there was no alcohol, zero drugs, lots of adults looking on; and it was over before midnight.

The following morning, threatening weather held off long enough for the flutes and the high brass to get their early practices in. Grant and Keith McCrorey worked with a dozen trumpet players while a third senior worked with a handful of mellophones and flugels. Laurie Schalliol drilled the freshmen girls, self-consciously pushing the brim of Grant's cowboy hat out of her face. Afterward, the group grabbed some food at Taco Bell and Arby's and brought it out to Oxbow Park for a picnic. The sky was leaden, the air warm and moist. They ate beneath a covered shelter, then ran around on the grass throwing and catching Frisbees. The freshmen still seemed so much younger than the seniors, so eager to get close to Grant. He was gentle with the beginning students, careful. And also relaxed. He still wanted to win another championship, and he wanted to win it the right way. He was giving eight hours or more that day to the band, and willing to give much more in the season's remaining two weeks. He seemed alive and happy, felt different—he wasn't losing himself in the band, as he had the previous year when he needed it to fill an emotional vacuum, or even as he had earlier that summer, when band had helped him stave off depression. He'd wanted marching season to be *great*, spectacular, the rousing finale to long years of rehearsal and grooming. It was happening later than he thought it would, but it was happening. Here he was at Oxbow, kicking back with the high brass, the band finally coming together. He'd taken Leandra out to breakfast that morning, and was still warmed by the memory of it. This was finally how he expected his final, triumphant year of high school to feel.

THE RAIN STARTED almost as soon as the full rehearsal that afternoon. It broke across them in waves, driven by the wind. Max pulled a raincoat and a hat out of his shoulder bag and put them on. He gave no indication that he was considering moving indoors. Without a word about the weather he continued the practice. Within minutes, the students' notebooks were drenched. Puddles spread beneath the piles. Any pages not inside the protective sheets were ruined. A blast of wind burst through the fence and over the practice field, spattering water from the chain links onto the kids standing near the front sideline.

The year before, they'd practiced once in such a downpour. By the end of that practice, they'd waded—it was impossible to heel-and-toe—through water several inches deep. Later that season, Max halted a practice only when someone ran out and warned them that tornadoes had been sighted at the county line and were barreling toward the high school. Now, though, Max had them play on. He had checked the radar and several weather reports beforehand; he knew that all they would be getting was hard rain. Nothing teenagers couldn't withstand. Except for the keyboards, even their instruments were surprisingly resilient. Tennis shoes squished on the flooding pavement. Jeans soaked up the moisture and turned dark above the calves. Water streamed off hat brims.

"Lovely day for marching band," Max said dryly.

Some of the students looked like they wanted to say, What is wrong with all of you? Get reasonable! Brandon Dascoli and Jim Schoeffler held themselves like wet cats shivering at the front door, but no one let them in. Grant raised his hands over his head, did a little rain dance. If anything, he looked more wired in the rain than two nights before. Someone else shouted out, "I *love* rain!" and suddenly kids were laughing as they sloshed around. They played hard, got through the practice together, and in the end seemed to have drawn closer. It was possible that the long run of fair weather that fall had delayed an important stage in the group's formation. The soaking might have been just what the band needed.

The next morning the sun was shining again. The day of the Homestead Invitational began bright and breezy, and cooler than in previous days, but the air warmed quickly. At the early practice, Max preached performing. "Practice it," he said. "Sell it." After a first run-through, he told them, "Make it obvious that all the rules are being broken right now, and we're gonna convince you that this is how marching band should be done."

But in spite of the bonding and the renewed energy and a lot of hard work on the field, critical parts of the show continued to fall apart. Max picked out timing problems between opposite sides of the field in

"Gabriel's Oboe." Near the beginning of "Africa," he saw Brandon Dascoli falling behind the tail end of the battery as it traversed the back of the field. To move sideways, drummers used a step called "crab-bing," crossing and recrossing one leg in front of the other at a pace that had only a mathematical relation to how quickly they were mov-ing their sticks. At the beginning of the season, Max had joked about how fast the drumline would have to crab in the show. Now Brandon kept lagging on the fast traverse, creating pile-ups and confusion in the tubas and baritones who followed, and it was no longer a joke. "Get going!" Max yelled. "You're five yards behind. C'mon Brandon, *move*. Get your legs moving. I don't care if you play!"

Partway into "Africa," Nick and the drumline fell off the beat and struggled to get it back up. The drumline captain strained to hear the drums around him even as he watched the hands of senior drum major Pat Doherty. Nick and Pat, together, were responsible for setting seven tempo changes in the eight-minute show: two relatively slow tempos for Amanda's ballad; roughly twice that for the beginning of "Africa" and a hitch faster for the end; back down to a swaying pace for "A Closer Walk" and up to a snappier one for "Saints"; and last, the 200 beats per minute—nearly three and a half beats a second—for "Swing, Swing, Swing." If the band had maintained concert formation the en-tire show, Pat Doherty would have set the tempo for each section from his high perch in front of them, Nick would have kept it, and there the matter would have ended. But they were a band on the move, and that complicated the matter significantly.

The physics of light and sound dictated how Nick responded to Pat's conducting. Because sound travels more slowly than gesture, when Nick marched on the far side of the field from Pat, he focused ex-clusively on watching Pat's hands and matched his feet and drumbeat to them. When Nick traveled near the front sideline, though, he had to ignore Pat's hands and listen to the sound coming from behind him. He had to catch the music sent by parts of the band half a football field away from the drum major, and send it on. If he watched Pat from too close, he rushed the tempo. If he listened to the sound from too far away, he fell behind. Either way, the band would split into warring tempos. The band's size made Nick's translation that much more diffi-cult. When the drummers in the battery stretched out in a long line, they had to work harder to hear one another. And certain parts of

Nick's chart existed right on the line between looking and listening. The tempo in "Africa" sagged exactly at one of those points.

They completed the run-through, and Max called down from the tower: "Africa was horrendous. Awful back in the battery. You lost time bigtime. We were down close to 120. We never got to 144. All we could do was try to recuperate. And then we never cranked it up. Every tempo I checked with the metronome was low." When he got around to the set drumming in "Swing, Swing, Swing," he praised Jen Bollero's energy but said, "The rest of you are just losers."

Nick Stubbs took all of it personally. He finished the practice stone-faced. By the time Max dismissed them to get ready for the trip to Homestead, practically the entire percussion section looked pissed.

On the bus to Fort Wayne, the drummers were mostly quiet. A few of them talked, though not about band. Someone mentioned the presidential election, less than a month away. Nick said, "I hate it when teenagers say America sucks." Matt Tompkins replied, "I hate it when they say America is the best." Their conversation devolved into a sarcastic routine on preparing for a nuclear holocaust, which they both thought equally possible under presidential candidates George W. Bush and John Kerry. Their checklist for the basement bomb shelter: *Bible. Check. Back-up Bible. Check. Contingency Bible. Check.*

Lisa Bennett, sitting in front of Nick and Matt, ate a second breakfast of Pop-Tarts covered with purple icing. "Lisa has the metabolism of a mongoose," Nick said admiringly.

The bus turned onto the streets near Homestead High School. Nick called out, "Machine time. Headphones off." In the quiet bus, he addressed his section, "This is about revenge. Last week, something was taken from us. I want it back. We all do."

At the high school, banners bearing the crested helmets of the Homestead Spartans flapped in the stiff breeze. Nick, probably alone on the bus, knew the story of how Spartan King Leonidas had sacrificed his life defending the Greek mainland against a far larger Persian army. Leonidas's heroism had long inspired Nick, who continued to view his role in the band as a proving ground for later battles. Nick had formally started the application process for West Point, and was waiting for the required recommendation from one of his senators or his congressman. He had been running in the mornings, still, even with the extra practices, preparing for the physical aptitude part of the application. He knew the odds were long: Only a tenth of the ten thousand applicants to the academy each year got in. On some level, he linked the fate of his West Point application with the success of that year's drumline. Starting with the Homestead Invitational, he had three shots left.

Concord performed last in Class B. The new, smaller tarp was making its first appearance that afternoon, along with the rescreened acacia-tree backdrop and the drumset covers.

Nick started the show behind the tree, so he had a great view of what happened in the final moments before Pat Doherty got things going. The heavy breeze caught the fabric of the scrim and filled it like a sail. The poles supporting the ends of the twenty-by-thirty-foot tree started to bend, like masts too weak before the gale. Jim Faigh, standing on the track, yelled, "It's gonna blow!" Mark Tack, who normally helped set up the pit, raced across the field, while other parents rushed around the track. By the time Pat raised his hands high for the first downbeat, several band moms stood at the front of each pole, more adults leaned in from the back, and band dads pushed in at the sides, an Iwo Jima tableau. Both poles were bent about ten feet up, but the tree stayed upright.

From the start of "Gabriel's Oboe," the wind whipped the color guards' flags and blew the music too fast past Nick's ears. But up in the high press box, judge Beth Fabrizio, seeing the show for the first time since Concord's invitational, let her tape run without comment for more than a minute. She had been unconvinced, three weeks earlier, that "Gabriel's Oboe" should include the 12/8 drumming. "I'm not saying anything," she finally said, "because I am feeling goose bumps up here." Their hard work on the opener—along with Max's gamble—was paying off.

"Careful, percussion, battery," she said as the band split into two sides for a couple measures. "Watch your tempo." Nick and the snare line reached the twenty-yard line, Nick just off the back hash—the boundary between looking and listening—and pulled it back together.

But in "Africa," the timing problems reappeared. "Tempo, tempo," Fabrizio cautioned, at a point where Nick and the snares were in outer Siberia, while Jon Faloon and the djembe drums were right below Pat's nose and following his hands only too well. "Boy, do you have an issue here because of the distance," Fabrizio said. "There's just no way." Nick would hear that on the judging tapes later, grateful that someone had acknowledged what the drumline had been asked to do. On the field, Nick could feel the tempo wanting to drag at every note despite his effort to hold it up. He was in nearly the same place on the field in "Africa" that he had been in "Gabriel's Oboe" when the band again threatened to fall apart. As drumline captain, he'd been put in an almost impossible place for the heartbeat of the band, like putting a human heart in an elbow and asking it to work at full capacity. Fabrizio called out again in warning, once again they made it through. But they missed the uptick to 160. Worse was yet to come.

Max had predicted that the pinnacle of the Concord show would be the surprise unveiling of the four new drumsets at the start of "Swing, Swing, Swing." The New Orleans medley would have done its work stirring the crowd, getting people clapping, starting the party. A normal marching band on a football field couldn't have done much to take the energy level higher. But Max wasn't a normal band director, and he saw no reason not to throw in a few swing-band drumsets and drive the beat faster—get people standing, get them *dancing*. "Swing, Swing, Swing" was the piece to do it. The John Williams score had been adapted from what was possibly the signature song of the Swing era: "Sing, Sing, Sing," written in the thirties and reworked into a classic by the Benny Goodman Orchestra. Goodman had discovered that with the right arrangements, his big band gave a swinging, lively feel to standard pop tunes, and crossed jazz over into white America, which couldn't get enough of the new music. Goodman's band introduced white audiences to what some called "hot jazz" and others called "killer-dillers"—fast-moving dance numbers with a strong, rhythmic beat. It was this hard-driving beat that made "Sing, Sing, Sing" memorable, and it was provided by an energetic, crowd-pleasing drummer named Gene Krupa. For the song, Krupa took a simple but extremely catchy jazz rhythm and played it loud, repetitively, and with a showman's flourish. His beat, and his energy, dominated the song. For a while, "Sing, Sing, Sing" closed every Goodman show. Krupa's solos required so much effort from the other musicians that some left the band.

Sitting on the stool behind his drumset, Nick Stubbs was in certain respects a Krupa heir. He couldn't remember when he'd learned to play "Krupa style." It was like trying to recall when he'd first counted to one hundred. Nick's own drumset contained a bass drum that he played with a foot pedal, three toms, and a hi-hat cymbal. All reflected Krupa innovations. Even the subtle style that Jeff Hamilton had taught

Nick on the ride cymbal derived partly from Krupa's experimentation in the 1920s and 1930s. Teenage drummers who practiced with visions of rock and roll stardom carried on the legacy of his "killer-diller" beat. Max, unwittingly or not, had brought music that had last been popular when his parents were teenagers right into the present, and, of all things, right into a marching band. And then to that centerpiece, he'd added a drum-corps-style flourish: a flashy segment in which drummers raced around a circle of bass drums, beating on them as they passed. Now *that* would be a pinnacle of a show.

But two problems had emerged with the concept. To start with, the timing at the beginning of "Swing, Swing, Swing" was extremely tricky. If Nick had been sitting behind the drumset in the Benny Goodman band, that would have been one thing. But the Concord band, of course, was 243 students spread from end zone to end zone across a football field. When Nick took off his snare to move to the drumset, he stopped being able to give the band its pulse. While he and the three other drumset drummers were pulling their sets into place and preparing to drop the curtains that hid them from the audience, Lisa Bennett and the rest of the drumline were bringing the band to the close of "Saints." At the start of "Swing, Swing, Swing," then, Nick had to look as if he was setting a swinging big-band beat. But for the song's first thirty-two counts, he had to listen back to where Lisa was, in the backfield, and follow the rhythm she set. For her part, she had to keep listening forward, making sure he was following her, at the same time that she and the rest of the line barreled toward the front sideline and their moment in the spotlight.

Second, on top of the timing challenges, judges the week before had complained that the drumsets had obscured their view of the circling bass drummers. All that visual energy and effect was being wasted. So Max had moved the bass drums in front, repositioning the drumsets in an arc behind them. The drumsets became the backdrop to the real action. Nick had felt the slight.

Now, at Homestead, Nick crawled into his drumset within the newly positioned arc, and discovered that the spacing was off. Because Mark Tack was back handling the crisis with the tree, the parents who stepped in to set up the pit and the drumsets had no way of knowing what to do, and that critical part of the show was set up incorrectly, off-center. The opening between Nick's drumset and Jen Bollero's was too small for the color guard to run through side by side. The girls hesitated, stopped briefly, bumped into each other, and finally ran through single-file. As he started the distinctive Gene Krupa rhythm, Nick could feel the drumset cart being jostled as the girls tried to squeeze through. He struggled to concentrate, to hear Lisa, to get his bearings.

Fabrizio noticed the spacing problem right away. She also could hear that the drummers weren't getting the Krupa beat down. "Keep that 2-4 swing feeling going," she said into her tape recorder. "Set drummers, make it happen. Make sure you're all maintaining the same tempo. It feels like a tug of war out there."

Despite all of it, the set drummers drove on. The crowd went crazy. The Concord section in the stands stood and clapped, and others stood, too. Max had seen a similar reaction on the Concord practice field. The beat was magnetic. Every time the drums played the pulsing rhythm, it pulled everyone toward it—the directors, students, band parents, spectators, and now judges, too. Up high in the stands, Beth Fabrizio seemed, at the end, to sit back and enjoy the show. "It's been nice to watch this program grow and develop. But even nicer to see all of these students who devote so many hours of their lives to this activity really enjoying what they're doing. And the crowd loves it, too—not just the parents of your children but all the parents in the audience. And that's what it's all about."

Concord won back the music caption, although by less than two points. And easily outscored the other bands from Class B overall.

As promised, Max kept them afterward to watch the Class A bands, the big bands with the big budgets and year-round practice schedules—bands that would be more like the ones they'd see in the state finals. They stayed to watch the Homestead band, bigger even than the Concord band, with its color guard in bright velour and its rows of alternates standing at attention in one end zone. Watching from the top of the stands, Scott Spradling nodded toward the end zone and quipped, "Bet there's a lot of learning going on out there." But the Concord kids were most interested in seeing Avon.

In 2002, Avon had beaten Concord for its second straight Class B championship. Some of the Concord kids felt the judges had got it wrong, and their sense of injustice had fueled some of the desire the following year. The only thing that could have made Concord's win in 2003 sweeter would have been beating Avon. But Concord didn't get the chance. The newly incorporated town of Avon had grown so rapidly that the Marching Black and Gold had bumped into Class A. Concord students had long seen themselves as a sort of northern Avon, and felt something akin to sibling rivalry. Except this sibling had somehow slipped past them and was spending its time with a cooler, fancier crowd. In its first year in Class A, Avon had won the state championship, again.

Avon's enrollment of 2,000 totaled only half that of the giant schools like Homestead, Penn, and Lawrence Central. Yet Avon had the biggest marching band in the state, marching just under three hundred kids. At the Homestead Invitational, the announcer's introduction of the Avon staff seemed to go on forever. It finally stopped after twenty-seven names.

And then Avon went out and put on a show. The name listed in the program—"Are you ready for some football?"—was only the start of the fun. The color guard was the cheerleaders *and* the football team. The band—playing fight songs from various colleges and well-known themes from TV sports programs—became an opposing team in one segment, spectators in another, and, in the middle of the performance, its own halftime show. Nick and a few of the other Concord kids noticed that the huge band marched conservatively—that sections moved in tight bunches, more easily hiding individual errors, not risking the exposure that Concord did with its end-zone-to-end-zone drill. And Nick noticed that even in a supposedly traditional marching band show, the vaunted Avon drumline was being asked to accent the music instead of being allowed to play like a traditional drumline. But everyone saw how good Avon was. The music bounced and pulsed. The show was sharp and clever and the crowd and judges loved all of it. Avon finished first among the Class A bands. Had Concord been competing head to head, Avon would have won every single category. It's what Max had wanted his kids to see.

MORE THAN THIRTY kids showed up at the party at Grant's house later that night. His mother's back was bothering her and she wasn't up for putting out her usual spread, so they ordered in pizza instead. Brent popped videotapes of the Concord and Avon shows into the VCR. Kids clustered in happy groups. Some played cards. Grant stayed up late with Cameron and Leandra. They played *The Lord of the Rings* Trivial Pursuit, and without Keith to give him some competition, Grant ruled.

He drove the next morning to West Lafayette, where Anne was in her last semester at Purdue. Anne had called their parents earlier in the fall to ask permission to do something big for Grant's eighteenth birthday. She'd learned that his favorite bluegrass band, Nickel Creek, would be playing at Indiana University right around the big day. Because the concert was on Sunday night in Bloomington, though, five hours away, Grant wouldn't be able to drive back safely the same night. He'd need to miss part of the school day on Monday.

A few years earlier, Jeff and Chris might not have let one of their children skip school for a bluegrass concert. But they appreciated the bond that had developed between their two children since Anne had gone to college. And it was a great way to celebrate a big birthday. So they agreed, and the college senior and the high school senior had worked out the details on their own.

Grant and Anne drove together to Bloomington. The two decided ahead of time that they'd be extravagant and stay only for the show they'd come to see. Grant was thrilled to see Nickel Creek live. The band played songs Grant knew, and their harmonies seemed even richer and more playful in person than on their recordings. The musicians on the stage weren't much older than he and Anne, but were polished beyond their years. The guitarist and violinist were brother and sister, too, which made the concert more special. Anne had introduced Grant to much of the music he now listened to, including nearly all the jazz he knew, and the Dave Mathews Band, which he'd hated at first, then grown to love. Earlier in the year, he'd taken her to see them in Indianapolis. They talked about the trip to Bloomington as part of a new birthday tradition.

After the show, he bought a CD for Leandra and a Nickel Creek T-shirt for himself. The siblings sat on a curb outside the performance hall, got a bite to eat at a coffee shop, and started back to West Lafayette. The trees reflected gold in their headlights. They talked about Leandra, as they had coming down and at the concert and the coffee shop. For Grant, it was a pleasure to talk about her without having to know how it was going to end, and to feel his sister's respect for how important Leandra was to him.

He found his sister a kindred spirit. Anne had switched majors several times at Purdue and had finally landed on teaching English, like Mrs. Greene. But that seemed like only a starting point. Who knew what might happen after a few years? Back on the curb in Bloomington, she'd talked to Grant about her job in a Turkish restaurant near campus. The manager there reminded her of him, she said, always talking about philosophy and the meaning of life. The manager had encouraged her to look into jobs teaching English in Turkey. We could go to Turkey together, Anne said in the car. Travel around Europe, Grant said. For a while, side by side, they imagined the adventures they might have. They looked into the future, into lives they couldn't even imagine there on the dark road in Indiana. Anne was good for him. Simply being with her reminded him to enjoy life, not to be afraid of what might happen next.

On impulse, they stopped at a White Castle and picked up four burgers for Mr. Jones. The oniony smell was so strong that they had to stop again to stick the bag in the trunk.

He spent the night on the couch in his sister's apartment, near a couple of his own paintings hanging on the walls. Her white cowboy hat, what she called her "thinking hat," was slung on the back of her desk chair. She'd gotten her hat before he'd gotten his, during a summer's trip to a dude ranch in Colorado. Grant would never have worn a white cowboy hat at home, but he'd been willing to slide in behind her bravado and continue the Longenbaugh tradition in the band. Not many of the current students knew he was copying his sister. Some saw his hat and copied him. Anne would find it funny, he guessed, if she knew how her idea had become Grant's signature.

The next morning, it took him longer to drive home than he'd expected. He had to pull over three times to keep from falling asleep and had to down a forty-eight-ounce Mountain Dew to help. He got to school having missed Government, Anatomy, AP English, and Spanish, but with enough time to spare before band to present the greasy White Castle bag to Mr. Jones.

He'd had trouble seeing past his anxiety about Leandra, God's purpose for him, and the jumble of emotions over the past weeks and months. It was with relief and new clarity that he entered the music wing. They could do this!

He finally dared to ask his director, "Is there still hope?"

11 ⋆ Closer Walk with Thee

While millions of teenagers around the country struggled to get out of bed and ready for school, an increasing number of Concord students set their clocks early to come in before classes began. On Monday and again on Tuesday, Matt Schnaars, the snare drummer who'd waited in vain for a ride the week before, left his house in pitch black and rode his bicycle four miles along unlit county roads to make the percussion sectionals. He joined the first students entering the music wing shortly before seven o'clock, a handful of minutes before sunrise. By ten after, the band room bustled with purposeful activity. Puffy-eyed students wordlessly opened cases and assembled instruments, expending no more than the minimum amount of energy necessary to get themselves ready. These were still teenagers, after all, perpetually sleep-deprived, the demands of their days and the rhythms of their nights in constant conflict. Three nights out of five, Brent Lehman and Brandon Schenk and a dozen other students in the band rehearsed for *Little Women*, the fall play. Others worked part-time in restaurants, at fast-food windows, as cashiers, grocery baggers, or stock-boys. They had papers to write and tests to study for, especially the seniors in Mr. Judson's AP English class, who were finding it hard to balance their early introduction to college-level coursework with the buildup to the marching-band championship. This year's juniors dragged themselves into Mrs. Greene's room, grateful for her hugs.

Max, who'd stopped being able to sleep past 4:30 for the duration of the season, was in his office every day now by six o'clock. From his window, he could look down on the band room at the gathering students, most of them unaware that he could see them.

Nearly all the students turned right around and headed back outside to the pavement to work through the toughest knots of marching, music, and movement. They wore winter hats, now, or pulled the hoods of their sweatshirts tight against the damp chill. On the dark practice field, pairs of flutes practiced marching backward on tiptoe. Brent drilled trombones on their melody line in "Swing, Swing, Swing." After Monday's break, Grant continued his practice schedule for trumpets, going over rotating blocks one morning, the trumpet flourish that accompanied the start of the Dixieland melody the next. Day arrived in shades of gray while they practiced. The winds had shifted, driving moist, cold air down from Lake Michigan. Fog now lay in dense blankets on the grass some mornings, or pulled thin gauze over everything, like a curtain. Still, the most dedicated members of the Marching Minutemen practiced, even when they could see only a few paces in any direction.

It was easy to forget that they were doing this for an academic class. And yet the early-morning practices didn't count toward their grades. Students reported to no adult or teacher.

They were, however, getting credit.

After the day had come on, Max usually took a little stroll. He peered over the top of the steep embankment above the junior high track. He walked through the student parking lot until he had a full view of the practice field. He made sure to observe all the sections at work, from a distance. Students who came in at the normal time would find him in his usual spot near the entrance, and wouldn't know he'd already taken attendance.

Alone among the senior leaders, Diana de la Reza kept her clarinet pod inside and focused on music. It had taken a few days, but Diana had learned that the best way to get the three freshmen to school on time in the morning was to pick them up herself. (Adilene's parents took the extra practices less seriously than official rehearsals and had been dropping her off later and later. Diana added her to the morning route.) Diana needed to leave at 6:05 to make her rounds. She didn't mind that she had to wake up before five—she was a morning person, anyway—but missed her daily caramel mocha. The coffee shop was still dark when she drove past, and by the time she'd crossed the railroad tracks twice and picked up Adilene, she was looking at her watch, anxious about the ground they had to cover, and how little time they had left.

At first, Diana had planned to rehearse "Gabriel's Oboe" one day, "Africa" the next, and so on through the four parts of the show, dwelling on trouble spots when they hit them. Right away, she had to revise her plan downward. Their first day together, the three freshmen barely made it through the opening measures of "Gabriel's Oboe." The pace was so slow that the lone sophomore stopped coming. Two mornings later, still on the show's first piece, they spent the entire session on measure 24: four notes. Diana took them through the notes one by one, walking around their small circle to reset their fingers if they played the wrong ones. She checked their intonation and drilled them on timing. When they didn't crescendo together, she explained the dynamics. At last, while they played their simpler part, she played the more complicated first clarinet part. In the entire half hour, the freshmen didn't play the measure correctly, together, even once. None had practiced enough over time to have developed good embouchures, the strong muscles around their mouths that helped them hold their notes and keep them in tune during changes in volume. Within the Concord band, the girls in Diana's pod were the musical equivalent of kids trying to play sports with no muscle tone.

Diana noticed that whenever someone else entered the band room where her pod was set up—and people came and went constantly—her little trio stopped playing. It occurred to her that they might be ashamed to let others hear how they sounded. On Wednesday morning, she told Adilene and the others to grab their music and instruments and to follow her. She led them through one set of double doors and stopped at another. She motioned for the girls to circle their stands in the small area between the doors. In that protected space, not much bigger than a bathroom stall, they could play without distraction or shame.

Nick Stubbs had continued holding his extra sessions every morning, but attendance remained spotty, even among the seniors. Fellow snare Derek Richard hadn't made it to a single early-morning practice. Of all the students on the Concord drumline, Derek looked, and acted, the most like a stereotypical drummer. He wore his hair long, curling on his shoulders, and his pants low on his hips. He was as insouciant about attending class or studying as he was about following the school's dress code—except when it came to band. Lisa Bennett, who worked in the front office during first hour, when attendance was taken, knew that Derek sometimes came to school only for fifth hour. And for that block of time, he shone. The rare praise Max gave the drumline was often directed at Derek, for his obvious pleasure in performing. He was easygoing, fun-loving, quick to smile. But his lack of extra effort irritated Nick. Early in the season, Nick had promised Derek that no matter what he said to him on the field, once they were off the field it he would stop being Nick Stubbs, drumline captain, and revert to Nick, friend. But back then, he hadn't anticipated being in the awkward position of having to ask a friend to step up. After Monday's practice, he made a point of scanning the group, looking into people's eyes if they let him. "For morning rehearsals," he said, "not a single person is good enough to miss."

For Nick, this amounted to a direct request. The rest of the group understood it as such.

Matt Schnaars said to the others, "You guys who are saying you don't have a ride, I rode my bike today, and I live, like, four miles away." Frost had coated the grass that morning. "It was *cold*." His outburst only earned him a round of ragging. As a sophomore, he had little sway in the group.

Nick shot another straight look at Derek, his request hanging between them. Derek only grinned in response.

Brandon Dascoli avoided Nick's eyes. Like Derek, he had yet to come to a morning sectional. Brandon's seniority made him the head of the tenor line, but in fact he was the least accomplished of the group. Both Max Jones and Amy Davis had taken the unusual step of instructing Brandon not to play at Homestead, to concentrate solely on his marching. But, not playing, he'd seemed to lose any sense of timing, and had moved about the field in his own world.

From the beginning of the season, Nick had considered Brandon the drumline's weakest link. During the summer, when they split into groups to focus on fundamentals, Nick had taken the tenor line and had seen close-up how slowly Brandon learned and how easily he shut down. At first, Nick had laid his best drum-teacher growl on the small group and the same sarcastic tone he used with his friends. Nick had accepted a similar rough education when he was a novice. But Brandon had simply gone vacant in response, and had stubbornly resisted Nick's attempts to coax him back out. The approach had cost Nick hours of lost time.

By now, the rest of the section had given up on the stubborn tenor. Nick sensed that Miss Davis had little energy left for him as well. But although Nick was almost out of ideas, he wasn't ready to quit.

Nick had read Sun Tzu's classic text, *The Art of War*. Tzu advised leaders not to get close to those they led. In spite of the ancient warrior's advice, and going against his own notions of leadership, Nick had recently started trying to befriend the section's weakest member. During practices, Nick noticed that no one talked to Brandon, except to correct him. If Brandon repeated a mistake, which happened often, the correction escalated. Nick knew how his own feelings curdled when Mr. Jones singled him out from the tower, and could imagine how much worse it might feel if everyone were criticizing him. He stopped trying to improve Brandon, and tried instead to connect with him. One day, Nick asked Brandon what car he was working on. Posters of favorite models covered the walls of Brandon's bedroom; the only reading he did outside of school was in car-racing magazines. With a big smile, Brandon launched into descriptions of engine parts and bodywork. Nick had two nearly simultaneous, intersecting thoughts. He realized that he had no idea when he'd last seen Brandon so animated. And he noticed that Brandon looked like a different person when he smiled.

That had been right before Homestead. Nick had gone out of his way since then to talk to Brandon about cars—he researched model cars online at night, so he'd have things to say—and about anything other than the drumline and the show. Nick was about to break a promise to a friend and push Derek Richard to come to the early-morning sectionals. At the same time, and without being able to explain why he was doing it, he decided not to push the one person in the section who most needed the extra work.

Nick also decided to ask Max for help. The percussion section needed a firmer hand and a tighter focus during the Tuesday evening sectionals than Nick thought Amy Davis could provide. By going to Max, Nick was in effect going over the head of his superior. The insubordination ran counter to everything he understood about leadership, but his ideas about leadership were getting murkier by the day.

Sitting across his desk from the slight drumline captain, Max agreed to head the sectionals. Nick sensed an understanding pass between them. He'd felt hammered by his director all season. Now he would be working in tandem with him to solve some of the show's deepest problems. Nick left the meeting feeling more confident than he had in weeks.

AFTER THE FIRST hour of rehearsal on Wednesday night, the band's focus moved to cleaning the show. It was about time—past time, in fact. For several weeks, Max had been trying to begin the detailed work that put a high gloss on a show and readied it for the Dome. The year before, they'd started cleaning with three weeks to go before state. Max had earlier believed they might have five weeks in 2004. Now they were down to eight practice days left to clean the entire show: to go through the show chart by chart and straighten every line, clarify every body angle, and run every form until not a foot was out of place.

Max never gave his bands enough time to clean. It had been years since he'd adhered to the "one week for each minute of the show" guideline that most directors followed. Cleaning late was part of his strategy: It allowed him more time to fiddle with music and choreography; it kept pressure on the kids; and at the same time, it kept their performance from growing stale. Between the high demands and Max's tinkering, Concord's shows came together late every season. Ideally, a Concord show acquired its final polish in Indianapolis on the morning of the state championship. Max's approach was similar to that of coaches who trained elite athletes to peak at the moment when the stakes were highest.

Of course the strategy carried risk. It asked the students to have faith in Max's system, and confidence in themselves. For Max, it meant calibrating the level of changes that his band and his assistants could handle. Cleaning late left little room for error or the unexpected, such as a drumline that couldn't keep time, or a percussion instructor who didn't know the difference between good tinkering and bad. Max's bands never peaked too early. The question that hung over every season was whether they would have time, in the end, to reach their peak at all.

Less than halfway through the evening practice, Max stopped them in the first measures of "Africa." "It's too dirty to clean," he said.

As if in an aside, he remarked, "We have Christine Fischer this year. She's marching in the trombone section as of today." The teenagers on the field cheered and clapped for the German exchange student. Max continued. "This drill is all new to her, and she's making fewer mistakes than a lot of you."

Christine had done remarkably well for someone who hadn't been able to visualize a marching band when she'd first arrived. *Playing instruments on a football field?* Max had enough experience with exchange students to know they could pick up the basics quickly enough to march in the show, but they usually needed some time to get their bearings. He had instructed the LC guys to write Christine into the drill starting halfway through the show. In just two months' time, however, she'd learned to march—her footwork was exquisite—and had memorized her music. She'd acquired a tan and an American swagger. That night she wore the latest in flute-section fashion—a bright pink T-shirt with "CONCORD FLUTES" in big block letters, and black sweatpants flashing neon pink "FLUTE" across her butt. She no longer stood out from the rest of the band as a foreigner or as a beginner.

The United States had been her fourth choice on the AFS list, after New Zealand, Australia, and Great Britain. But every would-be exchange student from Europe had apparently wanted to spend a year in the Southern Hemisphere. Some of her politically minded classmates had been surprised that she'd even consider going to the United States. She'd come to Elkhart expecting the fast food, the malls, the televisions and video games. She even recognized the high school, with its hallways and lockers, its cheerleaders and football players, from imported TV shows and movies. She had been surprised, however, by how much her experience in America seemed framed by competition. In her school in Germany, direct competition among students was frowned upon. At Concord, students tracked their own and one another's test scores and grades almost obsessively. She was still getting used to the expectation that students come to class with opinions they were prepared to defend. And she thought everything about marching band was geared toward winning. In America, it seemed, learning how to compete was one of the skills you were groomed for before you graduated from high school.

Christine, still playing her flute, would be marching in place of Jeremy Crawford, a trombone player who would soon withdraw from school after missing much of the trimester. Each year, a few kids got injured or became ill or overwhelmed and couldn't march their spots. Less often, students refused to abide by the rules of the school or the band and were kicked out. Either way, it meant marching holes, which didn't look good on the field and, like the gaping wounds they resembled, were sites around which other problems often developed. Steve Peterson was about to pull a kid for lying about missing practices, but he had a freshman who'd moved to the district late in the summer to put in his place.

Each situation was different, as was each student. But the ones who got kicked out usually had violated the single most important requirement of the Marching Minuteman Band: They hadn't tried their hardest. Max's system, with its structure and emphasis on personal responsibility, needed to work in concert with what kids were being taught at home. Some of those who came through the program lacking that congruence in their lives responded by making the band their home. But others made different choices, or needed more than the program could offer. And some students simply didn't find what they needed in marching band. Each year, a small number of students who started the marching season either retreated to indoor band for individual practice (where they could still get credit for the class and rejoin the group for concert band), or dropped out of band, and school, entirely. Still, with one week to go to before the season ended, only three students who'd started in July were no longer marching in the band.

Even for those who stayed, however, marching band wasn't a home for every kid. The other directors joked that Max preferred students who looked like him. While that wasn't entirely true, he did seem more comfortable around uncomplicated, clean-cut, easygoing kids. Max disliked untidiness of all kinds, including the untidiness of other people's lives. He was impatient with rebels, kids who asked too many questions, kids whose lives, for whatever reason, weren't under control. He didn't expressly dislike those kids. With them, he just seemed uncomfortable, and emotionally tone-deaf. Each season, a certain number of kids marched unhappy.

One of that year's unhappy kids, Jon Faloon, was slowly coming back into the family. Since having The Talk with Max, his interest and commitment had steadily increased, with some backsliding. He'd gone from leading disruptions in the pit to being a wobbly but positive leader. As if by design, both Max and Nick had given out exactly the kinds of rewards that made Jon want to work harder, Max by telling him that the younger kids in the pit looked up to him and needed him, Nick by giving him authority over the section. Jon had taken some pride in working with the other drummers on the djembes, goblet-shaped African hand drums, for their parts during "Gabriel's Oboe" and "Africa."

Now, with just a couple of practices left before regionals, he was given a further responsibility and honor. Max, continuing to look for ways to make it clear that the Concord show followed the African roots of American music, had asked Jon and his djembe to walk forward from the back sideline with Amanda at the start of the show. That evening, Max took the full band back to the beginning to try it. Jon emerged from the shade of the tall tree, straight down the fifty-yard line, holding the drum out in front of him. From the tower, Max explained to the rest of the band what Jon was doing. "We're presenting the African drum," he said. Amanda walked to one side of Jon and then the other, bowing and pointing to him and the drum. Although she would soon be featured, now was Jon's moment. "Cradle it like a baby," Max suggested. The bulky drum filled Jon's arms. He smiled widely above it.

And then they started working through the show again, with a flute player marching with the trombones, with clarinets who still couldn't play the entire show correctly, with timing issues everywhere. Just before the end of the practice, Max sprang the new ending on them.

He had felt that the show needed one final flourish to finish it off. The previous year, at the same late stage, Max had introduced "salad shooters" that propelled colored streamers high into the air to spice up the finish of "Malagueña." Now he introduced "L'il Liza Jane," an energetic, bouncy number that the band would sing along with two lead vocalists: Cameron Bradley and Brandon Schenk. The show would seem to end, Max explained, but they'd keep the party going. "I want people to say, 'Omigosh, I can't believe they did this!' No Class B bands have this much nerve, and only a few Class A, national bands. There hasn't been a band in Indiana that has had this much fun!"

On the field, the kids learned the tune and practiced singing along with Cameron and Brandon, up on the drum major podium. Grant and the Dixieland ensemble accompanied the entire group. It made no sense to be teaching a new song when the band hadn't mastered the rest of the show, but that was Max, and that was Concord.

For possibly the first time all season, the practice ran late. At nine o'clock, while Max was still working on creating the party atmosphere, two flute players made a point of checking their watches and walked away from the group. Others called out to them. The girls turned back and shook their heads. To the surprise of many, Max didn't boom down from the tower and order them to return. They were making a choice.

On Thursday, Max called Brandon Dascoli out of Steve Peterson's music theory class and brought him into his office for The Talk. Max told the young man that he had to see more effort. He reminded Brandon that he'd rebuffed many offers of help. "I'll pull you if you can't do it. All you need to do is show me that you're working 100 percent."

His talk with Brandon fresh in his mind, Max started rehearsal in the band room that afternoon by pointing to the numbered list that ran across the top of the students' weekly forms and the daily staff schedules. "You're still missing something," he told them. He read them number four on the list of reasons that people become members of a group: because they need to experience something bigger than themselves. "Socially, we're not state champions," he said. Of course they were working hard, he told them. Working like a state champion was hard work. Only a few people looked up at him as he scanned the room, so few had the chance to notice that his face wasn't angry but sad. And tired. "The only thing that can fix this band is in this room."

He went on, speaking low, his words bleached of anger. "I think you can be great. I think you can win. But if you win operating like this, I won't be excited."

Earlier in the week, Max had met with the seniors again. He'd repeated Grant's question to the forty-some seniors gathered around him: "Is there still hope?"

"This band could be turned around in five days," he told them. "Is there hope to be state champions? Absolutely. But time is dwindling down."

Now they were almost down to those five days.

BRANDON DASCOLI SHOWED up for the percussion sectional on Friday morning. The others accepted his presence without fanfare. Nick took him and the other two tenor drummers down to the junior high track and marched them around the small oval while they played "Gabriel's Oboe" and "Africa," "Gabriel's Oboe" and "Africa." It had rained overnight, and the fog was dense and heavy with moisture. Max on his rounds could barely make out three bulky forms moving in a line on the opposite side of the track, trailed slightly by a fourth. Senior drum major Pat Doherty had assigned himself to the percussion section. Though he worked the closing shift at a local Wendy's restaurant, he joined them at their morning sessions. He didn't know the first thing about drumming technique, but his presence kept the others on task when Nick wasn't there. Now Derek Richard was the only one left on the drumline who had yet to appear.

Grant's first class of the day was Government, where they were just then learning about the American electoral system. It was one of the classes Grant had stopped paying attention to, and his grade was suffering as a result. But it hadn't kept him from being elected president. The conceit of the class was that the students created their own government, mirroring the American system. (He'd won the election against a girl whose campaign slogan had been "Elect Kim, not him.") As president, Grant led the Pledge of Allegiance every morning, passed out papers, and greeted the class every Friday. His presidential portrait hung on one of the walls, last in a long line of other "presidents."

President Grant enlisted the help of his vice president, Cameron Bradley, and the chief justice of the Supreme Court, Jon Faloon, in his weekly greeting. The three band geeks had dubbed their effort "the techno preamble." Jon provided a syncopated djembe-style ground, over which Cameron scatted whatever lyrics popped into his head, and Grant made noises and faces. Each week they offered a new composition to the class. That Friday, Cameron had put some forethought into his lyrics. "Do you know the muffin man?" he sang, while Jon pounded out a soft beat on the edge of the desk, slapping the top here and there for extra emphasis. "It's Grant's birthday. Huzzah!"

The teacher wished Grant a happy birthday. Eighteen? Grant nodded. The real presidential election was less than a month away. Are you going to vote? the teacher asked. "Noooo," Grant replied, sheepishly. A girl who had been swinging a pink flip-flop from a crossed leg called out, "You're a bad president." Grant looked even more sheepish.

But he had more on his mind than a typical apolitical eighteen-year-old.

The back pain that had bothered Chris Longenbaugh since tearing out the wall in the basement hadn't gone away. The kindergartner-size desks that she'd always been able to squeeze into had sent her back into spasms, and visits to massage therapists and chiropractors had brought no relief. She'd started sleeping in one of the recliners, and recently, she'd needed help to get up out of it. A week earlier, after the pain finally forced her to quit her job—the job she loved, teaching kids to read—MRI results had come back that raised the possibility that the breast cancer she'd fought off six years earlier had returned to her spine.

On the day that Grant turned eighteen, his mom and dad were driving to Chicago to see a specialist. They'd be back in time for dinner and to celebrate the birthday. Grant had taken their reassurances at face value: Even if it was the cancer again, they would beat it, just as they had the last time. But the worry threw a pall over the day.

The rain that had threatened all week finally arrived for Friday afternoon's practice, adding to the grayness. Steve Peterson, Scott Spradling, and Bryan Golden joined forces to work inside with the brass sections on "A Closer Walk with Thee." Peterson moved quickly down the line of trombones, checking that they had the right notes and especially the right style. "Doo-VAH," he said to one, demonstrating the placement of the accent on the offbeat. He pointed to one trumpet player after another. Grant played his part along with the rest of the brass. His notes sounded warm, mellow, tinged with just the right bittersweet sense of life in its full round of joys and sorrows. The spiritual behind this version of "A Closer Walk with Thee" seemed close to the surface.

At Grant's party that evening, his aunts came over to bake the birthday apple dumplings his mother usually made for him. Leandra, unsure how personal to make her present, gave Grant a "Napoleon Dynamite" T-shirt. (Ten days later, equally unsure, Grant would give her the love poems of Robert Browning and Elizabeth Barrett Browning for her birthday.) Grant and Cameron acted goofy as always. They played 90s Trivial Pursuit. The party was mostly over when Chris and Jeff finally got home from Chicago. Jeff called Grant up from the basement, and told him the news that no one wanted to hear: The tests showed cancer, and possibly a kind worse than breast cancer.

The ISSMA regionals that year were held in Chesterton, about ten miles from Lake Michigan. Grant waited until the high-brass bus was almost there, then got up from his seat, asked the driver to turn off the music, and borrowed a microphone. His energy hadn't been met by the upperclassmen in the section, and he was growing frustrated. He had lost his patience for the mounting excuses he heard from kids who weren't coming to the sectionals or doing the extra work. He stood in front of all of them.

Then, in a low voice, for the first time, the most admired member of the Concord marching band talked about his depression. "I've struggled with this," he told them. He said he understood how hard it was sometimes to get up for band—that he had to make the choice, in fact, every morning, to get up and face the day. He didn't mention cancer, or medication, or crisis of faith. He simply empathized, and asked them to make a choice, as well. To go out and have the best performance of the season. To commit themselves to what it took. "I'm asking you to make the decision—today."

In the silence that followed—*Grant Longenbaugh? Depressed?*— Grant walked back to his seat, close to the front of the bus, to be with the freshmen and the weakest among them, the ones most in need.

At Chesterton, the wind blew hard and unforgiving across the football field. Max decided not to risk the tree scrim or the drumset covers. They'd have to go to the state finals without the covers ever having worked correctly, even in a practice, and having used them in competition only once.

In the stands, parents huddled beneath coats and blankets. Word passed quickly among the Concord group about Chris Longenbaugh's bad news. A band mom near the Lehmans waited for Dick to leave his seat for a few minutes before she told Jolene. She wasn't sure how Dick, who was sixteen treatments in for his lymphoma and not yet in remission, would take the news.

On the field, the wind was brutal. The color guard shivered in their light costumes. Feet froze, faces froze. They didn't play or march particularly well. Everything seemed hard. Between numbers Grant blew on his hands to keep them warm. He wore his new Napoleon Dynamite T-shirt under his uniform jacket but wished he'd worn long underwear instead. His lips were cold; he couldn't get a feel for the trumpet. He wasn't able to give the solo the emotion he wanted to. What he would most remember about the performance was not winning it, or qualifying again for state finals, which from the start had never really been in doubt. What he remembered was the sense of having gutted it out.

12 ★ A Beat Too Late?

With five days to go, Max drove to Indianapolis for a directors' meeting he didn't need to attend. For twenty years, ever since the Dome had opened, Max had made the trip and done the walk-through and heard what was expected from the directors of the forty bands that had made it to the pinnacle of the Indiana marching-band season. By now, he gained little new information by going. Still, he wanted to catch even the smallest revisions in the procedures surrounding the championship, be they new parking rules or a change in the flow between warm-up areas. And the meeting that year meant more to him than mere information. He knew it would be the last time he'd be a member of the most select group of band directors in the state. It was the last time he'd gather with his tribe.

Max timed the drive perfectly. He steered the school van to a particular spot in a nearby parking garage, pleased to show his passenger, Concord principal Dan Cunningham, how close they were to the entrance they wanted at the Dome. They had about twenty minutes to spare, enough time to locate the meeting room inside the cavernous building and still be early. Several other directors converged on the same entrance, timing their arrivals as carefully as Max had, and coming, no doubt, from their own special parking spots. They all hailed

Max, who returned the greetings with a big smile. Max introduced Cunningham, and one of the other directors said, "You'd never get my principal to come to one of these meetings." The crowd swelled during the wait for the elevators, each addition bringing more handshakes and hellos for Max and a bigger smile from him, until by the time the group reached the meeting room, he seemed to be the grinning magnet at its center.

The Concord director and principal seated themselves in one of the back rows. Greenwood's veteran director Jon Sutton leaned over a chair and shook Max's hand. The two men traded lighthearted insults. "Aren't you getting to be too old for this sort of thing?" Sutton inquired. Max suggested lunch following the meeting. He promised the meal would last until at least three o'clock. "My kids would think I was great if I could get Greenwood to miss a practice."

The room filled quickly with directors from every part of Indiana, from Fort Wayne, which had sent five schools in three classes to the finals, to tiny Paoli, where almost a third of the students marched in the band. A couple of the schools on Amy Davis's "north" list, North Harrison and North Posey, had come up from the south. The Lawrence Central directors walked in together, including Greg Hagen, who never had made it back to Concord for his promised third visit. They were among the regulars, from the schools that people expected to see every year at the Dome: Clay City, Norwell, Lewis Cass, Carmel, Ben Davis, Homestead, Avon.

It was no more a surprise that those schools had made it into their finals than it was that Concord, Greenwood, Jasper, and Northview had made it in Class B. Just before the meeting started, however, Sutton mentioned a surprise. For the first time in almost thirty years, Center Grove, a two-time national marching band champion, had not made it out of regionals. Max and Sutton both knew that Tom Dirks, Center Grove's longtime director, had retired a few years earlier. Neither man commented further, but it wasn't hard to imagine the two of them, edging closer to retirement themselves, silently calculating the length of time it had taken another great program to fall.

The older directors in the room followed a dress code of brightly colored sweaters, polo shirts, stretch dress slacks. The younger ones tended toward fleece and jeans; James Goodhue, the Jasper director, wore sandals and socks. Their style was too casual for Max's taste, but it was becoming the norm. Looking around the room, he saw the trend was clear.

The meeting started on time, of course; and of course no one arrived late. The burly white-haired ISSMA executive director, Charles Briel, known as "Rusty," asked first-timers to raise their hands. Two directors did so, one of them from Northridge. "New kids comin' up," an older director whispered back to Max.

Briel went over parking, staff passes, photography, parking, student privacy, traffic control, parking, ticket scams to avoid, parking. (Parking was always an issue, because of the Dome's central location and the Saturday schedule, and because the crowds turned over three times in the course of a day.) The directors listened to Briel with an attentiveness that was respectful but not full, tuned to pick up only what was new or different. Simultaneously, information passed among the Class B directors clustered in the back rows. Weather had kept the southern bands indoors most of the previous week. Jasper had won the southern regional in Class B, followed closely by Northview and Greenwood. Max told Sutton it had been much closer in the north than he had liked.

Rusty Briel had worked in music education almost as long as Max. He was the head of ISSMA; his role included preaching the band gospel around the state and reminding people of the history and importance of Indiana's music heritage. Just the week before, he'd shared his on-the-ground view of teaching music with students at Indiana University. He told the class that most music students were taking five years to get their education degrees, then teaching music for five years before leaving the field for other—often less demanding—work. "You're going to have days where you work fifteen hours, nobody cares, you go home and think maybe you've even made things worse," he told them. His final bit of advice boiled down to what Max and the other directors gathered in the room that morning had long since learned to do: "You need to give them something tangible to work toward."

Each year at the pre-finals meeting, Max saw fewer of the old-guard directors that he'd come up with. Many of them had started out at Butler or Ball State or Indiana State around the same time, had worked summer staff for each other, and had developed individual styles and strengths in part by watching each other. Most of them had won at least one championship; some, like Max and Jon Sutton, had reigned over dynasties. The directors who had successfully made the transition from track shows to field shows had presided over the creation of ISSMA and the current contest format. Their generation had built—in the face of economic and cultural challenges that had crippled arts education across the country—a statewide music system that had become the envy of educators everywhere. But more and more of the directors of that era were reaching the ends of their careers. The question hovering in the room was who would be the next to leave their ranks. None of the others knew yet that it would be Max.

Briel started to talk about the new rules relating to shows. The energy in the room perked up. More than a few people turned around to look toward Max. Max had a long, interesting relationship with the ISSMA rules and rule changes. He had helped compile the original manual. He'd pushed to improve the educational quality of contest judging and the competing experience. The old State Fair contest, with its emphasis on pleasing crowds (and enhancing gate receipts), had followed a tick-list approach to judging that came straight out of the military. Bands back then started with a certain number of points. Each infraction—a misstep, a missed note or bungled rhythm, even a dirty uniform—counted against the total. The band with the most points left at the end won. The ISSMA judging system that Max helped create tried to measure a show's educational quality for the students and to give points for educational reach as well as follow-through. The more subjective system was continually being refined.

Still, as they all knew, directors wanted to win. And there was a persistent impression among some of his competitors that Max Jones continually pushed the edges of the rulebook he'd helped create. A Concord show often seemed to inspire rule revisions the following year aimed at closing yet another loophole that Max Jones had managed to exploit (as the complaining directors saw it) or that moved the system back toward the old tick-list (as Max saw it).

Two of the revisions Briel mentioned at the meeting derived directly from the previous year's state championship. In putting together the "Guitarras Españolas" show, Max and the LC guys had arranged the pit instruments on and around the raised platforms that formed the neck and frets of the huge guitar. Matt Tompkins, the guitar player whose solos gave the show its name, was to step up and perform on the highest of the platforms. However, the setup crew had quickly realized that something inside the Dome was interfering with Matt's cordless microphone. The band's technical director ran out onto the field to troubleshoot. When his back-up channels didn't work, he went to a second back-up plan. That failed, also, and with time ticking down, he was forced to plug Matt directly into the Concord sound system. By the time he ran off the field and the announcer was able to say, "Drum majors, the field is yours for state finals performance," the standard three-minute setup limit had passed, plus another minute. When it came time for Matt's guitar solos, the upper platform was empty. Unless you looked carefully at the musicians arrayed below and noticed Matt standing next to the amplifier, you might wonder, as many did, whether the music you were hearing had been pre-recorded.

Inevitably, there were inquiries after the competition, especially after Concord won. Skeptics were reassured that Matt's solos had not violated performing rules. But others questioned the excruciatingly long setup time. It had clearly gone past the standard specified in the ISSMA manual. But it had not, in fact, broken any rules. The recommended breakdown was three minutes for set-up, ten minutes to perform, and two minutes to clear the field, but the rules specified only that the band could not go over its ten-minute performance time, nor over the total allotment. Concord had played within the rules.

Briel spelled out new rules that, not surprisingly, clarified the three-minute limit for setup. They also specified that all adults had to be in transit off the field at the three-minute mark. As a member of ISSMA's executive committee and its current past president, Max knew that the clarifications were coming. He accepted them, as he'd accepted a rule the year before that required sound-system levels to be set by students. Did the people who asked for such rules really think that keeping a Concord director from turning those dials on the field would make it harder for Concord to win? Max still had one of the best and most well organized technical directors around, a member of one of the best music staffs in the state. He thought the other guys should spend more of their time developing their own great systems instead of trying to neutralize his.

When Briel finished, he looked up from his list and scanned the room. "Does anybody else have a question for Max?" he asked.

Max and his principal walked along with the others for the tour of the Dome. None of it bored him. He didn't mind seeing the judges' boxes again, or hearing Briel try to put a positive spin on the Dome's acoustics: "What you hear at ground level is nothing at all like what you hear at the judges' level." The Dome was showing signs of its age. Rumor was that it would soon be demolished to make way for a new stadium.

Max ate lunch with an old friend, Bob Medworth, the director at Northview. As Max and Dianne had done for many years at Winchester and Concord, Bob and Ruthann Medworth ran their band as a husband-and-wife team, Ruthann handling the color guard. The two men had been friendly rivals for years. Northview had thought it would win the 2003 title but had come in 4th; some of Medworth's band parents were undoubtedly among the people who had complained to Briel following Concord's win. The two directors talked about their seasons with a frankness that might have surprised those parents and the students in their bands. Medworth said the Northview show wasn't his style, not his music. But the kids related to it, and they'd been willing to work hard. He was happy with it. He and Max talked about old shows, old times. They shared a history and an approach, though they came at their work from different perspectives. On the Monday following the finals, Medworth would switch roles and become the girls' basketball coach, just as Max was going straight to his work with Concord's concert band.

Max lingered in the city after lunch. He drove every route the buses would take the following Saturday morning, timing the drive and checking for construction that could affect his tight schedule: out to Ben Davis, where the band would squeeze an hour's practice between dawn and Dome on Saturday morning; backtracking to the hotel on the outskirts of the city where the band would spend Friday night. Everything checked to his satisfaction. He made one last stop, a shopping mall, where he picked out a new shirt and tie to go with the new suit he'd bought for his final appearance at the Dome.

Driving back to Elkhart, the director and his principal talked for a while about the band and about the school; then the conversation trailed off. They finished the trip back to Concord in silence, each alone with his thoughts.

———

WITH FIVE DAYS to go, the band room began to feel crowded in the early mornings. The practice field turned into an asphalt continent of small countries, each flying the flag of its native instrument, each with its own customs and government, each trying to outdo the others. A sense of excitement, or urgency, or fear, pushed the optional attendance higher. Good work was getting done. It set the tone for the final week.

Chris Longenbaugh returned to Chicago for a bone biopsy. Grant kept quiet about his mother's cancer. They didn't know everything yet. There was still a round of tests and confirmation ahead of them. He could tell that his mother was worried, though, and that his father, behind his reassurances, was worried, too. But for now, as he did with lesser family concerns—whether there would be enough food for a gathering, whether they'd make it to an airport on time—Grant took the positive view. They'd beaten breast cancer before. They'd do it again. He focused his attention on his playing and his section. They had a championship to win. There was still a shot at creating a dynasty. Those around him saw all his usual focus and effort, and had no idea that a part of him had turned numb.

Ideally, during the final week of rehearsals, the band would concentrate completely on cleaning the show. But learning the music came first, and the week had to run in two modes: intensive work on "Swing, Swing, Swing," and detailing and cleaning everything else in multiple run-throughs.

It had been clear at regionals that the show's big finish still exceeded the grasp of too many students.

One afternoon, Scott Spradling set up the trumpets, flugelhorns, and mellophones in an arc on the stage of the Beickman Center to work through it. With its rapidly ascending and descending runs for every horn part, all of it in syncopated swing time, "Swing, Swing, Swing" asked a lot of his section. He positioned the horn players as far away from each other as possible, until they could hear only themselves while they played. "Practice for the Dome," he said tersely. He pointed to one student after another in the arc, listened to each play the phrase. Point, play. Comment. Point, play. Again. To some, he said, "Good." He said to Laurie Schalliol, playing second part, "Keep your air coming. You want to crescendo all the way through." To those who couldn't get the run after two tries, which meant many of the seconds and nearly all the thirds, Spradling jerked his thumb toward the exit.

The three amigos lingered at the doorway to pick off the students one by one for rapid-fire individual work sessions. Craig Searer bent over the music in the middle of the hall with one of the small freshmen and showed him where he'd been fingering incorrectly. "We're gonna lick this lick," Craig told him, "if we have to do it note by note." Grant steered a tall, lanky freshman who was having trouble with all of it—the notes, the rhythm, the tone—to the men's bathroom. "It's got great acoustics," he said with a grin as he pushed the skeptical boy ahead of him, "just like singing in a shower at home."

As soon as someone had licked the lick, the amigos sent the student back to the arc and grabbed another. The seniors got giddy with the pace, or with their power to change things so quickly. One amigo clapped the syncopated rhythm while his student played the run of notes. Another slowed down the two measures, making clear how C went into C-sharp and on to D. Grant ran a kid through repetitions of a single note, sounding for all the world like Max Jones: "Play it again." "Play it again." "Again." "One more time." "Again." "One more time." "Good."

When it was nearly time to go onto the field, Spradling brought them all together to play the tricky section. "If you can get it," he said, "that's great. Otherwise I gotta change your part." He listened to them play through it. "That was much improved," he said. Big smiles spread all around, the feel of a good round of work. There might be time yet.

Diana de la Reza continued her early-morning practices between the fire doors with a rising sense of impotence. Two of the girls remained opaque to her. They were willing to let her pick them up every morning, but one complained her way through the short practices, and the other barely spoke a word. Only Adilene seemed willing to do the work, but Diana wasn't even sure if Adilene would be ready by Saturday. At times, she felt like a babysitter.

Adilene's progress might have been slow on the field, but her experience in the band and with Diana was showing up in other places. She was taking her homework seriously for the first time. Her math teacher, Mr. Rolon, the only Hispanic teacher at the high school, had watched her change from an invisible student to one who raised her hand and asked questions. Her grades heading into the end of the first trimester were higher than anything she'd earned in junior high. Less than ten weeks into the school year, she'd already been transformed.

At the moment, such perspective was beyond Diana. Her frustration mounting, she yelled at her twin sister one day for not staying to help lead a sectional. Steve Peterson tried to gather the clarinets together after a rehearsal, but discovered that, other than Diana, they'd already dispersed. He called the stragglers back. "This is state finals week," he said in exasperation. "This is the best you can do?" Later, with night coming on, Diana burst into tears walking to her car. "We don't deserve to win!" she screamed into the nearly empty parking lot. "NO ONE IS HELPING!"

After thirteen weeks of trying to do the right thing, Brent Lehman had succeeded in getting his section to work but still hadn't moved the other upperclassmen's opinions of him—and Brandon Schenk was talking about quitting. Brent was feeling the old sense of isolation, even more so as the presidential election drew near. He'd taped a picture of Jesus to the back window of his car, above the words "Jesus was a liberal." More than once, he'd had to remove angry notes stuck beneath the windshield wipers, some of which he knew had come from classmates in the band. His section was still out on the practice field early and late, but as a leader he was out there alone.

Yet each afternoon, the small countries grew larger, their customs more pronounced. One day the flutes wore halos and wings. The trombones practiced in thrift-store suits and hats. The saxophone sweatshirts arrived. Pat Doherty, who played saxophone in concert band, wore one that said, "Get Milk!" on the back. (Everyone caught the reference to the championship's biggest sponsor, the Indiana Dairy Farmers.) Cameron Bradley's said, "Get Angry!"

Max listened to them play through "Gabriel's Oboe" and called down from the tower, "That was the first time all season I heard the high G, first trumpets. But where are the seconds and thirds, to make it a deep, dark sound?" Grant, down below, called out, "Keep doing it, guys."

They played the piece one more time. Max said, "OK, that was goosebumps." He sent them back to Chart 8. Someone yelled up to the tower, "I *love* Chart 8!"

The saxophones held their first morning sectional. Cameron, who hadn't been one of the kids getting up early, excitedly pointed out the colorful sunrise. Nearby, Jared Nymeyer, working one of the rotating trumpet blocks in eight-count segments, looked and grunted, as if to say, We've seen plenty already, buddy. But he joked, "Let's work all the way through first hour!"

Over in the percussion section, the morning walk through the fog became part of the banter. Nick took a line, Pat took another, and if they had three lines going, there were plenty of volunteers to take that one. Brandon Dascoli made it almost every day. No one had thought it possible, but he'd started marching and playing his part at the same time—and enjoying himself! The sullen boys in the pit had straightened up beneath Jon Faloon—Nick's delegating had worked. Max had stepped in just in time. Nick was managing the delicate balance of leading from both above and below. The risks he'd taken were paying off. One by one, the challenges that had seemed insurmountable were being solved. Except for Derek Richard, who remained outside of Nick's reach, the entire drumline was playing with new energy, new esprit. In two weeks' time, the section had gone from being the most picked-on in the band to becoming what Nick had always imagined—the elite, the proud. Even Mr. Jones noticed the change and complimented them. They weren't just setting tempo now; they were setting example. "We have forty-five seconds left," Nick said one morning. "Let's play 'Africa' to the end!" Everyone stayed, everyone played. They were using every second, trying for a miracle.

People crowded the fences, now, to watch the band practice. Girls from Northridge came over one evening to watch Concord's color guard. Kids heading to basketball tryouts stopped and watched from the back sidelines before going in the gym.

Band parents washed the tarp and retouched it. Moms had taped sheets of paper to every band student's locker—"Proud Member of the Concord Minuteman Marching Band"—and framed them with twists of green and white streamers. Friends of Adilene's had scrawled "Go Adilene!" and "We're proud of you!" on hers. Posters lined the music hallway. As the pep rally drew near, "decorating moms" dangled green cutouts in the shape of Indiana from the ceiling tiles, one for each student and member of the music staff.

The Thursday evening before state finals was windy and almost too warm for the season. Dark clouds rolled in. The good weather was finally coming to an end. Parents and friends arrived in cars and vans sporting soaped-on slogans—Flutes Rule! Win State!—while the band worked away on the practice field. Kathy Peterson, visibly pregnant, holding Adam's hand, watched below the tower where her husband stood.

On the center tower, Max said, "We could be a great band. We've been a good band all season. We've grown every week. We have not had a great performance yet. Two days. Here we go."

Just before eight-thirty, he called them to set up the full show on the varsity football field. Max told the staff to let the show run as it would at the Dome. No comments, no gestures.

Jeff and Chris Longenbaugh found seats in the grandstand close to midfield, where they could have a good view of Grant during his solos. The pain from the collapsing vertebrae in Chris's back was so severe that she had to steel herself even for the short ride from their house to the high school. She wasn't sure she could survive six hours in a car, or even a couple of hours on an unforgiving stadium seat. She hardly recognized herself. She had spent so much time imagining her youngest child's final marching season, the crescendo of his high school career. Ever since Anne's tumultuous senior year, Chris had thought of the last year of high school as how God helped parents let go of their children. But the pain was causing her to let go of Grant early, and that knowledge was as hard to bear as the pain itself.

On the first run-through, the set-up took too long. The drumsets resisted being pushed onto the uneven ground. The wind picked up one edge of the smaller tarp and lifted it clear of the ground before the band dads could catch it and bring it back to earth. In front of the parents, Max and Jim Faigh had an angry blowup.

They played the show twice. Both times the timing fell apart. Both times Grant tried to shout encouragement to the people around him, and in the high-brass huddle between performances, he urged his section to keep believing. In themselves, in the show, in all of them together. But he felt the energy and the hope draining away.

Over the course of the week, his dedication and focus hadn't lessened, but dark circles had appeared under his eyes; he looked gaunt, worn out. Without realizing it, he had become part of the band's timing problem. He was losing himself in his solo for "A Closer Walk with Thee," trying to put all of his swirling emotions into the notes, wanting so badly to send that prayer up to God. And the harder he focused, the more he slowed down the time for the rest of the band. He'd stopped listening to the others around him, and couldn't hear the problem.

Now, he heard others around him yelling at younger kids who messed up, really ripping into them. It was exactly what he was trying to change. What had happened to being servant-hearted?

And it wasn't only the students doing the yelling. Max yelled at them, again, and Grant thought, *We can't change right before State. This is as far as we got. Can you find something in us to appreciate?* Even deeper, he asked, *Can't you see all that I'm doing? I've given everything I have.*

They walked off the field, and Grant already knew the criticism that would come when they got back to the band room. He reached the track on the far side of the field, and then he couldn't go on. He staggered out of line, waved off help, and leaned heavily against the fence. He sobbed for his bone-weariness and for his frustration and the burden he'd shouldered too much alone. He sobbed for his mother. He sobbed because he felt harshness from God.

He stayed there until the stands were empty. Then he gathered himself, picked up his trumpet, and made his way inside. He lingered by the doors of the band room where Max was talking. He knew what Max was saying in there. If he heard any more, he would break. He still had the pep rally to go to. The packed auditorium, the raucous energy from classmates and well-wishers. His parents would be looking for him.

THE DRUMLINE HELD its last sectional the day before the finals. After the timing fiascos of the night before, Nick hadn't needed to push the others to show up. With efficient movements, they put on carriers, strapped on drums, and headed back outside. By now, Nick had such a well-tuned ear for Mr. Jones's criticism that he recognized the progress the drumline was making. He knew they were *this* close to pulling it together, across the entire show. Two weeks earlier, Nick wouldn't have guessed that he would feel so pumped twenty-four hours before the state contest.

It had rained overnight. Water pooled in places on the dark pavement. Fog settled thickly over everything. They'd just started when Nick sensed something moving in the grayness. His first thought was that Mr. Jones had come out to say something to them at their final practice. But the shape wasn't right. He looked harder and saw his friend

Derek Richard emerge from the fog, like a ghost, like a developing photo slowly gaining form and color. At the last possible moment, in his own time, Derek was joining them. And the final piece was in place.

Max had awakened at 3:27 a.m. Knowing that he'd get little sleep the coming night, he tried to turn off his mind so everything else could get some more rest. But of course he worried. Now he had a headache behind his eyes and puffy bags below them. He had worked through one decision, though, there in the dark. Everything in the show had improved—some things dramatically—but the new ending remained rough, and there simply wasn't time to polish it. "Li'l Liza Jane" would come out of the show. As for the rest of it, there wasn't much more he could do.

The afternoon light was fading as the students boarded the buses idling in line along Minuteman Way. Drivers swung cargo doors open and threw in overnight bags. The instruments had been loaded onto the semi and the fifth-wheel, along with the drumsets and the pit carts. The band dads had divided the tasks and given them silly names. (The nose packer had crawled above the cab to pack up that small space; the nose picker would unload it in Indy.) But the usual joking between the dads and the kids was absent. Parents, boyfriends and girlfriends, families hovered near the buses, saying good-byes. The mood seemed charged, almost tense, like the night before battle.

That's what Jeff Longenbaugh saw when he drove up. He found Grant, just in time, about to step onto the trumpet bus. Jeff pulled his son off to the side and talked urgently to him. He hugged him hard, extra long, then, wiping at his eyes with his coat sleeve, watched him get on the bus.

The caravan pulled out together and made a slow, careful circle through the parking lots. On the buses, band moms handed out battery-powered lights and old-fashioned crepe paper to string along the windows. On the low-brass bus, Brent Lehman gave bags of candy and personal notes to all the trombones. The freshmen saxophones turned the tables on the seniors by presenting them with a card and asking them to share their advice and their memories of previous state finals. Cameron Bradley handed a letter to every person in the saxophone section. Near the end of it he'd written: "We're not doing this show for fame, or glory, or a ring, or a banner, or for people to remember us, but for each other. . . . Get it right for that person next to you. That kid's counting on you. Love, love, love this. It's the best thing you can do—better than winning."

On the high-brass bus, Craig Searer and Jared Nymeyer scored the back seat. Craig yelled up to the front of the bus: "Only sixteen hours, fifty-one minutes, and fifty-four seconds until we perform in the Dome!" Ten seconds later he called out an update.

Grant chose a seat in the middle with the seconds and thirds. For a moment, he wished he could allow himself to sit in the back of the bus, too.

The doctor had called just as Grant's father was heading out the door to join the band. It wasn't breast cancer, but something more serious—multiple myeloma, an incurable cancer of the blood more common in older African-American men than in middle-aged white women. Jeff had given Grant the news outside the bus. He told him they wouldn't be coming to watch the championship, after all. And Grant knew for the first time that it was serious. "I need to stay with Mom," his father said.

The caravan—eight buses, three vans, a semi-trailer, a fifth-wheel, dozens of decorated cars—pulled out from the high school onto County Road 20, where it was joined by a police cruiser and fire truck, lights flashing and sirens spinning. The procession traveled slowly past the nearly deserted Concord Mall, where lighted signboards in front of Arby's and Taco Bell wished them luck, past churches and convenience stores, past El Paraiso grocery store and its handwritten Spanish signs, past the shade trees screening the Mennonite Seminary. Houses thinned and gave way to industrial parks. Oversize warehouses for the RV industry sat squat and square behind tall chain-link fences, bathed in the orange glow of sodium-vapor light. Near the township line, the first farmland opened up, dark in the flatness, and the caravan turned down County Road 19. The cruiser and the fire truck pulled off onto the shoulder at the cloverleaf entrance to the I-80/90 bypass. The buses honked and kept going. Inside them, kids flashed green and white lights and hung crepe paper, and the buses pointed south, toward Indianapolis.

13 ★ Swing, Swing, Swing

The upperclassmen had been there before, but not enough to get used to it. They stood in front of the immense west entrance of the RCA Dome and felt awe. A thirty-foot-tall poster of local hero Edgerrin James, running back for the Indianapolis Colts, rippled down one of the wide concrete pillars. The poster captured James running full tilt over the same field that the Concord students would soon step onto in search of their own moment of glory. Above the splash of color loomed the nineteen-story stadium, the gray colossus near the heart of Indiana's capital city.

The scale was so unlike anything back home in Elkhart that some of the kids gaped up at it with mouths open. And to know they weren't merely spectators, but belonged there, their arrival at one of the great doors in the Dome's side officially anticipated, invested them with pride and accomplishment even before the competition began.

Their caravan of buses had passed the building's main entrance on the way in from the dawn practice at Ben Davis. Students had seen the line for tickets snaking nearly halfway around the Dome before angling back again. By now, the doors were opened and the line was moving quickly. The first band of the day wouldn't start playing for another ninety minutes, but the competition for the best seats had already started.

In loose ranks, the band followed Pat Doherty and the other drum majors up a long ramp and stood at the entrance to Hall F. An enormous overhead door had been lifted partway for them. Standing erect in their gold-braided uniforms and their white-plumed shakos, they looked like a small battalion of soldiers massing before the gate of a gray fortress. ISSMA officials in red sweatshirts and orange vests held the group briefly at the door, checking watches. At precisely 9:03, the officials waved Max and the drum majors inside. Pat Doherty and Amanda Bechtel smiled as they filed past. Behind them, many of the faces entering the arena appeared nervous, or afraid, or focused.

Climbing the ramp, Adilene Corona bit her lower lip and blinked back tears. The morning's practice at Ben Davis had gone badly for her. She'd missed chart changes she'd made consistently for weeks. Early in "Gabriel's Oboe," she'd discovered herself out of step without a clue how it had happened, and she'd just plain forgotten to think about spacing. Once again Mr. Jones had called out her mistakes. Before she boarded the bus for the drive to the Dome, Steve Peterson clasped her shoulders and told her not to worry, to remember to breathe, that she knew the show, she'd do fine. But now that she was here, Adilene wondered how that would be possible.

The practice at Ben Davis had been disastrous for others besides Adilene. They'd run through the show twice, and played scared both times. Entire sections missed their marks; the tempo, again, fell apart at crucial moments throughout the show. "You're already letting the place overwhelm you," Max told them.

Inside the Dome, in the fluorescent light of a cavernous function room, the Marching Minutemen had twenty-four minutes to stretch and loosen up and another twenty-four minutes to rehearse the music one last time, somehow forget the morning's mistakes, and find whatever greatness they had inside them. On the other side of a portable dividing wall, the Jasper Marching Wildcats, the second-biggest Class B band in the finals, started their music warm-up. People who knew bands around the state often mentioned Jasper and Concord together, pairing them for their directors' high musical standards and willingness to attempt complex scores in their shows. Both bands had performed Leonard Bernstein's *Mass*, Aaron Copland's *Appalachian Spring*, and operas in the Dome. But where Max pushed the envelope of a tradition he loved, James Goodhue, the Jasper director, pushed against a tradition he didn't much care for. Goodhue would have preferred to set up his musicians in traditional concert formation and let them play beautiful music for a willing audience. He understood, though, that even in a state that supported music education as well as Indiana did, he wasn't going to get fifteen thousand people to listen to his band play, say, the music of iconoclastic American composer Samuel Barber. But he could trick them into hearing Barber, anyway, as long as he added color guard and drill.

Jasper's entire program that year was Barber's "Second Essay for Orchestra"—a little-known composition that a season-ticket holder might not hear over five seasons at the Chicago Symphony. Plenty of Jasper band parents could hum the whole piece from memory. A lush woodwind sound rose over the thin divide between the two bands, a full sound the likes of which Concord had not encountered in competition all season.

The Concord sections drilled one last time on placing heels first, guiding down a diagonal, twisting torsos to play to the box—the consistent marching problems in the Concord show. The trumpets and the trombones sang their parts. An ISSMA official, watching for possible rulebook infractions, made sure none of them put a horn to his lips for even a single note. Band moms wearing fanny packs stuffed with supplies flitted among the moving students like tick-birds tending to a herd of rhinos. A mom fell in step behind a student who was marching backward and unzipped the back of his jacket. Changing direction as he did, she reached in, tightened each shoulder strap with a practiced yank, and zipped him back up. She gave him a little pat on the back to let him know she was done and moved on, tucking stray hair up under a shako here, pulling up the back of a jacket to rearrange a cummerbund there.

Grant Longenbaugh walked over to one of the band moms to get some water. He gulped down two half-size bottles from her backpack. A few minutes later, he left the high-brass warm-up for more water. But even after guzzling another cup, his mouth and tongue remained dry, and he knew he must be nervous. He was aware that part of what he was feeling had to do with the news of his mother's cancer. But he pushed his feelings down, and focused on the one thing in front of him.

Drum major Jeremy Parker came over to him and asked if they could pray together. The two found some space between the moving sections. Jeremy, who planned a career as a youth pastor, slung an arm around Grant's shoulders, closed his eyes, and prayed, "God, please give Grant peace. I can't imagine how hard it would be not to have your parents here, your senior year, at state." It was the last thing Grant wanted to hear. And at that moment, he didn't want to take the praying seriously. He said, "We're all anxious and nervous. But we know this show. God, let us kick everyone's butts."

Scott Spradling gathered the high brass around him for some last-minute advice and wisdom. Music pounded through the wall from the Jasper band, so loud that only the students pressed in closest to Spradling could catch more than a few words at a time. A thunderous final drumroll ended in silence, and suddenly the high brass could hear Spradling saying, ". . . and that's what it's all about."

But he went on. He said, "You're one of the best bands I've ever had." The high-brass director had wanted to say this to his section for some time now. His relentless pushing made it seem as if he shared Max's negative perception of the seniors and the band, but in fact he believed that Max had misread the band, and that his insistence on perfection may have kept them from getting the most out of that group of kids.

"You're already one of the best bands in the state," he told them. "You could be number one in the state. Don't think you have to do something superhuman. All you have to do is what you've done all those times it's been almost perfect." Who knew if they could hear him, or if it was too late? He said, again, "It doesn't have to be perfect."

They set up for their run-through in wide arcs. It was their one chance that day to blend sound as a concert band. Max had a checklist of issues to focus on, but when he climbed a couple of steps on the portable podium, his megaphone in one hand, and looked out at them, he changed his mind about the list. For nearly forty years, he'd stood in front of bands in the last moments before a state finals performance. He could sense fear or panic; he knew when to soothe or encourage. There had been years when a band had faded in the final days before the championship and had to be reinfused with energy. A year earlier, standing possibly in that same spot, Max had seen a band that was spinning off its axis and needed him to center it. Everywhere he looked now, though, he saw serious expressions and determined faces. Going over the list, at last, would be extraneous. "I'd tell you to be focused," he said, "but you already are."

The sound overwhelmed the small space and carried back over the divide to the Northridge band, next in line. The drummers led them into "Swing, Swing, Swing," and it sounded like the Paramount Theatre in 1937, like the dance had already started. The students in the band whooped and hollered as they had been taught, but the mood was so infectious, so real, and the release of all that killer-diller nervousness so welcome, that many of the parents watching, and Bryan Golden and Amy Davis, even a couple of the ISSMA guys, whooped along with them. Max refrained from yelling, but his left knee was popping like crazy, and his grin couldn't have been wider.

Max's last words to them before they moved into position for the field were nothing about winning, nothing about their competitors, nothing about a dynasty. He stepped back onto the podium, just high enough to see the faces of the students packed in tightly around him. He started quietly, conversationally, as he had in a hundred practices that season. "You know what they say," he said. "Third time's the charm. We had our first show over at Ben Davis. It was pretty good. But, you weren't in charge." Then, referring to what they'd all just heard, he said, "*That* show was incredible. Now it's time for the charm. When we go in there, it's just a carpet. It's our practice field. It's yours. It's yours for the taking. Give it everything you've got."

After weeks of missing with the band, of not knowing how to motivate his students, of not recognizing how he undercut some of his best leaders, he had regained his balance. He didn't go on too long. If anything, some of the newer parents were surprised by how little he said, and by his matter-of-fact tone.

"Take the show," he said. "Line up." The students cheered and some pumped fists in the air, hardly aware that Max, efficient as always, had already put them into motion toward the air lock.

The pit carts and the four drumsets led the way. The band dads guiding the carts were nervous. At the beginning of the summer, before band camp had started, back when Jim Faigh had believed they could work ahead of Max and avoid last-minute scrambling, he and another band dad had driven to Indianapolis expressly to measure the two doors between the warm-up room and the air lock. He couldn't have guessed then that there would be no roots among the props, and that they'd have drumsets whose covers had yet to work properly. Faigh wrung his hands and worried out loud.

The carts slipped through the first doors with an inch on either side, the blue fabric billowing in the rush of air that met them. The band dads gave a small hurrah. A small hurrah, though, because directly ahead of them was the second, smaller door. If you looked at eye level, you could see clearly that the drumset was much too wide—by a good half foot on either side of the door. But the dads weren't looking at the fabric covering. They were looking down at the carts, and smiling. There was no clearance to speak of, but the carts could slide through. One dad slowly nudged the first one through the door while another felt through the fabric for the drumset frames, and squeezed. "It's why we made 'em flexible!" one cried.

The band was so big that Max had to turn the ranks in a tight U to get everyone inside the dimly lit tunnel. Another door opened, and air roared past them, loud as a jet engine: the sound of the giant fans that kept the Dome's canvas roof inflated. Kids tried to slide hands under their shakos to cover their ears. Two solidly built men walked through the tunnel without acknowledging any of them. Football equipment and duffel bags bearing the Colts' blue horseshoes were briefly visible through the door, reminders of whose house this really was. The Colts would play Jacksonville the next day in front of nearly sixty thousand spectators.

They reached the massive folding doors that opened out from the tunnel onto the floor of the Dome. On the other side, the Jasper musicians played Barber while the color guard, bright in yellow velour cat-suits, danced and threw flags high into the air. Jasper had come in second to Concord the previous year by less than a point. A tiny plexi-glass window, less than a foot square, gave the closest students a view of the vast curved ceiling. The day before, Steve Peterson had prepared students in the woodwind section for the moment they'd see it. "I want you to look up at the ceiling," he'd told them. "Every performance that has ever been given in the Dome is up there under the roof. Last year's championship show is up there. Yours will be, too."

And then it was their turn.

The doors opened, folding back against the sides of the tunnel. The Concord students walked slowly forward. Their eyes were drawn up the steep blue walls of seats, up to the gray billowing ceiling. It was impossible to resist staring up into it. It arched over them like heaven itself.

One of the Concord parents had hung a sign from a railing high up on the far side. It said, "We love you, Concord!" Loud cheers swept down from the crowd that filled row upon row of seats.

The impossibly bright green turf confirmed where they were and reminded them of what they had come to do. It grounded them. Each wave of students went through a similar progression from awe to focus as they emerged from the tunnel. For some, the sequence went quickly. Others seemed stuck to the spot where they had looked up and had to be prodded along or hugged and brought back to their shared purpose. The first of them made their way around to the back sideline.

Up in the stands, Leandra Beabout and her parents sat with Keith Yoder, who had met them in the long line for tickets and offered to find them good seats and guide them through their first state finals. They were right on the fifty-yard line, about halfway between the field and the press box. "Best seats in the house," Keith assured them.

Leandra was there to watch her sister Kelsey, a freshman in the flute section, as well as to watch Grant. During the season, her sister had complained when Leandra talked about the band at the dinner table, or that Leandra went to Grant's parties when she wasn't even in the band. Leandra understood her sister's irritation: She hadn't learned to march, couldn't play an instrument, and wasn't down on the field getting ready to lay it out there in front of thousands of people. Still, Leandra had been to enough practices and competitions during the season to know the trouble spots. She'd seen the show come together. Band had also given Leandra a group of friends. When she walked down the halls now, in a school that had been a foreign place a year earlier, kids in the band raised their hands in greeting and smiled at her. At lunch, she often joined Grant at the band table.

Until today, however, she hadn't fully comprehended the world that Grant and her sister entered when they competed. She'd watched only two bands so far, but already she realized that everybody there in that enormous indoor stadium—the thousands of spectators, the teenagers marching on the field below her—cared passionately about marching band.

It didn't matter to her that all this passion was happening at ten o'clock on a Saturday morning, inside a concrete stadium with a huge white football helmet painted in the middle of the performance field, with banners for the Indiana Dairy Farmers hanging all over the place. Or that a new band was trotted out every thirteen minutes. The production-line feel and the location and the time of day fought each other, robbed the event of some of its glamour, like holding prom at breakfast.

She knew, too, that although the Concord cheering section was one of the biggest that morning, maybe the biggest among the ten Class B finalists, if the football team or the basketball team came down to Indianapolis to compete for a state title at the Dome, the stands would be swamped by Concord students, Concord teachers, Concord parents, truly the whole community. None of that mattered to Leandra, though. She felt part of something big.

She picked out Grant down in front, doing his sound check. She and Keith yelled together, "Go, Grant!" Grant looked up and waved vaguely into the stands, as if he wasn't sure who'd called his name.

Above where Keith and Leandra were sitting, Gavin Jones had run ahead of his mother and eighty-three-year-old grandmother to save them the best seats in the house—he'd assured them—right on the fifty-yard line as high up in the stands as they could get before reaching the press-box overhang. His father had taught him that this was the closest way to see a performance the way a judge would see it: the best mix of sound, the best overview of forms on the field. Anne Longenbaugh, who'd driven down from Purdue with him that morning, helped spread coats over seats for Gavin's family and for George and Shirley Dyer.

Gavin, who had been raised with the Concord band, had come to state finals every year of his life, often for all four classes. When he was little, his mother had occupied him during the fourteen-hour days with Ziploc bags filled with Cheerios, crackers, crayons, toys. He'd been on the field with his dad to hear Concord win its first state championship, and had also watched as they fell just short—all before he started high school. He'd wanted desperately to be one of his father's champions, but during his four years playing trumpet at Concord, the band had never placed higher than third. More than once during those years, he'd begged his father to play the game to win. Gavin had absorbed his father's approach and biases from the beginning, but it had taken him a while longer to appreciate his father's higher goals.

Normally, Concord's third position was not considered a good slot in the line-up. It was always better to go late in the program, ideally last. The judges, then, wouldn't be tempted to hold back from giving high scores in case something better came along. But it was also helpful to perform right after your biggest competitor, at least if you were better. Following Jasper might have been the best thing that could have happened for Concord that morning. Gavin was pleased when the Jasper show seemed flat.

All around him, he heard the Concord call-and-response—"Give me a C!" "C!" "Give me an O!"—and he saw his father striding across the field below them for the last time.

"Our next band in Class B is the Concord Community High School Marching Minutemen." The announcer's booming introduction ricocheted around the stadium.

Musicians and dancers took their places. Grant walked slowly to his spot and kneeled on the AstroTurf, surrounded by the other trumpets. He leaned forward until his head nearly touched the ground, and breathed out. Amanda stood in front of the wide-limbed tree. Its African sun glowed behind her in bands of tan and orange, the African sky a brilliant indigo. Her flute hung at her side, inside a linen sheath sewn by one of the band moms. She bent her head and waited.

The stands fell silent. The announcer gave them their final cue. "Drum majors, the field is yours for state finals performance." They'd heard nearly the same sentence in every contest that season. Now, however, honoring the achievement of making it all the way to state finals, "performance" took the place of "competition."

The timpani rumbled. Amanda glided toward the arc of blue and orange tarp at the front of the field, circling Jon Faloon, who cradled the djembe. Flutes and clarinets emerged behind them in curving lines, bringing the roots forward. On either side of the tree, trumpets, tubas, trombones slowly rose to full height and reached for the sky, spread their arms wide, brought palms together.

Amanda lifted her flute. She was ready, eager, unafraid. She felt no nervousness, only pleasure and the desire to play for all the people gathered there. The melody flowed freely from her, notes and rhythms changing as the music welled up inside. Jon beat out a rhythm on the djembe that moved to either side of Amanda's notes as she had weaved around him. Behind them, dancers swayed, unwrapped scarves from around their arms and held them out like gossamer purple wings. And then the flute was soaring above the other instruments, like a nightingale, an aria, the hymn above the thunder.

The solo ended, and Amanda became the point where two lines of flutes converged. She stepped back and was swept into the moving line, and immediately blended in with the rest of the band. Now the field became a kaleidoscope of forms that curved and merged and reshaped. Like clouds across a summer sky, the band flowed into circles, flowers, a humpbacked animal with an arched neck and long tail, an eye, all curves in motion. Diana and Adilene marched side by side through Charts 9, 10, anchoring a long arc just behind the pit, near the forty-yard line. Diana was ready to call out a warning or a reminder as needed, but the freshman was hitting all her step-offs, all her chart changes. They came to the tough one, Chart 11, and Adilene played the notes just as they'd practiced so many times, big-small-big. She strayed toward the clarinet on her other side, and Diana called out, "Stay close to me!" Adilene stepped back into position, kept going. Diana kept playing and watching, too preoccupied to notice the blossoming next to her.

The music rose, fell back, and rose further, like swells growing before the tide. The seconds and thirds added their voices. The flugelhorns sounded their eighth note. The rich, deep chords that Max had tried to draw out of them all season now filled the Dome. Four descending notes—the product of at least a thousand collective hours of work on accents, dynamics, phrasing, tone, breathing—led to one final sustained note. Every horn, every bell pointed up. The final chord vibrated, shimmered, became almost visible.

From the moment Pat Doherty had turned and faced the band, Nick's eyes hadn't left Pat's face. They'd stayed locked on Pat all during "Gabriel's Oboe," even during the drumline's exile to outer Siberia between the twenty-yard line and the back hash mark. Nick had felt the two of them moving the band, together, toward that shimmering ending. Pat broke into a smile, and Nick felt himself smiling as well. They rolled into "Africa." The uncanny sensation of being locked together continued. Nick could feel the tempo inside him and could hear it coming from him. He could see it as Pat conducted it. It seemed to him that he could edge it faster or slow it down at will, and Pat would know what he was doing as he did it. The drumline returned to its place of exile on the field, to the place where they'd lost the tempo more times than Nick ever wanted to count. And they were by it. Not even a wobble. Nick's smile turned into a grin. He saw that Pat was grinning, too. He didn't know who was responding to whom, but it didn't matter. His grin widened. Man, had he worked long and hard. But it was worth it. Every bit of it was worth this shared feeling.

Grant felt the momentum building. All around him the long snaking lines of "Africa" dissolved and re-formed seamlessly into two blocks. He sensed the change in himself, saw it mirrored in the faces under the white-plumed hats going by him. Relief had replaced tension and was easing into something that looked like delight. Now they were ready for the funeral, and he would lead them there.

He heeled-and-toed toward the middle of the field, skirting the Colts helmet. Brent Lehman moved along with him just off his shoulder. One beat, two beats. Grant broke out of the marching step and into a stroll. Amanda held the last note of her reprise, and Grant slid in under her, in the slow, mournful notes of "A Closer Walk with Thee." He stepped into the middle of the fifty and laid back into a yearning blues he felt he understood, despite being a white boy from northern Indiana.

> Just a closer walk with Thee,
> Grant it, Jesus, is my plea.

He and the Dixieland ensemble played it like no hymn Grant had ever heard at stodgy St. Vincent's or at Nappanee. They played it like countless New Orleans musicians had, full of soul and sweetness; they played it like Ella Fitzgerald sang it at Duke Ellington's funeral. Grant added grit. He smeared. He scooped. He missed a note, but he didn't care.

His prayer was simple: *O God, please let my mother live.*

> Daily walking close to Thee,
> Let it be, dear Lord, let it be.

He heard the applause that audiences always give soloists, even bad ones. There was a glitch with the banjo: Matt Tompkins, under a sound-system curse at the Dome, had neglected some step in his sound-check, and might as well have been playing air banjo. It didn't matter.

They moved into the faster, syncopated rhythm of "Saints," starting the celebration after the funeral. Grant heard scattered cheers, and then a noise he'd never heard in the Dome before. Clapping, in unison. It was as if all the people who'd paid twelve bucks a ticket were thrilled to recognize a song and joined in.

> O Lord I want to be in that number
> When the saints go marching in.

The color guard twirled black umbrellas over their heads and sauntered between fast-moving rows of musicians. In the clarinets, Diana de la Reza stopped playing and kept one of her other freshmen in line, shopping-carting her through the maze of Dixieland. Brent Lehman shouted out the counter-melody. Everyone was moving faster, playing faster. Grant could feel energy ripple up into the audience and back down to the floor. They rocked the house. Up in the stands, in one of the swaths of Concord green, Anne Longenbaugh held out a cell phone so Chris and Jeff could hear the ruckus from home.

The rest of the show was a romp. The crowd cheered again when the disguised drumset covers—finally, almost miraculously—fell in unison for "Swing, Swing, Swing." Jim Faigh and the other band dads pumped their fists from the sideline benches. The driving beat passed seamlessly between the drumsets and the bass drums barreling toward the front. Brandon Dascoli, who had marched a great show, stood behind Nick and pounded on the tenor drums. Anybody noticing him for the first time would never guess how close he'd come to being pulled from the show. The drum-break came, and in the flashing of drumsticks and that unstoppable Krupa beat, it happened. The drummers leaping between piled-up bass drums, the drummers on the shiny blue drumsets, the tenors behind—each heard the whole as one. The entire drumline locked.

The saxophones came in, the high brass, 41 clarinets, 29 flutes, 8 tubas, kids in size 50 uniforms, weak marchers, timid freshmen, sullen pit crew, the seconds and thirds—243 Concord High School Marching Minutemen joined the party. The crowd cheered right through the drum break and the crashing waves of trombones on the shore of the sideline and the screaming high notes of the trumpets. After the last note, Grant punched the air with his instrument and held the pose, sweating and breathing hard. He was aware of dirty marching here and there, and some forms that hadn't quite meshed. But he knew they'd played their hearts out. It was the best performance they'd given that year, the best performance in all his four years. Grant looked up and saw thousands of people in that partisan crowd rising to their feet, standing for the Concord show. It was enough to make him think maybe they'd win after all.

Leandra had leaned forward on her seat during the entire performance. She'd teared up listening to "Gabriel's Oboe." Her heart had ached while Grant played his solo, and tears had filled her eyes again at the end as she rose to her feet along with everyone else. Keith had been moved as well. When it was over and the band had filed off the field, he said, "I have nothing to say." A few seconds later, he repeated, "I have nothing to say."

Gavin hadn't seen the show since the summer, and he was blown away by it. Of the dozens and dozens of shows he'd watched in the Dome over the years, not one topped what he'd just witnessed. But he'd also grown up hearing his father say, We control our performance; the judges control the score.

Down the row, Gavin's grandmother called her son on his cell phone. On the other side of the stadium, over the crackle of static, Max heard, ". . . incredible!"

Walking around to their seats on the back side of the field, the Concord students held an impromptu celebration. "We did it!" kids shouted. "We won!" The other shows passed in a blur of euphoria and nervous anticipation. While they were settling into their block of grandstand seats on the backside of the field, their families and friends across the stadium cheered for neighboring Northridge. Two bands later, Greenwood gave its usual highly polished performance. Cameron noticed how conservative the drill was, that the marchers kept to the middle of the field. "Look," he said to his neighbor, "they're blocked twenty-five to twenty-five." Other bands came on, exited; the Concord students applauded each performance, excitement growing. Then they saw Northview.

Marching ninth out of the ten bands that morning, Northview put on a startlingly different show. Based on the movie *The Matrix*, the show's heavily themed spectacle showcased a top-notch color guard and drum-corps–style choreography. Its black trench coats and edgy, atmospheric music were the dark to Concord's light. One of the Concord drummers saw trench coats on the Northview drumline and complained, "That's cheating—the judges can't see their feet." Up in the cheering section, Leandra said to Keith, "It's cool."

"Yeah, but it's not hard," Keith said.

But everyone saw it was clean.

When it was all over, the ten finalists returned to the field and lined up in the order they'd performed. The crowd, there to see a champion crowned, stayed in its seats. During the brisk countdown, Grant stood at the end of a row in the trumpet section, scanning the Dome. He found Anne sitting with other band alums in the Concord cheering section. Seeing her made him suddenly more hopeful.

The names ticked down to eighth, seventh. Nick stood in the middle of the snares, his championship ring from the year before tucked in an inner pocket, for luck. Sixth. Half the trophies (the smallest ones) that had lined tables near the fifty-yard line now stood arrayed and accounted for in front of five sets of drum majors. Fifth. A woman representing the Indiana Dairy Farmers took the caps off six small bottles of milk, each decorated with a single note of music. Someone whispered to Brent that Mr. Golden had crossed his fingers behind his back. Fourth: Greenwood. Third. The Concord lines tensed, held one breath. It was Jasper! Now it was down to two: Concord and Northview. Two strong programs, run by two long-time, revered directors. Two electrifying performances, two shows that couldn't have been more different.

The announcer started in on a long preamble, his syntax as muddy as the Dome's acoustics—"An end comes to all things, and let's give a well-deserved recognition to this year's outstanding runner-up . . ."—and then paused. In the reverberating echoes that passed for silence in the Dome, in some confluence of acoustics and community, thousands of dreams and untold hours of work and love squeezed into a single moment. Grant barely caught the announcer's next words. "The 2004 runner-up in Class B is Concord. . . ."

Grant felt the air leave him. In the vacuum, he felt crushing disappointment. But also, a sense of confirmation. He knew they'd waited too long to want to win—waited, in fact, until the last possible moment. No matter how hard they'd tried out there that morning, all the other days of holding back still showed. Grant's first complete thought was *I have no regrets*, followed by *Two's still pretty dang good*. It was only when he saw so many others crying, including some whose tears surprised him, that he felt anger. *Why are they crying now?*

Diana stood motionless in line with the clarinets, tears tracking down both cheeks. Adilene cried out of relief and exhaustion, and because she'd wanted to win for Diana. Brent cried, not ready to stop trying. Nick, who had wanted to win for so long and with such passion, stood stoically, surprised that his elation from the show held even as he heard the Northview Marching Knights announced as the number one band in Class B. He held his jawbone parallel to the ground, his chin high, his eyes ahead. The Concord way.

The finalists exited the Dome in the order of their final placement. While the Concord students waited their turn, Max taught them one last move. "We're gonna go out of here in style," he said with a sly grin. He called for the snappy roll-off to "Li'l Liza Jane," and told the band to break out their party poses for eight counts, wave to the stands for eight counts, then fall into the regular cadence, and heel-and-toe on out of there. The smiles looked forced as the drums started up, but the beat was irresistible. Even before they turned off the turf, many of the faces had lightened. It was a classy exit, made even classier by stopping in front of Northview, the new state champions, so the Concord drum majors could shake the hands of their counterparts. Max and Bob Medworth did the same.

The band stalled in the stuffy, close air lock for the east entrance. Heavy rain and cold winds raked the outside of the Dome. Grant allowed a band mom to take his trumpet from him. Another helped him pull a plastic poncho over his uniform. He said thank you but didn't register their extra tenderness. He tucked his trumpet under one arm, under his poncho, and followed the others outside.

Parents and families, friends and former band members lined the walkway to Pan Am Plaza, applauding as the band sloshed past them. Water ran off their umbrellas in torrents. Grant heard "Good job! Go, Concord!" but the words didn't cheer him. For more than a decade, Max had walked his bands across Capitol Street from the Dome to the brick-laid terrace to wrap up the marching season with a few words and one last performance. An unusually big crowd huddled together in the driving rain. People had been calling the music office for weeks, wanting to know if this was Max's last state finals, and wanting to be there if it was. Shirley Dyer, answering the phones, couldn't tell them what she knew, and nothing was definite yet. Still, many sensed that they were seeing the passing of an era. Some of Gavin's and Anne's classmates had flown in from around the country for the reunion. A few former students from Winchester had made the trip as well, even though their time with Max Jones had ended more than thirty years before.

Grant found his sister and hugged her. A straight shooter as always, she told him, Northview deserved to win. They were cleaner. And then she was gone, off to greet friends.

Leandra had come out of the Dome expecting the world to be different somehow, the city buzzing with news of the finals. She looked for Grant in the plaza. She wasn't normally effusive, but when she found him, she immediately launched into how much she'd loved the show. She almost told him how proud of him she'd felt, but fell silent when he responded with single words, seeming distracted, even angry.

All Grant wanted, right then, was to see his parents. He ached to hug them.

Max stepped up onto a cement apron with his portable megaphone in hand, his coat rain-darkened at the shoulders. Someone tried to hold an umbrella over his head, but he waved it away. "Look around this plaza," he told the students assembled below him. "This is what it's all about. Look at all the people who supported this band." Then he spoke to the parents. "Obviously, all of you adults know, it was the process of getting here today, it wasn't the placement. You also know—and the kids know—they gave the performance of their lives." He turned back to his band. "You need to know what you really did out there. You need to be really proud of it."

He quickly summarized the judging. There was no reason to linger; no lessons needed to be wrung from the numbers for the coming week. Concord had come in third in music and third in marching, in both categories behind Northview and Jasper. "But we were first—big-time—in GE," the general effect category. One of the GE judges had given them the single highest score of the contest.

Later, parents congratulated Max on his positive take on the finish and the season. Gavin, watching alongside his mother, saw something different. He saw his father, gray-haired, wet, being true once again to the educational experience of marching band. *You learned. This was your chance. Here's what you did with it.* More than that, Gavin sensed his father's deep emotions. He was bidding farewell to the

Dome, to the tribe, to the work that had been at the center of his world for forty years.

Max cued the drum majors to lead a reprise of "Swing, Swing, Swing." It was a chance for all in the band to play simply for the love of the music and the community surrounding them. "C'mon, make some noise out there!" Max shouted as the killer-diller beat started. And they did, swinging one more time together. Trumpets grabbed the chance to play those rapid runs without worrying about messing up. Grant could lay back and play without leading, without obligation. But the notes stayed locked in his throat.

The celebration and the season ended there, in the cold rain. The families drifted away. Indiana's 2004 Class B runners-up slogged back toward the buses. Grant lagged behind, wandered around the plaza. He didn't know what he was waiting for, or even that he was waiting. When he saw Max turn to leave, he started running.

Max didn't see him coming, just felt Grant charge into him. The best student leader Max Jones had ever had wrapped his arms around the slight director and slumped against him. Max, taken by surprise, caught a glimpse of Grant's red-rimmed eyes and quivering chin before he was hugging him, holding him up. Grant laid his head on the older man's shoulder and cried.

The rain streamed down. "Thanks," Grant managed. He held on.

Max had received thousands of hugs from band kids over the decades, but never one quite like this. Later, he would remember what he thought in the next moment: *That felt like an end-of-the-world hug.*

Too soon, Grant felt a loosening on Max's part, a telegraphing of discomfort and then a more direct *let's get going* squeeze, and he understood: The rest of the band was getting too far ahead, the buses needed to be loaded, there was the drive to Kokomo, the stop at White Castle. Grant wheeled away. The clear plastic of his poncho clung to his wet uniform. A gust of wind pulled the plastic free and filled it. For a moment, it looked like the outstretched wings of a large bird that had mistaken the plaza that dark afternoon for a refuge. Grant strode through the puddles toward the buses, alone.

14 ★ Where Is Your God?

The Marching Minutemen returned to Concord with a trophy that was two inches shorter than the one they'd brought home the year before. A couple of years earlier, many of the same students and parents had been thrilled to call themselves runners-up and to bring home the band's first banner in eight years. But the hope, the promise, and ultimately the challenge of the 2004 marching season had revolved around winning again—building a Concord dynasty, brick by brick. Grant held one last post-contest party at his house. Chris Longenbaugh was determined to honor her vision of Grant's final season, even though it now seemed unspeakably distant. She tried to extract what sweetness she could from the moment. She carried two trays of Blizzards down to a subdued group in their renovated basement.

In his theory class on Monday, Steve Peterson gave up trying to teach his students, all but one of them in the band, how to notate major and minor keys. Some of the students were adamant that Concord had been robbed of its title, that the judging must have been rigged, or incompetent. Peterson finally said, "You sound really sore, but you don't know what you're talking about." He turned to the whiteboard and quickly wrote out their new lesson for the day:

1. They're a really good band.
2. You're a really good band.
3. It's out of your hands.
4. You rocked the house.

A kid who had played tuba in the band said, as if in response, "Yeah, but now I'm just another student."

Each student reacted differently to the end of the season. Brandon Dascoli, who had been as hard to reach in music theory as in the drumline, entered the class that day with a smile. For possibly the first time all trimester, he raised his hand to answer one of Peterson's questions. He seemed to be on a new trajectory. Jon Faloon put his head on his desk and kept his eyes closed for most of the class.

Max heard from his share of people who were shocked that Concord hadn't won. His first assistant at Concord, Gay Burton, who had started Concord's jazz program, e-mailed Max that she'd listened to the show from the stands and was amazed that he'd been able to get almost 250 kids to play swing style. "They play better than some college jazz bands," she wrote. Over the following weeks and months, people in the band world—directors, parents, teenagers—would dissect the Concord show the same way Hoosier football fans endlessly discussed Notre Dame's recent upset of Michigan or the chance that a Purdue Boilermaker quarterback might actually win the Heisman Trophy. Parents and students wished online and in print that their bands could play such entertaining music. Directors shook their heads over how Max had managed to have it both ways, earning points for his show's march through American music while getting everyone—even judges— to tap their toes and clap along. It appeared that once again a Max Jones show had changed the way people thought about marching band.

Max and the rest of the Concord staff performed their own dissection of the season. In many respects it had been a repeat of '93. In spite of Max's warnings on the first day of full camp, too many students had possibly been content with *having won* the state championship; they knew only too well how hard they'd have to work to keep winning, and chose not to. Max had been warned by his first principal at Winchester that it was harder to win the second time. Because his Winchester band had gone ahead and won, and kept winning, Max hadn't fully appreciated that wisdom at the time. He'd learned the lesson since then, but he'd truly believed that in the Class of 2005 he'd found the critical mass of students who were willing to work hard enough to begin a new dynasty.

He looked at the Class of 2005 again. Now he saw them as nice kids, especially nice kids—but not special. Not enough of them had stepped forward to lead and motivate the rest of the band. Before the start of the season, Max had identified students in the baritones, tubas, clarinets, and saxophones he thought had the ability, the charisma, and the desire to become strong section leaders. In every case, he'd been disappointed. The large group of committed seniors—half a dozen, a dozen, more—that he'd envisioned at the start of the year had never materialized.

Some other students, not the class's strongest musicians or marchers, had nonetheless contributed where they could. Diana de la Reza had made exactly the sort of commitment to her pod of weak beginners that Max had hoped all the seniors would make. Her heroism of the everyday, the heroism of seemingly small acts that change lives, had embodied every important principle and value in Max's system. That week, a band dad showed Max a picture of her crying after the announcement at state finals. Max commented, "She earned those tears. She's one of the only ones who did."

As the sole senior in the trombones, Brent Lehman had been given a difficult leadership challenge. Max had half-expected Brent to complain and lose his temper: It was how Brent had acted the previous year, it was how his brother had acted before him. But Brent had continually impressed Max with his work ethic and his humility. Max's disappointment in the trombone section focused more on the juniors, whom he'd expected to help Brent much more than they had.

Nick Stubbs had come through in the end, but Max had needed to push him hard to become the leader he'd needed. Max would say to Nick, in the coming weeks, "Nice job—the last month," leaving Nick feeling as if he'd just received a final jab from his director.

And Grant. Grant had done everything Max asked a leader to do. He'd served his section selflessly, from the first day of band camp to the final ride home on the trumpet bus. He'd taught with knowledge and humor. He'd shown extraordinary patience with the beginners, with the sophomores who followed him like puppies as they learned to lead, with the juniors who left the leading to others, with the awkward seniors who didn't play or march that well but craved a way to make a difference, with the dos amigos who'd been good leaders in the old mold. He'd never complained. He'd taken care of business, he'd taken care of the least of these, the seconds and thirds, he'd led from behind. And he'd done all this under the difficult circumstances of family illness and depression. Grant had done everything for his band except light a fire under it.

But maybe that's what the band had needed most. The year before, Evan Jarvis had provided the spark. Max had hoped that Cameron Bradley would play that leading role in 2004, had assumed that Cameron and Grant would form a team and a plan, create something even better, now that they were seniors. Unaware of Cameron's silent rebellion, Max couldn't understand why Cameron hadn't stood out on the practice field on some Wednesday night when the band wasn't paying attention and used one of the dumb jokes he was known for to get them fired up to work. Max only knew that it hadn't happened.

Maybe the nice Class of 2005 had needed a spark in the form of a different kind of rebel. The former director at national champion Center Grove, Tom Dirks, had kept an eye out for rule-breakers and rebels because he often found his most outstanding leaders among them. When he succeeded in rechanneling their troublemaking impulses into the band, they became the catalysts for greatness. Max could have used some of the volatile, creative energy he felt least comfortable with.

Was it possible that Max had simply overreached? Had he picked the wrong hand to shoot the moon with?

There was another possibility, another way to look at what had happened. It was the wrinkle at the center of Grant's attempted legacy, and to some extent, of Max's as well. There hadn't been enough people motivated by just doing the right thing, either by Max Jones's lights or by God's.

As he'd done with every other authority figure in his young life, Grant had taken Max's system, its goals, and its challenges completely to heart. To him, what Max wanted the program to be, and to honor, was the acting out of faith in the world.

Grant had been able to lead, to do the work that Max's system and his own understanding of living out one's faith required—in spite of everything—because he'd internalized the principles guiding him. Grant understood that Max Jones's system gave the students at Concord the opportunity to win. He'd believed that if the students in the band practiced the Sermon on the Mount on the marching field, they would be Max's champions and Champions for Christ, both. He had believed that whoever would be first must serve. He had wanted to serve, and to win.

But it's hard to do what Jesus would do. It's hard to know what those actions are, in the first place. And even when they seem clear, as they had to Grant, it's hard to carry them out. It's hard as a parent to give children full-hearted love and attention; hard to love family and friends without expectation or strings; harder still to take care of the least among us in all their sad profusion of trouble and want and need. And if you're a teenager, worried about how you fit in and who you are, how much harder is it to see the glory in taking care of people who are (pick your category) dumber, uglier, slower, poorer, less talented, less popular, less coordinated than you are? How much harder, even if you're only being asked to stretch yourself over a fourteen-week season—not all that long a time, taken in the context of a full life.

At the leadership workshop in February, Dr. Tim had said that 10 percent of the people in any group are positive leaders. Grant had taken that number as a challenge. But that's about what they'd had, as it turned out, in the 2004 marching season. And they'd needed more.

Max and the other directors didn't fully appreciate that Grant had been trying to live out his faith on the marching field over the past three seasons. They had no inkling of the religious questions he was wrestling with. What they did decide was that Grant Longenbaugh had blinded them to the average qualities of the Class of 2005 as a whole. Grant's leadership, combined with his intelligence and musical talent, had shone so brightly that it included the entire class in its radiance. It hadn't been Grant's fault, but the Class of 2005 had, possibly, grown complacent in the glare.

Grant, on one level, saw the season as a struggle between the students and their director. He knew that Cameron had decided to fight Max, and sensed that others had, too. He thought that still more had given up or pulled back under Max's constant criticism. It would have helped, he thought, if someone had given in. Even a slight easing on either side—enough students who said, We don't care if he thinks we're bad leaders, we're still going to do the right thing; or Max asking them, Hey, what's going on? and waiting for their answers—could have made the difference.

Unless Max and Grant could institutionalize their beliefs and make them appeal to a wider range of people, it would remain the rare group of students who overcame inertia, self-centeredness, apathy, fear, anxiety, internal division, arguments with authority; the rare year they became champions. It was a fundamental problem of both perfection and faith, when those were the goals expected to motivate entire groups.

Or maybe, as Christine Fischer had wondered, Americans needed to compete, to establish winners and losers. And whatever other categories Max Jones's band fit into, it was an American band. If it took a state championship to motivate the majority of kids in an American band, then they'd just have to accept the possibility that they'd end up losers.

Concord lost the championship by two points on a 100-point scale. In that tiny margin, how much could be traced to the LC guys, who had gotten their drill to Concord late, and Greg Hagen, who had never completed the final detail work on the choreography? How much did it matter that Scott Spradling had been absent during a critical period in the Dixieland segment and "Swing, Swing, Swing"? What was lost in the multiple rewrites of the percussion score? How much could be charged to Max's growing generational distance from his students? To changing demographics, changing families, even in Concord? And what about the capriciousness of judging in such tight competition? What did it mean that many considered the final show in 2004 even stronger than the show put on by the champions of 2003? If all the factors had somehow reconfigured to give Concord a bare three more points in the finals, would that suddenly say something fundamentally different about the senior class, and the band? About perfection and faith?

LIFE WENT ON. In the days following the trip to Indianapolis, the band viewed the state finals video and listened to judges' comments, recorded their music to put on a CD, and marched the show on the practice field twice more so half the seniors at a time would have a chance to view it from the towers. Max's staff directed back-to-back concerts with the junior high and beginning bands.

The students in the marching band were now joined by students who'd stayed in indoor band. Before the end of the first trimester, in one week's time, the directors had to assess them all and separate them into four levels of concert band. For three months, the focus had been on including everyone: "One band, one sound." Now students were being not only divided, but ranked.

For a week, band members cycled through the practice rooms to sit in front of an assistant director and play short exercises by sight. Students needed to hand in audition tapes of eight short pieces in different keys and one of four tempos, starting with the standard B-flat concert scale in quarter notes and ending in an exercise in D-flat and 12/8 time.

Grant made his audition tape late one night in the basement while his mother half-dozed in the recliner nearby. He repeated each exercise until he was certain that he'd done it perfectly.

The night before the audition tapes were due, Adilene stayed up past midnight finishing hers. She'd had to borrow a tape recorder from Diana de la Reza and then ask her parents to buy her some blank tapes. Camelia Corona wanted her daughter to get enough sleep on a school night and urged Adilene to stop. "I'm sure it's good enough by now," she said. The sharpness of Adilene's response surprised her. "It's not good enough! I'm not going to stop until I get it right!"

Max posted the line-ups for the four bands in the music department hallway on the second Monday in November. As expected, Grant Longenbaugh sat first chair in the trumpet section for the top concert band, as did Amanda Bechtel in the flute section. Surprisingly, it was a freshman, Robin Bortner, who earned the first chair in the trombone section, not Brent Lehman. Tucked in the four lists was something that would have shocked everyone involved only three months earlier. Listed second among the clarinets in the fourth-hour band, ahead of several juniors and a number of the other freshmen, was Adilene Corona. The next week, the Coronas stood in back of the band room before the start of rehearsal for the symphonic band. They'd picked out a potted plant from the nursery where Juan worked and written a card and come to school personally to thank the senior clarinet who'd made such a difference in their daughter's life.

Without marching band, Grant lost a focus to his days. He looked depressed again. He supposed he was. But from the inside, he felt focused on what mattered, and a lot of what mattered was spending time with his family. He was still shaken by his mother's diagnosis. He consciously didn't look up information about multiple myeloma. He learned enough from observing how seriously his parents and their friends took the disease. The week after state finals, his grandfather, the former principal of Concord and Elkhart high schools, died after a long diabetic decline. Grant played "Taps" at the service. He and Anne agreed that they'd want livelier, New Orleans–style funerals for themselves. Later that week, he stayed home and cooked pancakes with his parents instead of polling his neighborhood with Cameron and Jon Faloon for their Government class.

On November 2, Indiana again turned red on the national electoral map before any other state. In Elkhart County, George W. Bush carried the popular vote two to one.

On a sunny afternoon later that month, Nick Stubbs took a physical aptitude exam for his application to West Point. While a Concord PE teacher recorded his scores, Nick completed nine pull-ups, fifty-five push-ups, a long jump, a basketball throw, and, finally, shuttled as fast as he could between two cones set twenty-five yards apart, six times. Then he threw up.

Five days later, the Concord Marching Minuteman Band flew to California. Brent Lehman hadn't signed up because of the uncertainty and expense of his father's cancer. But with his father finally in remission and a spot in the trombones open after Jeremy Crawford's withdrawal from school, he was able to slide in at the last moment. After some discussion, Adilene Corona's parents had decided to put the money they'd earmarked for Adilene's quinceañera toward the Hollywood trip. The day after Thanksgiving, the Concord students marched together for the last time, three miles through Tinseltown, past Grauman's Chinese Theatre and the white sign high on the hills, and then—especially once they turned off the main drag—past tawdry storefronts and convenience stores and crowds of the town's citizens, most of them African-American and Hispanic. Hollywood, it turned out, was not that much more glamorous than the rest of America, or Concord.

Grant received his first A minus, ever, in Government, and suddenly it was no longer clear that he would be valedictorian after all. Grant could earn nothing less than an A in every class for his last two trimesters. It was nothing more than he'd done all along. But he found it increasingly hard to push himself merely for a grade.

In mid-December, Anne graduated from Purdue. This time the entire family celebrated together. She finished her student teaching and stayed on in her apartment in West Lafayette, still working nights at the Turkish restaurant. Chris Longenbaugh left Grant a note on Christmas morning. In her clear cursive, she wrote, "I promise you, today, that I will be the biggest fighter (with God's help) so that I can experience, with you, all the wonderful things awaiting you in your life. I love you."

At a service at The Connection in early January, Grant painted to the music of a praise band. Praise painting, you could call it, and it did feel that way. Setting up his easel on the side of the stage, Grant brushed in a scene of trees in winter during the first part of the service. Then he turned the canvas upside down and the winter scene into a picture of Jesus ascendant, the branches of the trees becoming his thorns and a new day dawning behind him. Grant had finally talked with Pastor Terry about some of his questions. Terry Bley took Grant's crisis seriously, talked about it as "wrestling with the darkness of the soul," and asked the youth group to pray for strength for Grant, and for God to light his way through the darkness. Over the holiday, Grant and Leandra kissed for the first time.

With the start of the new year, Grant continued to skip school, come late to class, and turn in half-filled practice sheets for jazz and concert bands. Max and Steve Peterson saw that his lack of practicing was trickling down to others. They decided, unbelievably, that the band's best leader needed The Talk.

ONE AFTERNOON IN the middle of January, Grant was watching a video about Russian history along with the rest of the Fine Arts team when a voice came crackling over the intercom: "Grant Longenbaugh, please proceed immediately to the music office." Max Jones and Steve Peterson were both waiting for him in Max's office. They told him that that his sister was in the hospital. Grant's first impulse was to laugh, but it wasn't a joke. Anne was in a hospital in West Lafayette in serious condition. His parents, trying to locate him, had called the music department for help. Max dialed the phone for Grant. Anne has bleeding in the brain, his mother told him. Please come home.

Grant, Chris, and Jeff rushed down Highway 31 to West Lafayette. A light snow was falling. Chris and Jeff had been at the doctor's earlier that day, where Chris had received encouraging news about the treatment she'd been undergoing for the cancer. There was a good chance she'd be able to get a stem-cell transplant the following summer, and that a remission should follow. But now, with no warning, their healthy, vibrant daughter had a brain aneurysm. Because of where Anne's blood clot was located, the doctors decided to send her to Indianapolis. Grant drove behind the ambulance. In the middle of the night, a winter thunderstorm rattled the windows of their hotel room.

When Grant and his parents walked into Anne's hospital room the next morning, they found her in the center of a group of Purdue friends. Other friends from high school were on the way. Over the next day, after several scans of the clot, the doctors became increasingly concerned. The surgery started at six the next morning.

Grant passed the time in the waiting room reading a book that Keith Yoder had recommended. It was called *A New Kind of Christian*, and it talked about something called postmodern Christianity. The doctors came out and said the procedure was tougher than they'd anticipated; the aneurysm was next to the brain stem. They moved Anne to another floor. Grant read in another waiting room.

At some point after the day had turned, the head surgeon met with the Longenbaughs to explain that they were placing Anne in a phenobarbital coma in the hope of reducing the pressure on her brain. Over the next hours, it became clear that Anne would never come out of it. Leandra was at youth group with Cameron when Grant called with the news. They would get a ride to Indianapolis with Mrs. Greene the following morning. A dozen of Anne's friends squeezed into her room on the last night of her life. Jeff asked them to tell stories about her. The next morning, Chris and Jeff officially requested that their daughter be removed from life support. They held her hands, stroked her face, and told her to fly away.

Grant talked to Anne in the waning moments of her life. He told her she'd be in heaven soon. He spun a description of it as if he were telling her a bedtime story. He finished by saying he couldn't wait to see her there. His father almost vaulted across the hospital bed, nearly screaming, "No!" It had sounded to Jeff as if Grant was announcing his intention to leave this world as well.

Grant couldn't have explained the emotions behind what he said any better than he could explain other intense images and insights that started during the vigil at Anne's bedside and continued in the days following her death. He'd been unable the past two months to more than glancingly contemplate the possibility that his mother could die prematurely. But now death had come to him, and he'd never felt so alive. In the same whirl of emotion, he felt as if he were drowning in grief. But when it became too much to bear, he touched bottom. And just he had done dozens of times on gravel beds of Boundary Water lakes, he pushed off the solid ground he found there. He surfaced bursting with the certainty of God's love, filled with grief still, but also with joy. It didn't make sense. It made perfect sense.

They returned from the hospital to an outpouring of love and support. People brought them casseroles and pies until there was no more room in either the kitchen freezer or the one in the garage. Grant seemed to find unlimited energy. After so many weeks of lethargy, his response seemed a strange sort of grieving to his parents. But Grant felt completely clear. There was nothing else he needed or wanted to do, other than give his sister the celebration she deserved. He painted a new picture of her. He insisted that her viewing include videos of her playing saxophone at Jazz Café, of her performing in plays at school and at church, of her goofing around in the backyard with a broomstick microphone. Nearly a thousand people came to pay their respects.

They held the memorial service for Anne Longenbaugh on a dull January morning. The freezing fog of Elkhart winter hovered above gray slush. Heavy, wet snow fell intermittently. The Lutheran church that Chris and Jeff now attended filled quickly. Chairs needed to be set up in short rows at the back of the sanctuary. It was a crowd that might have filled even Nappanee. Chris and Jeff and Grant sat in the front pew, along with other relatives. Next were friends and classmates of Anne's from Concord and Purdue. Teachers that Chris worked with, teachers who'd taught Anne in school, dozens of band parents past and present took their places behind the rows of young people. Max and Dianne Jones sat with the Dyers and other directors while Gavin sat up front with Anne's friends. The pastel that Grant had created of Anne in her white cowboy hat sat on an easel at the front of the church, the hat itself balanced on the lectern.

Grant had written the program for the service with several of Anne's friends. On the cover were two verses from Psalm 30: "You have changed my sadness into a joyful dance. You have taken away my sorrow and surrounded me with joy." Friends of Jeff's and Chris's had found the lines written on a slip of paper on the desk in Anne's apartment. They rose and sang hymns. "Come Thou Fount." "On Eagle's Wings."

Cameron Bradley, guitar in his hand, told the packed church that Anne Longenbaugh was the only person who'd listened to every song he'd ever written. He'd based the second song, which he sang as a duet with another Concord student, on Psalm 30. Cameron sang in a full, clear voice while he picked the melody and strummed the chords.

> All my days
> Seem to slip away from me
> And all my time
> Is simply thrown away to please my mind

He gave the call, and the young woman sang the response:

> So hear my cry of desperation
> Take from me my sorrows and all my woes.
>
> Put another cry in me of love and your salvation
> Take from me my dreams, for they are yours.

They repeated the chorus, now mingling their voices. She gave up her dreams, gaining love and salvation; in harmony, he asked to have his sorrow lifted from him.

For the first time, the Concord directors heard Cameron play guitar and really heard his singing voice, which was surprisingly mature and clear. For the first time that year, they heard Cameron play music with all his heart, and were moved.

Friends stood at the lectern and spoke of Anne's spirit. In some fundamental way, she was still alive for them. Her vitality pulsed through their stories, which hadn't become fixed in memory yet. In their youthful faith, they raised their voices to praise Anne, but also to bring her home. Many ended their remarks assuring the community gathered before them that Anne Longenbaugh was with God now, in heaven. They danced her death as a consummation with God.

But one look around the church said something different about the adults. They were gathered to mourn Anne's death and to support her family, especially Jeff and Chris. They held themselves as if they'd been gut-punched. Their faces sagged in grief. *One of our children has been taken from us.* Even the pastor's recurring insistence that God gave his son to be crucified—the ultimate sacrifice, she said—seemed in that context simply another parent's worst nightmare.

Near the end, Grant got up to speak. He'd written out his remarks in a flurry early that morning. "When we consider heaven," he said, "we forget heaven."

Behind every sentence in front of him lay memories of Anne, but also his own struggle over the past months to understand what God wanted of him. Anne's death had thrown his crisis of faith into relief, brought him to a new place. The essay—a sermon, really—tried to explain the gift that his sister's death had given him.

He said, "The heaven we believe in—the 'church-all-the-time' heaven—and the heaven we desire are two things." He wouldn't have said that a year earlier, but he saw now how true it had been for him. The closest to heaven he'd felt over the past half year had been lying on the grass in Oxbow Park, holding hands with Leandra.

He said, "Heaven is not the perfection of our behavior or a reward for being good or a manifestation of the well-to-do." It also wasn't "the self we're told we should be, the self we're told we can attain if we follow the seven steps to a purposeful life or complete a checklist of the traits of 'good Christians.'" This was all his Type A Christianity rolled up together. He'd craved the sense of certainty that came with believing that if he did this and this and this, he would be saved. He'd wanted to hear the voice call him perfect. He'd wanted to feel special, chosen. Now he realized that perfection was all around him, in the God-filled imperfection of life itself. He didn't need to make himself over, or better. He saw, too, the fearfulness at the heart of his earlier approach. He'd held on so hard to being perfect that he'd forgotten that having faith meant being willing to take risks. To leap.

"Forget the being good and prudent," he said. "Just start being loved."

The voice that had tormented him with doubts, with his lack of faith, continued even in the hours following Anne's death. It had insisted that he give up Leandra. He'd known in a flash that God would never do that to him, not in his grief and need, not ever. He'd been on his way to figuring that out on his own, even before Anne died. But her death had made it clear.

In the months to come, he'd feel the finality of her death more keenly. For days at a time he'd be able to see only the loss and feel only the grief. But standing in front of their community, he wanted to give all of them, too, the gift she'd given him.

He walked to the back of the church, where Brent Lehman and Matt Tompkins waited with trombone and banjo, and picked up his horn to lead them all into the parade after the funeral. The notes of "Saints" swung through the church. A few band parents clapped. But even though Grant had hoped that the entire church would erupt into celebration, as Anne would have surely wanted, the faces in the pews did not lighten, and nobody danced.

MAX MET LATER that afternoon with his staff and George Dyer to formally announce the plans for his sabbatical. He would be at Purdue during the 2005 marching season, would return to lead the music department for the rest of the year, and graduate from teaching high school students with the Class of 2006.

The following month, Max pulled Grant out of jazz band and said, "Come up to my office."

Max knew all the sorry details about the missed classes, the empty practice reports, about work not being done in other classes. But he didn't say a word about any of it. Instead, he said, "You don't seem like yourself." He wanted Grant to remember that he had a great life waiting for him. And he wanted Grant to know that he cared about him. They embraced. This time, Max let Grant choose when to end the hug.

Grant graduated sixth in his class.

At the ceremony, the Longenbaughs took their places in the bleachers directly above the spot where Grant was sitting on the floor of the gym. They were proud of him for reasons that went beyond class standing. Over the past months, he had taught them the difference between happiness and joy. Chris was thin and frail; she still gave the impression that the slightest jostling might shatter her, but also that she was determined to hold those shattered pieces together by will and a sort of social grace. Jeff seemed hollow and aged. His hair had gone gray. Their grief still radiated out from them. Other solemn-faced parents came up to them. Jeff and Chris rose and hugged, received hugs, talked, sat back down, Chris carefully, Jeff solicitous of her. They resumed watching Grant, their remaining child. Their son.

Chris said during that time, "Our plate is to the brim. One more drop, and it spills over."

Postlude

Max spent the spring preoccupied by the question of succession. He'd held on for a long while to the hope that one of his own staff would take over the program, as if he were handing on a family business. But at some point, he pragmatically turned his attention toward finding someone with the same strong commitment to kids and to music. He bluntly told George Dyer, "You need to look outside."

For Dyer, the same months held overtones of the period following Joe Beickman's death. He and school board members received dozens of calls from parents and former band students who wanted the school corporation to understand how seriously they took the hiring of the new head director. The phrases "only the best" and "don't lose what's great about Concord" echoed back across the decades. And yet, what accomplished director would come in only for the marching season, and then work under Max Jones for the rest of the year?

So when the new director of music for the Concord schools was announced, ten days before graduation, the community was stunned by the obviousness of the choice. In retrospect, it seemed inevitable—so inevitable, in fact, that some suspected Max Jones of planning it that way all along. In the days following the announcement, he seemed never to stop grinning. He happily told people that he felt like a proud papa. As far as he was concerned, the new director was his child in every way but birth. If the name of the successor came with the whiff of nepotism, it also came with the force of a coup: Gay Burton.

Gay hadn't taught in the seven years that she'd been away, but few at Concord questioned her credentials or her ability to take over the program that Max had created. From the community's point of view, she was the perfect outsider: an insider who was returning after having been bigger places. Since leaving Concord, she'd been raising her daughter amid the swirl of big bands around Indianapolis, where her husband had been an assistant director at Center Grove. From Max's point of view, no one knew his own vision and his values better: Gay had been a part of the dynasty at Winchester, a member of the class that had accepted nothing less than a championship four years in a row; she'd done her student teaching under him at Southport; she'd ridden out the tough first years at Concord with him; with him, she'd laid the groundwork for what the Concord music program was now. Her family life, with its shared careers in music and one child, even mirrored Max and Dianne's. Max did think he'd pulled something off. Everything he'd hoped for in a transition could now happen. He thought Gay had it in her to take the music program at Concord to an even higher level, whatever that might look like.

No drill book could have outlined the right steps for following a legend like Max Jones, but from the start Gay Burton hit her marks. She came up to Concord immediately after the announcement, during the last week of the school year, when the music department put on one event after another, starting with Jazz Café, the simulated evening at a jazz club that she had created fourteen years earlier. The event had grown so popular that all thousand tickets had sold out in thirty-five minutes, just like a rock concert. In the packed, transformed gymnasium, the school's food services "catered" the food, and clean-cut teenagers played the jazz—yet the quality of the music and the vibe in the room made it feel like the real thing.

Orchestra and choir dinners followed, and the "pie-and-cry" band banquet, where band moms put out scores of pies and Gay listened as each senior spoke, often tearfully, about coming of age in the band. The crowd included parents, teachers, fifth graders about to start beginning band, eighth graders poised to become the marching-band's newest members, and the band's newest leaders, the Class of 2006.

Amidst all the events, Gay and Dan Burton started looking at houses in
the area. In the fall, Gay's daughter would go to East Side Elementary
School.

TWO DAYS BEFORE graduation, Gay walked into Room 406 to
talk to the students in the band. The seniors were already gone, taking
their annual dispensation to skip the final days of school; but Amanda
Bechtel, curious about the new director, made a special trip in to hear
her talk. As Gay Burton stood in the front of the room, it was easy to
see similarities between her and her mentor. She was petite, and fash-
ionable in a no-nonsense way. Her hair was blunt-cut at her shoulders;
she could, if necessary, climb the tower in the black pantsuit she was
wearing. She spoke quietly, in a husky drawl with more south in it than
people were used to hearing around Elkhart, and she instantly commanded the attention of everyone in the room.

Mr. Jones, she said, had told her that things hadn't changed much
since she'd been gone. She shook her head slightly. "Things have
changed a lot." She spoke fondly of each of the other directors, subtly
reminding the students gathered before her of the depth in the Concord
program apart from Max Jones. "Seven years ago," she said, pointing
up at the banners hanging from the ceiling, "the marching band didn't
have this kind of consistency."

But then she did something surprising, at least to students used to
the ways of Mr. Jones. She shared her personal life with them. "The
things I've been doing in my life over the past seven years make me a
better teacher," she said. "Having a child has completely changed the
way I look at things.

"I know my priorities," she told them, and then she listed them:
First came her faith in God, then her family, and then "all you guys." It
was hard to imagine Max Jones ever talking about his personal beliefs
with his students, and hard to imagine the band as anything other than
first on his list of priorities. The faith part moved Amanda, and clearly
resonated with many of the others.

Gay met separately with the incoming seniors after class. The group
moved to the lobby of the performing arts center, where Max had held
so many of his senior meetings during marching season. She seated herself among them, with Grant's picture as a backdrop, Anne Longenbaugh

and Gavin Jones perpetually playing "It Don't Mean a Thing (If It Ain't Got That Swing)." The students, unsure of what their new director expected of them, didn't respond immediately when she asked for questions.

She prompted them, "I want you to think about your role in the band." The students took it as a preview of a talk on the dunes. The first person to venture an answer said he just wanted everyone to have fun, and to avoid all the bickering from the year before. If Steve Peterson and Bryan Golden had been there, they would have exchanged rueful glances. Gay Burton responded to each person with a variant of the same question: "What are you going to do about that?" Only at the end did she speak at any length. By then, some of the upcoming seniors seemed wrung out from contemplating the prospect of leadership. They settled in to listen, heads bowed as if in prayer. "To me," their new director told them, "great leaders are leaders by example." Leadership, she said, "means I prepare myself so I can take care of others." The clarion phrase Gay Burton used was familiar to many of the students, but not in this context: servant leadership.

MAX TOOK GAY to Indianapolis and introduced her to the LC guys, but it was her meeting to run, as it was her show to put together. Max would still arrange the music, but Steve Peterson had come up with the themes and selected the music for a show that was, in wry honor of Max, all about trains. Max, the almost-railroad engineer, had never found train-themed music he liked well enough to build a show around. But Peterson had been digging deeply into the work of Duke Ellington, and had discovered a treasure trove of such music there; the top Concord jazz band had recorded "Happy-Go-Lucky Local" for the Essentially Ellington contest earlier that spring. The Marching Minutemen would combine that melody with "Night Train," a better-known song that had borrowed the same theme, plus add another Ellington and Strayhorn standard, "Take the A Train," for an all-out jazz show. The irony of honoring Max with jazz music was not lost on Peterson and the other directors.

The LC guys, for their part, were determined to give Max Jones a proper send-off. The show they put together for Concord was knowing, entertaining, and full of humorous references to Max. In a nod to

Max's past and future in marching bands, they marked out drill in recognizable shapes—the encircled X of a railroad-crossing sign, the word TRAIN—and added choreography more commonly found in college show-band performances than in "serious" competitions. It was American cornball and ambitious, both served up in large portions. Gay went along with all of it.

One of Gay's first official requests as the new music director was to have a spiral staircase built for the central tower. She also asked several members of the Class of 2005 to come back as summer staff. Grant Longenbaugh, Amanda Bechtel, Craig Searer, and Nick Stubbs worked with their former sections, now as teachers of music, teachers of leaders.

Nick immediately liked the young percussion instructor Gay Burton had brought up from Center Grove to replace Amy Davis, who had left Concord, the Midwest, and teaching in the schools altogether. The new instructor was the leader Nick had yearned for, and Nick was thrilled to work with him even after the fact. By midsummer, though, Nick's excitement was muted by the silence from West Point. He reluctantly sent in a deposit to Ball State. A few days before classes were to begin, a letter finally arrived from the military academy. He had not made the final cut, it said, but the letter encouraged him to try again. From his dorm room in Muncie, he sent in a new application request on the first day that West Point accepted them. As he'd learned on the drumline, good things might happen if only he kept trying. He held his chin high.

Brent Lehman was disappointed not to be asked back to help with the trombone section. He couldn't help but feel that his early years in the band had branded him, possibly for life. He had matured tremendously over the past year, but wondered if any of the directors had noticed.

But then, there was much they didn't know. After Robin Bortner won the trombone's first chair in the symphonic band, Brent didn't haze her, or ignore her, or mount a challenge, as seniors had done to him as a freshman. Instead, he congratulated her, then asked for the name of her private trombone teacher. A few weeks later, his father drove him north across the Michigan line for his first lesson. Dick Lehman watched from the car and through a plate-glass window as the man talked, and talked, and talked. Dick felt rising irritation on behalf of his son, thinking the guy must be so full of himself that he wasn't going to let Brent play even a note. Eventually, finally, he saw Brent lift the instrument and play. Afterward, Brent bounded out to the car, full of excitement about the teacher—how he played with the very same make and vintage trombone as Dick (and Brent), how he promised to help Brent with tonguing, with breathing, with learning to *hear* the music on the page, with everything.

Dick had done much more listening himself since the cancer, had focused more on being quietly present with the people he loved. He refused the easy, arm-around-the-shoulder version of cancer as a learning experience. He wanted the freedom to hate it for what it took from him and his family. But he was in remission now, and grateful for that. So he smiled at Brent, soaking in his son's enthusiasm, cherishing him. And he smiled to himself, reminded even by that small moment how little he understood.

Brent was starting to find positive role models all around him, including, increasingly, his father.

He would keep up the trombone lessons through the rest of his senior year and into college, and persuade others in the section to take them, as well. And—though there was no longer anything in it for him—he passed on everything he'd learned and was learning to the section's rising seniors. During the spring, over ice cream, Brent asked them about their plans for the section for the coming year. Like Gay Burton, he kept bringing them back to specifics: What will you do? Who's responsible? How will you make sure it happens? He encouraged them to learn the names of every incoming freshman, to delegate to sophomores and juniors, to be sensitive to others. Especially, he reminded them that raising their voices wouldn't accomplish anything. The voice of experience, he told them "It just shuts people down."

Brent drove over to the practice field a week or two into the new season and handed out green bandannas to everyone in the trombone section. Watching the section work together, he could already tell that it was on its way to an even better year, with Brandon Schenk at its heart and several other strong seniors to share the responsibility. He felt a mentor's pride as he watched. He had done his best, and now they would take what they wanted from his words and his example, and move on.

He e-mailed Bryan Golden and asked what he could do to improve his chances of joining the band's summer staff the following year. Gay

Burton, on Golden's recommendation, would invite Brent to work at the band camp the next summer, and Brent would happily accept. He didn't stop there, however. He surprised his directors and his classmates by becoming the only member of the Concord Minuteman Marching Band from the Class of 2005 to make it into a drum corps—and the world-champion Cavaliers, at that. He made it playing a new instrument, the baritone, and by working hard after narrowly missing the cut the first year he tried out. It was possible to see him and see Max Jones's hopes (". . . the best job, the best marriage, the best grades . . .") coming to life.

Back on the pavement, Grant, Amanda, Nick, and the other recent graduates worked among the ranks with the same shared language and lineage, but with a new voice coming down from the spiral-laddered tower. Where Max had never spoken explicitly about religion, Gay frequently mentioned God. For some, the change went unremarked. Gay merely reflected so much of the community. Others, like Amanda Bechtel, felt thrilled to hear someone in authority so matter-of-fact about her faith and so bold about expressing it. There was something comforting in her approach, at least for those who shared her beliefs.

Gay made a point of leaving school early enough, most days, to spend time at home with her daughter. The other directors with small children collectively breathed out and began doing the same. Steve Peterson's wife had had another boy. He and Scott Spradling, in particular, felt liberated from their roles as Max's "children." They were Gay's peers, and she treated them that way. She asked for their advice and included them in decision making in a way that Max never had. She even admitted to mistakes, and apologized for them. The staff, which had been in denial for so long, and then grown increasingly scared when it became clear that Max was really leaving them, couldn't have been more relieved. The mood around the music office became collegial, warm, and even giddy. It would have reminded Max of Southport.

FOR THE FIRST time in forty years, Max Jones didn't learn the names of incoming ninth graders. In August, he put on the gold-trimmed uniform of a Purdue Boilermaker band director. The college students called him "Max"—even, after some hesitation, Craig Searer, whom Max had recruited for the trumpet section of the All-American

Marching Band. But Max wasn't quite finished changing lives at Concord.

Every year, some number of seniors in the band talked to him about continuing with their music. Max had no problem telling students they should pursue other fields if he thought they lacked the talent or the personality. He encouraged the best of them to become teachers, partly for the security, but mostly for the nobility of the calling. And when he saw something special in one of his students, there was no end to the help he'd give.

He'd been glad to hear that Amanda Bechtel was applying to Indiana University's demanding music program. On the national stage, Indiana's strongest music institution was held in the same high esteem as Juilliard. Only one or two flute students were accepted into the school's performance program each year, and not many more into music education. Amanda didn't think she had much chance of getting into either program, and chose music education as the safer bet. Max helped her schedule lessons with a flute teacher in South Bend who was respected by the IU faculty, pushed her to prepare carefully for her audition, pulled out the stops for the student who had always come through for him. When she learned that she was one of six flutes accepted into the program, she was briefly disappointed: She'd started making plans to pursue Jewish Studies. But she took her admission as a sign from God, and felt her love for music deepen. She didn't question. Israel would happen, too, but in good time. After one year in music education, Amanda switched programs. She followed God and her heart into music performance.

Max worked the same kind of magic for Matt Tompkins, the banjo player in the Dixieland ensemble. Max had pegged Matt as yet another talented musician without the drive to do something with it—until he heard Matt's original composition, "Master P," at Jazz Café. Matt had worked on "Master P" much of the year and named it partly for the pun on "masterpiece" and partly in honor of his jazz director. The composition was a catchy and sophisticated blend of jazz and funk. Max, the master arranger of music, knew a good composition when he heard one, even when it was jazz, and he started to work on Matt's future. Matt hoped to go to the Berklee College of Music, the best place in the country to study the music he was most interested in: jazz, fusion, funk, rock—cutting-edge, whatever name it went by. But it had a reputation for being as hard to get into as Harvard, across the Charles River from Berklee's Boston campus. Max had never sent a Concord student on to Berklee, but he knew about auditions, he knew about scholarships, and most of all, he knew about music. He organized a scholarship audition for Matt and watched the young man—dressed in a rumpled corduroy jacket, his ubiquitous black high-tops, and a knit cap—completely win over the staid committee. Matt would go on to win the scholarship and entrance to Berklee in guitar performance for the following fall. He would shake his head, thinking of how close he had come to quitting band before his senior year, and of all the chances he'd given his director to give up on him. Instead, he counted Max Jones as his biggest influence, a mentor, and a friend.

AT PRECISELY 11:29 A.M. on the third Saturday in October, the clang of a sledgehammer striking metal carried high into the RCA Dome. Seconds later, it was followed by the loud whine of a drill. Max had been watching the 2005 marching-band finals from the press box, along with Dianne and the Dyers, but when the Concord Community High School Marching Minutemen started building a railroad on the field far below him, he couldn't stay seated any longer. He felt the emotions of a parent who was finally letting go—pride, anxiety, a sense of helplessness. He stood and paced. After four decades of doing, all he could do was watch.

Nick Stubbs watched from the press box, too, along with his father. Wayne Stubbs had been hired as assistant superintendent of the Concord schools on the same day that Gay Burton was hired as music director: another part of the transition, another signal that the high level of music at Concord would be sustained. In most places, the naming of an assistant superintendent wouldn't even be noteworthy. But George Dyer was also approaching sixty, and no school music program anywhere—despite the directors, despite the parents, despite the tradition—could thrive without a champion in the administration offices. Wayne Stubbs, like George Dyer, understood that music was not a sport or an extracurricular activity, and that it held a singular place in the Concord schools. In that place, learning was inextricably tied to an academic subject, but then was extended beyond the classroom into the community. Wayne could now wear Concord green all he wanted.

Down below the press box, Camelia Corona watched Adilene holding her clarinet as if it were a railroad spike, while other students pantomimed pounding it into the ground with their instruments. What *was* it with these shows, she wondered, that her daughter's expensive instrument always seemed in danger? Camelia spent her days educating teachers about the Hispanic community, and thought the band could do a better job of reaching out to parents who worried about expense and time commitment and their children being accepted. In a year's time, when Adilene was a junior and Esau a freshman, Candy Yoder would eagerly accept her offer of help, and Camelia Corona would become an official Concord band mom.

From the sidelines, band dads wearing matching engineers' caps heard the musicians in the pit bang out the sounds of a working railroad, some of them on instruments the dads had built with their usual scrap-heap, Home Depot ingenuity. An air compressor drove a bolt into the side of a fifty-five-gallon trash can. Tire irons, crowbars, hammers, and a wheel all created what the dads had dubbed "industrial instrumentation." They had put in the same crazy long hours as always, and put up with the same rework and revisions (some things, apparently, weren't going to change); the same last-minute crises. It was their show, too, and they wouldn't relax until it was over.

Brandon Schenk sang out to the audience, "All aboard!" and the train took off. Duke Ellington had set an ambling rhythm to the composition, which recaptured his band's leisurely train swings through the South. The LC guys had added jazz-dance steps—pliés, relevés, tondues—the sort of choreography that Max had believed the boys in his band would never accept. The kids were making all the moves, though, and smiling up to the stands as they did. All of it was bold and difficult and entertaining, from the choreography to the jazz. If anyone wondered whether Concord would continue to push the edges of marching-band performances, they had only to watch the opening minutes of the new show.

Jeff and Chris Longenbaugh sat among other parents in the Concord cheering section. After a stem-cell transplant over the summer, Chris was in remission. With the start of school, she'd gone back to the classroom, back to folding her long body into the kindergarten chairs and bringing home stories of the children with whom she spent her days. For the first time in more than twenty years, she had no children of her own at home. Grant was at the University of Michigan, which had offered the National Merit Scholar a generous award in its combined arts and humanities program. All of them still saw everything through the prism of Anne's death. The smallest moments had become almost unbearably precious; things that had once seemed big now struck them as completely unimportant.

Down on the sidelines, real railroad-crossing lights flashed, and an air-horn train whistle gave three sharp blasts. The sound of home for the Concord crowd.

Grant sat not far from his parents, with Cameron, Brent, and Leandra. He and Cameron and Brent had driven out to the Pacific Coast and back before the start of school. But he no longer talked about taking a year off to go to Europe or out west. In the end, he'd chosen a college close to home, partly to be near his parents and partly to be near Leandra.

College so far had disappointed him. He hadn't found his classes challenging. He was turned off by dorm-hallway talk of partying, and painfully aware that bringing up Anne—who was always on his mind—was an immediate conversation-stopper. He'd gone to Ann Arbor wondering if Concord would seem small in comparison, his high school friends not that special, but in fact, the reverse seemed to be happening. His friendships with Keith and Cameron—and increasingly, with Brent—seemed deeper, and his friends themselves more interesting, than anyone he'd met since leaving home. He continued to rely on them. He came home often on weekends, sometimes getting together with old high school friends, always wanting to see Leandra. She was deferring college for a semester and was about to leave on a six-week mission trip to Uganda.

The band slid into "Take the A Train," marching just as fast as they had the year before. The forms split and rotated and rearranged themselves, 234 kids spread end zone to end zone, the marching as exposed as the music. The timing sounded clean. Everything looked clean, confident. Grant knew what magic felt like, and he could tell it was happening down on the field.

Since reading *A New Kind of Christian*, he'd discovered the work of other committed but disaffected evangelical Christians. They voiced some of the ambivalence he'd felt at Nappanee and showed him other possibilities. Somewhere in there, he'd discovered a book by Rob Bell, whose artful videos he'd seen at youth group at Nappanee. Rob Bell was a charismatic former indie-rocker who in his late twenties, along with his wife and some friends, had started a church. They called the church Mars Hill, and put it in Grand Rapids, Michigan. By the standards of many, it soon qualified as an evangelical mega-church: More than ten thousand people attended every Sunday, and there was lots of talk of following and praising Jesus.

Grant started driving to Grand Rapids each week. The Christianity at Mars Hill seemed familiar but strange and exhilarating at the same time. Gone was a focus on being saved, staying saved, converting others; gone were the checklists, the never-ending plans for self-improvement. Instead, Grant heard that Jesus had called those who would follow to care for the poor and oppressed, work for justice, sacrifice for others, live for something bigger than themselves. It was the path Grant had tried to follow in the band, now writ as large as the world.

Grant had felt a weight lift from him when he read one of Rob Bell's stories. The story was a simple one, about the joy of jumping on a trampoline with his young sons. Bell wrote, in so many words, that when we want someone to join us on the trampoline, we don't set up a bunch of conditions ahead of time. We just say, Hey, c'mon up! It's a blast!

Bell described "brickianity" as a sort of counter-metaphor: the notion that faith was built on a series of beliefs, and that each belief—Jesus is the son of God, the world was created in six days—was a separate brick. Bell said that if you think of faith this way, it becomes a sort of wall. And not only does the wall divide believers from nonbelievers, people become scared to have any one of those beliefs questioned, because if they take one brick out, it destabilizes the entire wall.

On some level, Grant had understood the rigid teaching at Nappanee as "brickianity," and hearing Bell describe it, he felt freed from having to know exactly what was right to believe. For the first time, Grant sensed a spiritual home that encouraged him to think for himself—in fact, that urged him to question. He wasn't supposed to be perfect. He was just supposed to do his best to live the life that God had called him to lead—and to enjoy it. Celebrate it to its fullest. Jump like crazy on that trampoline.

The sermons at Mars Hill made it clear that being a Christian didn't take away the pain and suffering of life. If anything, they warned that following Jesus tended to make life harder. The message would comfort Grant in the coming year, when his mother went out of remission just as the family was getting ready to leave on a trip to Alaska. The new cancer was so aggressive that doctors weren't even sure Chris would survive the ambulance ride home from the hospital. But they underestimated her strength. She lived long enough to say good-bye to Grant and Jeff, and graciously received dozens—hundreds—of visitors, who for ten days, turned the Longenbaugh house into the social center of Concord one more time. Keith, Cameron, and Leandra moved into the basement, and Grant spent much of his time there, too. In the evenings, after the guests had left, they sometimes came upstairs and played music for her, Keith on the piano or Cameron on guitar, Grant and Leandra sitting quietly by her side. When she died, Grant and Jeff held her hands and told her Anne was waiting for her.

All this was in the future. Sitting in the stands at state finals, there was still the hope that the cancer would be held at bay for several more years, at least. Grant and Leandra were still months from clarity about their future, months away from enrolling together at Calvin College, a Christian college in Grand Rapids, months away from being engaged to marry.

But Grant had already started thinking, almost unwillingly, about the ministry. He didn't know how it would work, but he wanted to put all his gifts together, toward God. He knew that he was loved, and he knew that the time would come when he would be ready to serve.

AFTERWARD, THE BAND gathered in the plaza to celebrate the end of the marching season, just as it seemingly always had, surrounded once again by the Concord community. Members of the Class of 2005 now stood on the sidelines. Max Jones watched from the crowd and listened to his former student, now his replacement, talk to her band. Gay Burton wrapped an arm around her daughter; Adam Peterson and Alejandro Spradling ran around the edges of the plaza, a new generation growing up in the shadow of the Dome. As she hugged her daughter, Gay told the newly crowned Indiana Class B state champions, "You've been a special group from the beginning."

The kids in the band looked up with bright faces; some of them still showed the traces of the tears they'd cried when the championship was announced. Some of the kids hugged. The crowd in the Dome had responded to Concord's show with another standing ovation, and this time, several of the judges had joined in. How could one see that show, and the response, and the gathering on the plaza, and not believe that Max Jones might have started a dynasty, after all?

And not just that: behind Gay Burton's congratulations were the way the seniors had enlisted the sophomores and juniors in leadership, the way lessons in caring for one another had been passed on, the efforts of many to become servant leaders. Grant felt that he'd failed to leave the legacy he'd so fervently hoped to. But who was to say that his mission hadn't been successful, as well?

Late in the season, when the final push was on and every practice turned crucial, Laurie Schalliol came up with an idea for T-shirts for the high-brass section. She and several others had worn them down to the Dome. The shirts said, "What Would Grant Do?"

Author's Note

This is a book of narrative nonfiction—that is, an ordered narrative of facts and reported details, told as a story. Some practitioners of the form call it "immersion journalism," and no true story of any community as complex as a high school marching band could be told without extraordinary access and long hours immersed in the details of the characters' lives. To be able to tell this story, I lived in the Concord community with my family for six months in 2004. During that time, I observed nearly every practice of the Concord Community High School Marching Minuteman Band, plus numerous smaller, student-led rehearsals, every competition, and a number of band- and music-related events in the Concord schools. To more fully understand what the students experienced, I marched with them in the Elkhart Labor Day parade (playing a trumpet badly) and took Steve Peterson's music-theory class—two examples of the kind of reporting that gives immersion journalism its depth and its clarity. I was a constant presence around the music department and the high school, where I was given unrestricted access. I kept the directors' early hours and the teenagers' late ones. I accompanied the students to their classes, their churches, their gatherings, their homes, and Disneyland. Over three years, I made six additional trips to Concord, and filled in the stories that appear in this book with hundreds of hours of detailed interviews.

This particular narrative relied on personal conversations, innermost thoughts, and ongoing explorations of spirit and belief. I was present for much of the dialogue that appears in the text. In places where I reconstruct dialogue, I use the following conventions: Where I confirmed the specifics of a conversation with multiple sources, I use quotation marks. Where I could confirm the substance of a conversation but not the specific dialogue, or where accounts differed, I recount the conversation without quotation marks. Italicized thoughts are always based on interviews, and confirmed by the person to whom they're attributed.

When I first talked to the students in the band about this book, I told them that it would chronicle their season, but that I would provide my own context and interpretation for it. I hope that the students in the 2004 Concord Marching Minuteman Band feel that this book faithfully portrays their experience. This is their story filtered through my perspective.

As I worked on the book, I kept in mind that I was writing about teenagers whose lives are still being formed. I reviewed appropriate sections of the book with the students whose lives are most intimately portrayed in it. The book owes a tremendous debt to their honesty and thoughtfulness, and their willingness to risk opening their lives to me.

Acknowledgments

This book would not have been possible without the cooperation and support of a great many people, starting with Max Jones. His passion for music and teaching and his candor were all gifts for a writer, and his willingness to be part of this project set a tone that made my work with everyone involved with the Concord music program easier. He granted me complete access—even going so far as to give me the keys to his office so I could let myself in during off hours and read through twenty years of correspondence—and complete freedom in what I wrote about him. I will never forget his example or his kindness. Max and the rest of the band staff—Amy Davis, April Duffey Oppenheim, Shirley Dyer, Colleen Piekarz Molnar, Scott Preheim, and especially Bryan Golden, Steve Peterson, and Scott Spradling—were generous with their time and knowledge. Gay Burton graciously kept out the welcome mat. Dan Cunningham opened the halls and classrooms at Concord Community High School to me. Bob Bieber, Matt Furfaro, Kathy Greene, Chris Judson, Laura Livrone, Seth Molnar, and Lalo Rolon let me observe their classes at the high school, and George Dyer, Dianne Jones, Mary Amador, and Kevin Caird filled in my understanding of the Concord school district.

I owe a larger than usual debt to the families who also shared their time with me. Grant, Jeff, and Chris Longenbaugh let me into their lives and let me stay there even as those lives were being ripped apart. Their trust and openness informs every part of this story. Grant Longenbaugh did not want to be at the center of this book, but he kindly let me put him there anyway. I am also grateful to Wayne, Jackie, and Nick Stubbs; Adilene, Camelia, and Juan Corona; Laurie, Larry, and Robin Schalliol; Phil and Vicki Miller and Diana and Daniela de la Reza; Dick, Jolene, Brent, and Scott Lehman; Mary, Dianne, and Gavin Jones; Fred, Candace, and Amanda Bechtel; and the Yoders—Darrel, Candy, Keith, and Kim, who appears much less in the book than the other members of her family, even though she was the one who actually marched in the 2004 band. Leandra Beabout, Cameron Bradley, Brandon Schenk, and Matt Tompkins endured numerous additional questions with humor and grace. Many other members of the 2004 Concord Marching Minutemen and their families shared their experiences with me, and I thank them all.

Band dads and band moms Mark and Chris Tack, the incomparable Jim Faigh, backlot engineers Rick Rhude, Dave Lux, and Rick Nymeyer, Dave and Denise Sanders, "Mama" Moskowitz, Teri Schenk, and other parents whose work went on behind the scenes showed me how communities work. I'm also grateful to Dave Engbrecht and Terry Bley at Nappanee Missionary Church; Jeanne Rhodes at the Elkhart Public Library; Irvin Beck of the Elkhart County Historical Society; Steve Bibler and Jodee Shaw at *The Elkhart Truth*; and Cynthia Clopper, who explained the Northern Cities Shift and other elements of Indiana dialects.

The fuse for this book was lit more than thirty years ago when I marched in the (state champion) Richmond Red Devil band. After a 25th high school reunion at which I and other former band members shared the real stories behind our high school years and roundly agreed that band had transformed our lives, I called my former director, John Parshall, who told me that I wouldn't believe how much bigger band had become than when I was in it. Tom Dirks, former director at two-time national champion Center Grove, gave me my first foray into this new world by agreeing to be the subject of an article that appeared in *Indianapolis Monthly* magazine. He later organized a meeting of more than a dozen of Indiana's most experienced band directors for a half-day discussion with me about the history, trends, and future of marching bands in the state, a forum that was a reporter's dream, and which led me to Max Jones and Concord. Dr. Tim Lautzenheiser, Scott Mc-Cormick, George Parks, Lyndsay Rapp, and Andrew Boysen, Jr., extended my understanding of bands in other parts of the country; Rusty Briel and Ron Bell of ISSMA, Lissa May at Indiana University, Connie Dirks, James Goodhue, Bob Medworth, Jay Webb, Rich Breske, and Stan Garber added to my understanding of music inside Indiana.

Writing is a lonely endeavor, and writing a first book an anxious one, but Robert Shepard made it much less so. The critical talents he brought to this book were surpassed only by his humor, kindness, and integrity. I am extraordinarily lucky to have him as an agent.

Erin Moore and Bill Shinker, editor and publisher at Gotham Books, were both enthusiastic supporters of the book. Erin championed the book from both sides of the Atlantic; a writer can't ask for a more sympathetic reader. At Gotham, I'm grateful to Jessica Sindler; copyeditor Paula Reedy; Sabrina Bowers, who designed the book; Amanda Walker; and everyone inside the company and in the field who has helped make the book a reality. Gary Mailman's review of the manuscript sharpened its thinking while sanding its rougher edges.

When I first started thinking about a book on marching bands, I was surprised by how little has been written on this part of American history. One notable exception is the authoritative and expertly written *The Music Men: An Illustrated History of Brass Bands in America, 1800–1920,* published by the Smithsonian Institution, from which I drew some of my information about the history of marching bands and band-instrument manufacturers. I also drew on *Elkhart's Brass Roots,* a commemorative history of the Conn Company by Margaret Downie Banks, and on Paul Bierley's work on John Philip Sousa. My reading ranged through music education, the history of musical instruments, Dixieland and jazz, the history and culture of the Midwest, the psychology and sociology of adolescence, immigration and acculturation, and American religious movements. A handful of books deserve particular mention. Reading *Middletown* as a college freshman gave me language and tools for analyzing my own upbringing. Returning to it thirty years later, as I started writing this book, introduced me to the Center for Middletown Studies in Muncie, Indiana. Among the books I discovered there was *The Resilience of Conservative Religion: The Case of Popular, Conservative Protestant Congregations,* by Joseph Tamney, which drew on contemporary "Middletown" studies to explore the interplay between conservative and modernizing forces in society, and gave me a framework for understanding the Christianity in places like Concord. *Bowling Alone* by Robert Putnam helped me think about community, and Judith Wallerstein's *The Unexpected Legacy of Divorce* was an unexpected place to find a metaphor for successful parenting. I wrote my undergraduate thesis on narrative techniques in the works of George Eliot; I thought then that the "middle" in *Middlemarch* applied equally well to the Middle West. I still do.

No one has written more evocatively about marching bands than Barry Hannah in his novel *Geronimo Rex*. The book opens with a young boy watching "a fanatic man named Jones" who risks everything to form the perfect marching band. Jay Heinrichs introduced me to that book and encouraged me early on to broaden the scope of the story.

Mel Allen's advice continues to ring in my ears. Mark Kramer and Madeleine Blais gave me some especially sharp tools for narrative nonfiction. Dorothy Heinrichs, Leslie Sonder, and Kristen Fountain fed us and watched children. Others provided support, sustenance, and feedback along the way: Jon Berry, Jean Weiss, Julie Dunfey, Nancy Davis, Erick Laine, Peter Laine, Hilary Lombard, Dave Marcus, Caroline Levy, Bruce Jacobsen, Page Pless, Mike Berni, Marianne Jones, Amanda Cook, Patrick Henry, Les Norman, the women of the Seattle writers' group, the women and men of Dresden, the Dirt Cowboy in Hanover and the Daily Grind in Elkhart, Peter Dale, Edward Hoagland, and Gary Snyder. Kristen Fountain, Leslie Sonder, Whit Symmes, and Philip Koch read drafts and helped me see the story with fresh eyes. Thanks to the fabulous Allen sisters—Melissa, Chelsi, and Kate—and to Ian Burnette for joining our family at different points along the way.

Most of all, I am grateful to the three people who shared every step of the journey: Ursula, who edited me, drew me book covers, and lays claim to the book's title; Virgil, who reminded me daily, and sometimes through the night, of where my life was grounded; and Jim Collins, my partner in a project-based life, who took over the work of the family, never lost heart even when the money ran out, and has shared the music and the dreams, "hand in hand with wand'ring steps."